KENTA-(REALLY SHY!)-GIRLFRIEND

1

DING DONG

REIJI MIYAJIMA
ART ASSISTANCE: YUKA KINAMI

CONTENTS

 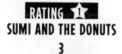

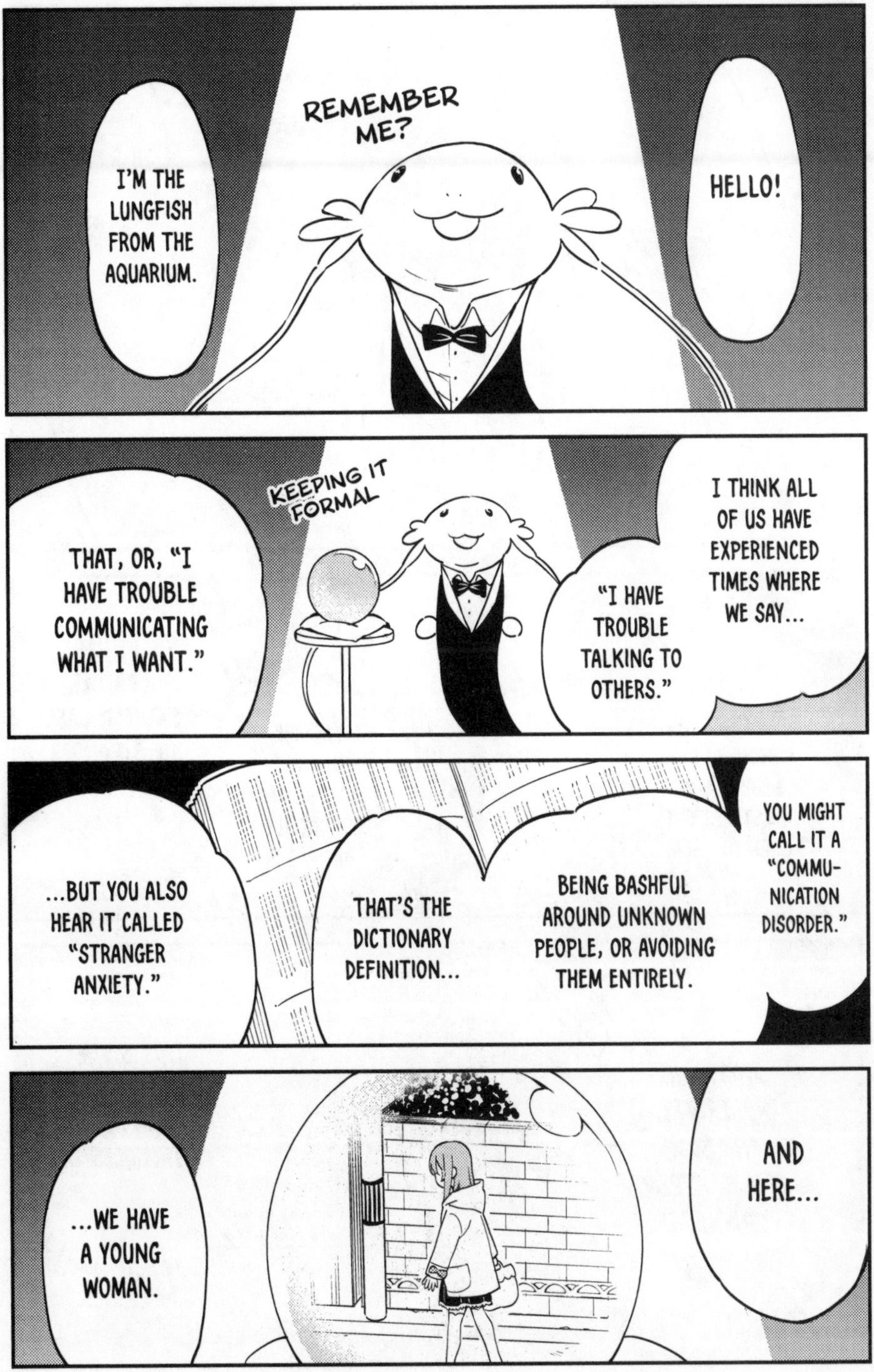
HELLO!
REMEMBER ME?
I'M THE LUNGFISH FROM THE AQUARIUM.
I THINK ALL OF US HAVE EXPERIENCED TIMES WHERE WE SAY...
"I HAVE TROUBLE TALKING TO OTHERS."
KEEPING IT FORMAL
THAT, OR, "I HAVE TROUBLE COMMUNICATING WHAT I WANT."
YOU MIGHT CALL IT A "COMMU-NICATION DISORDER."
BEING BASHFUL AROUND UNKNOWN PEOPLE, OR AVOIDING THEM ENTIRELY.
THAT'S THE DICTIONARY DEFINITION...
...BUT YOU ALSO HEAR IT CALLED "STRANGER ANXIETY."
AND HERE...
...WE HAVE A YOUNG WOMAN.

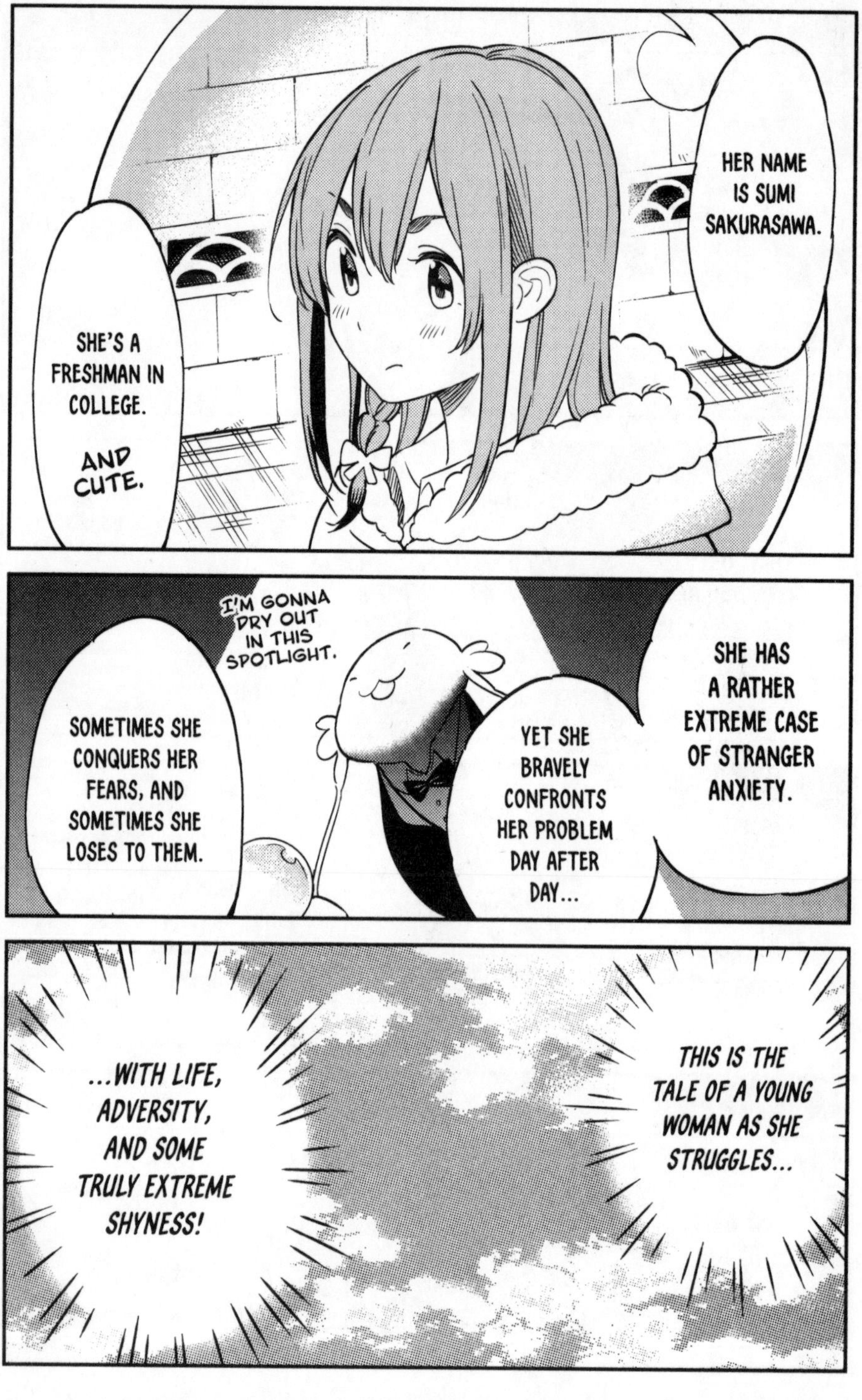
HER NAME IS SUMI SAKURASAWA.
SHE'S A FRESHMAN IN COLLEGE.
AND CUTE.
SHE HAS A RATHER EXTREME CASE OF STRANGER ANXIETY.
YET SHE BRAVELY CONFRONTS HER PROBLEM DAY AFTER DAY...
I'M GONNA DRY OUT IN THIS SPOTLIGHT.
SOMETIMES SHE CONQUERS HER FEARS, AND SOMETIMES SHE LOSES TO THEM.
THIS IS THE TALE OF A YOUNG WOMAN AS SHE STRUGGLES...
...WITH LIFE, ADVERSITY, AND SOME TRULY EXTREME SHYNESS!

RATING 1 SUMI AND THE DONUTS

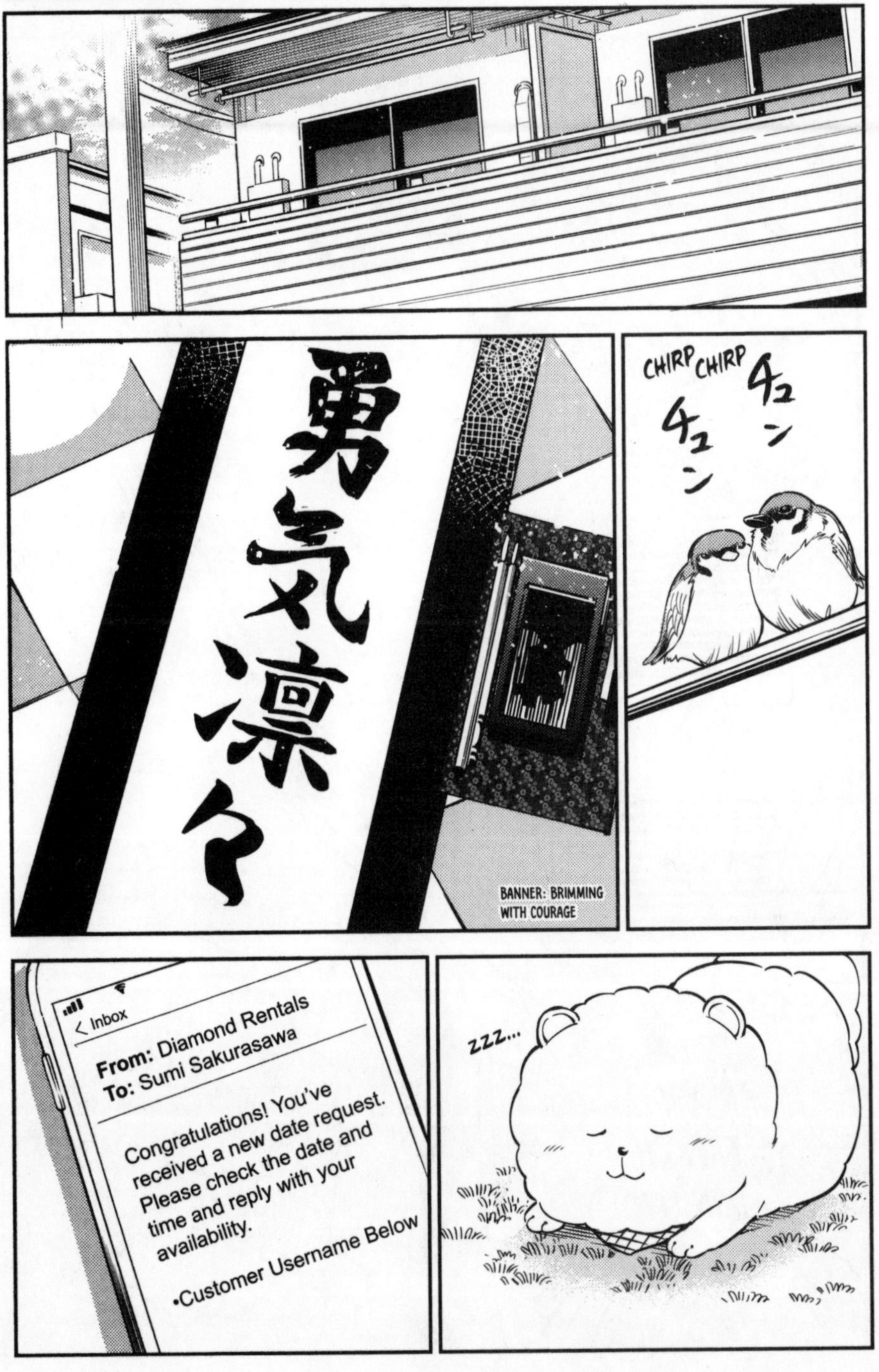
CHIRP CHIRP
チュン チュン
勇気凛々
BANNER: BRIMMING WITH COURAGE
zzz...
< Inbox
From: Diamond Rentals
To: Sumi Sakurasawa
Congratulations! You've received a new date request. Please check the date and time and reply with your availability.
•Customer Username Below

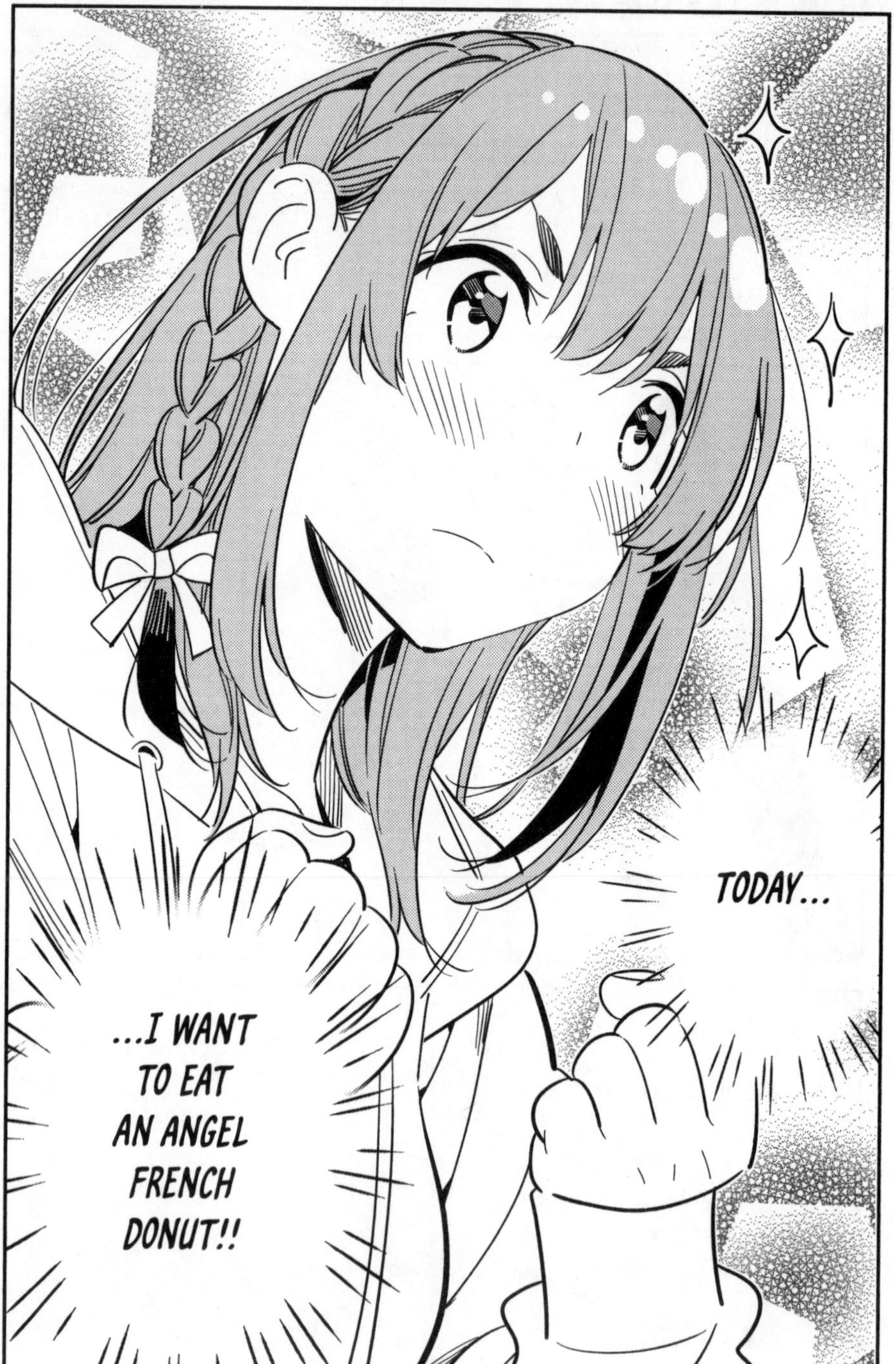
TODAY...
...I WANT TO EAT AN ANGEL FRENCH DONUT!!

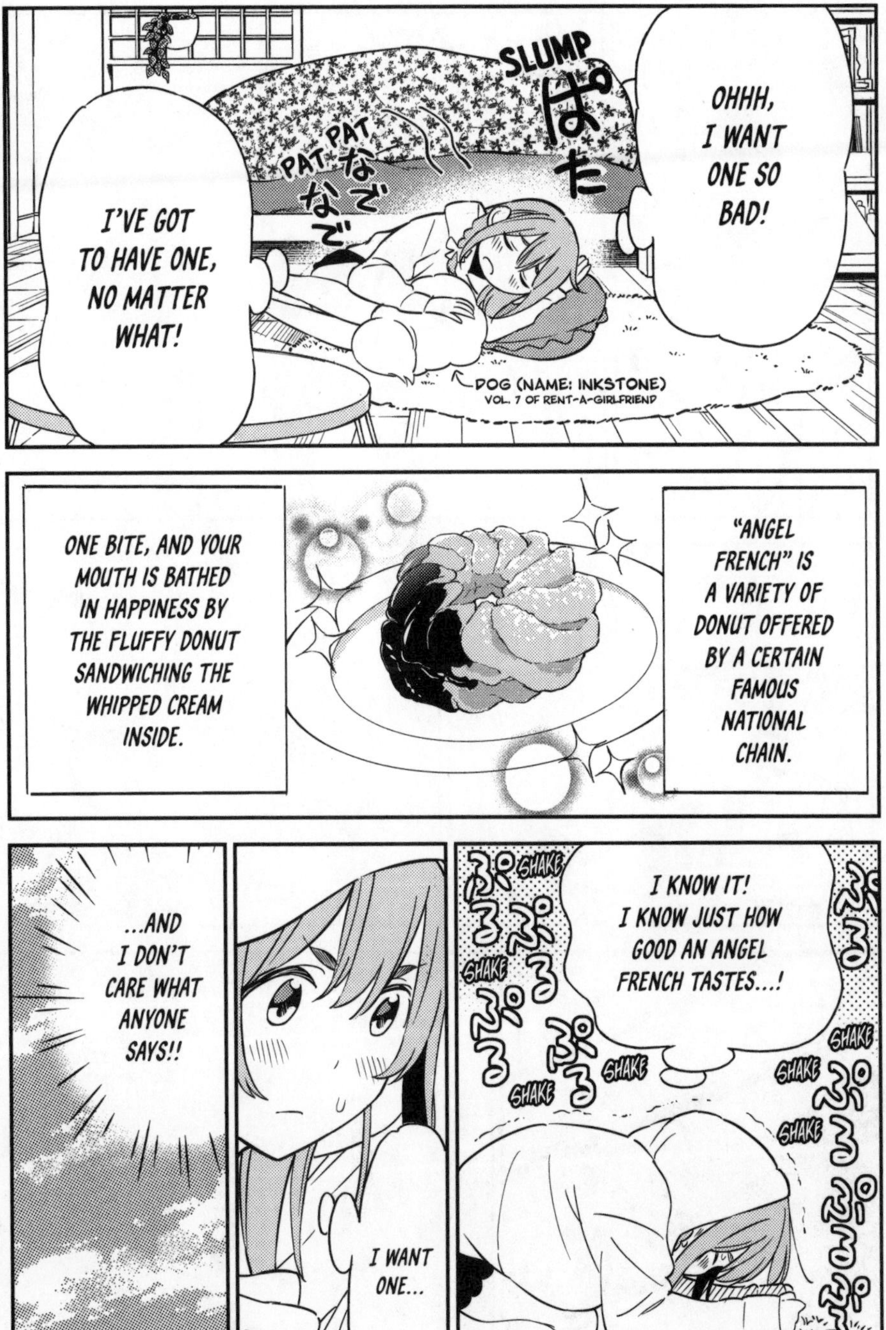

OHHH, I WANT ONE SO BAD!
SLUMP
ぱた
PAT PAT
なでなで
I'VE GOT TO HAVE ONE, NO MATTER WHAT!
DOG (NAME: INKSTONE) VOL. 7 OF RENT-A-GIRLFRIEND
"ANGEL FRENCH" IS A VARIETY OF DONUT OFFERED BY A CERTAIN FAMOUS NATIONAL CHAIN.
ONE BITE, AND YOUR MOUTH IS BATHED IN HAPPINESS BY THE FLUFFY DONUT SANDWICHING THE WHIPPED CREAM INSIDE.
I KNOW IT! I KNOW JUST HOW GOOD AN ANGEL FRENCH TASTES...!
SHAKE SHAKE SHAKE SHAKE
ぷるぷる
SHAKE SHAKE SHAKE
ぷるぷる
I WANT ONE...
...AND I DON'T CARE WHAT ANYONE SAYS!!

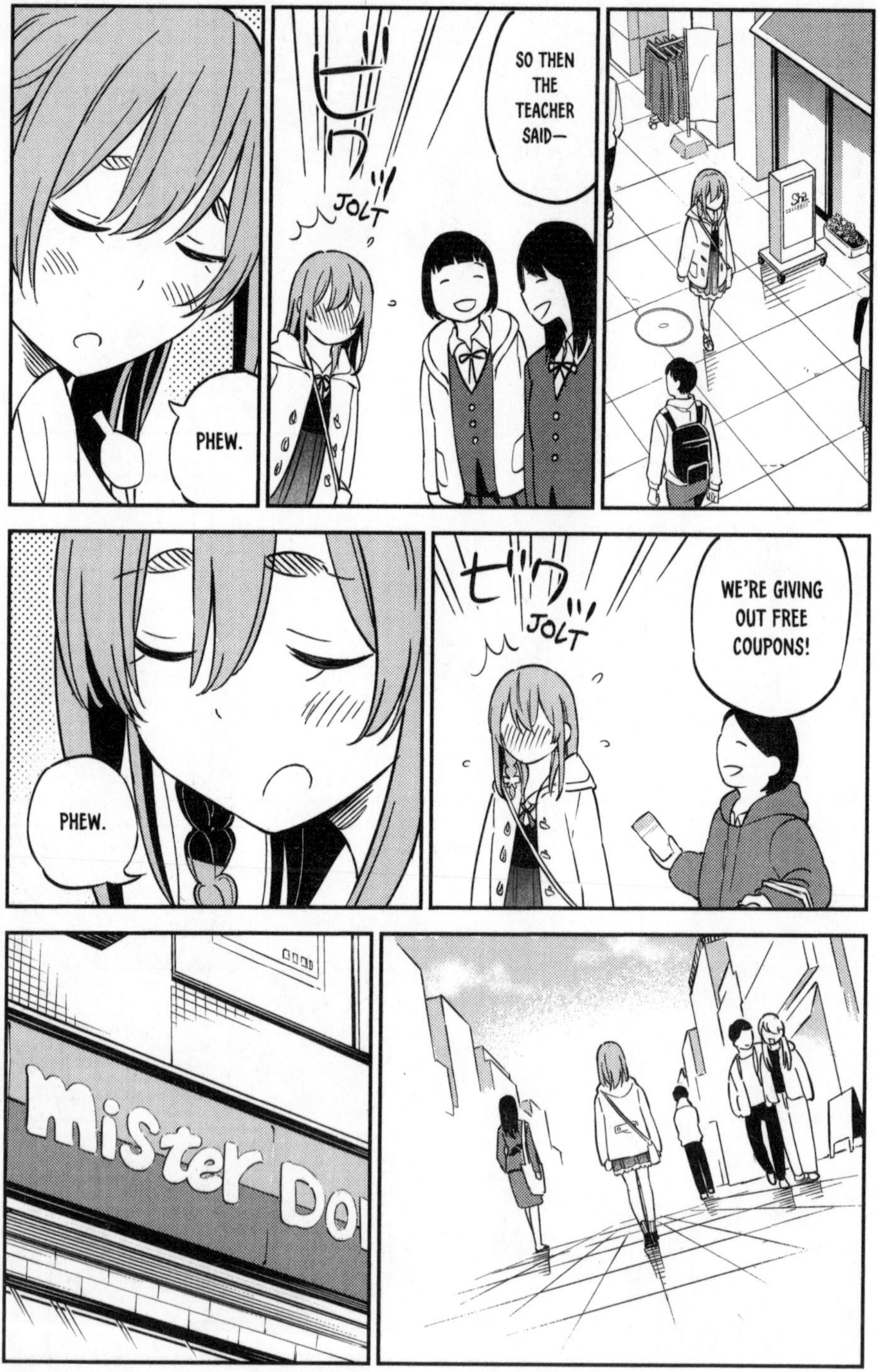
SO THEN THE TEACHER SAID—
JOLT
PHEW.
WE'RE GIVING OUT FREE COUPONS!
JOLT
PHEW.
mister Do

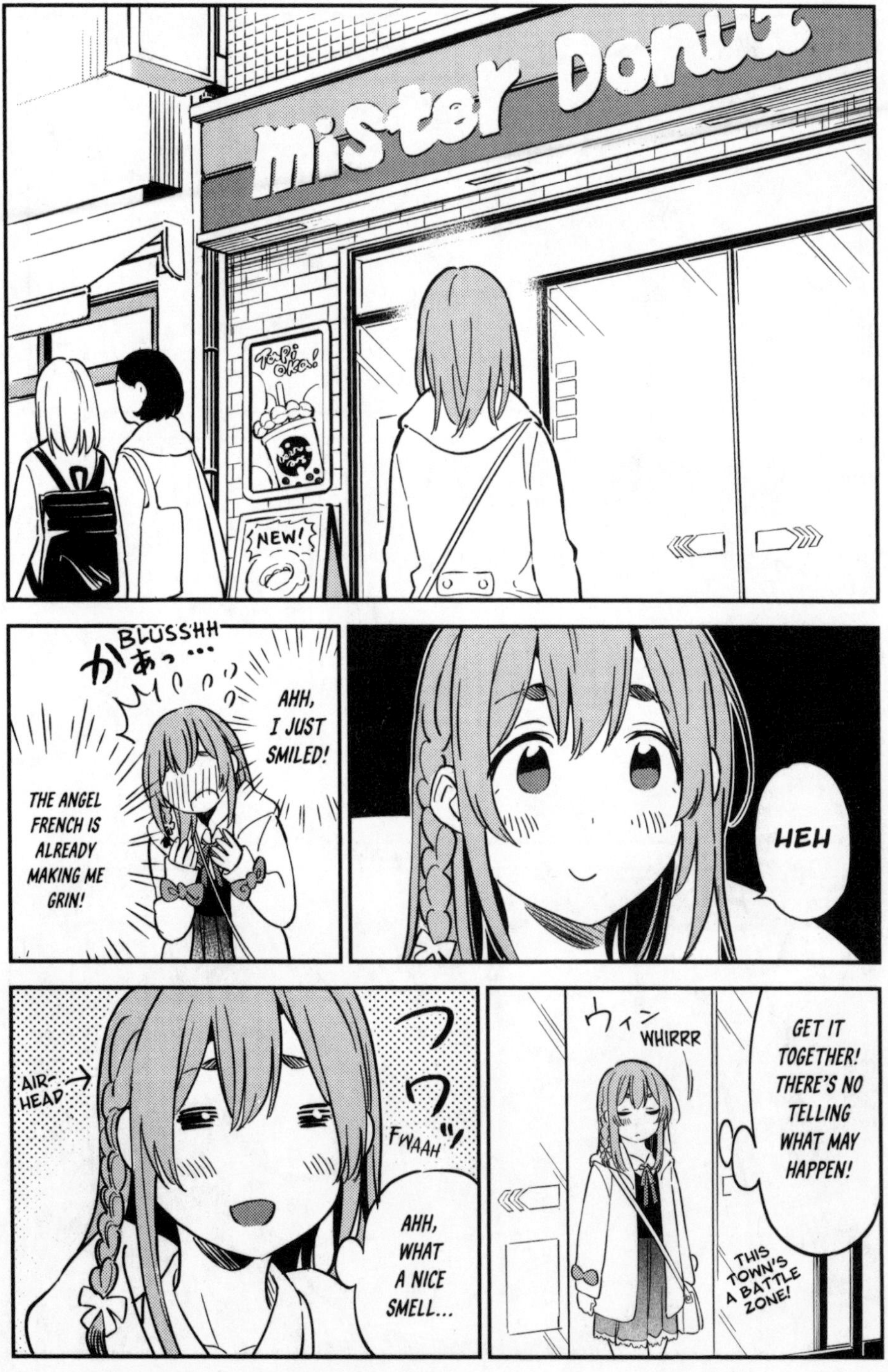
Tapi oka!
NEW!
HEH
かあっ…
BLUSSHH
AHH, I JUST SMILED!
THE ANGEL FRENCH IS ALREADY MAKING ME GRIN!
ウィン
WHIRRR
GET IT TOGETHER! THERE'S NO TELLING WHAT MAY HAPPEN!
THIS TOWN'S A BATTLE ZONE!
AIR-HEAD
フワァ
FWAAH
AHH, WHAT A NICE SMELL...

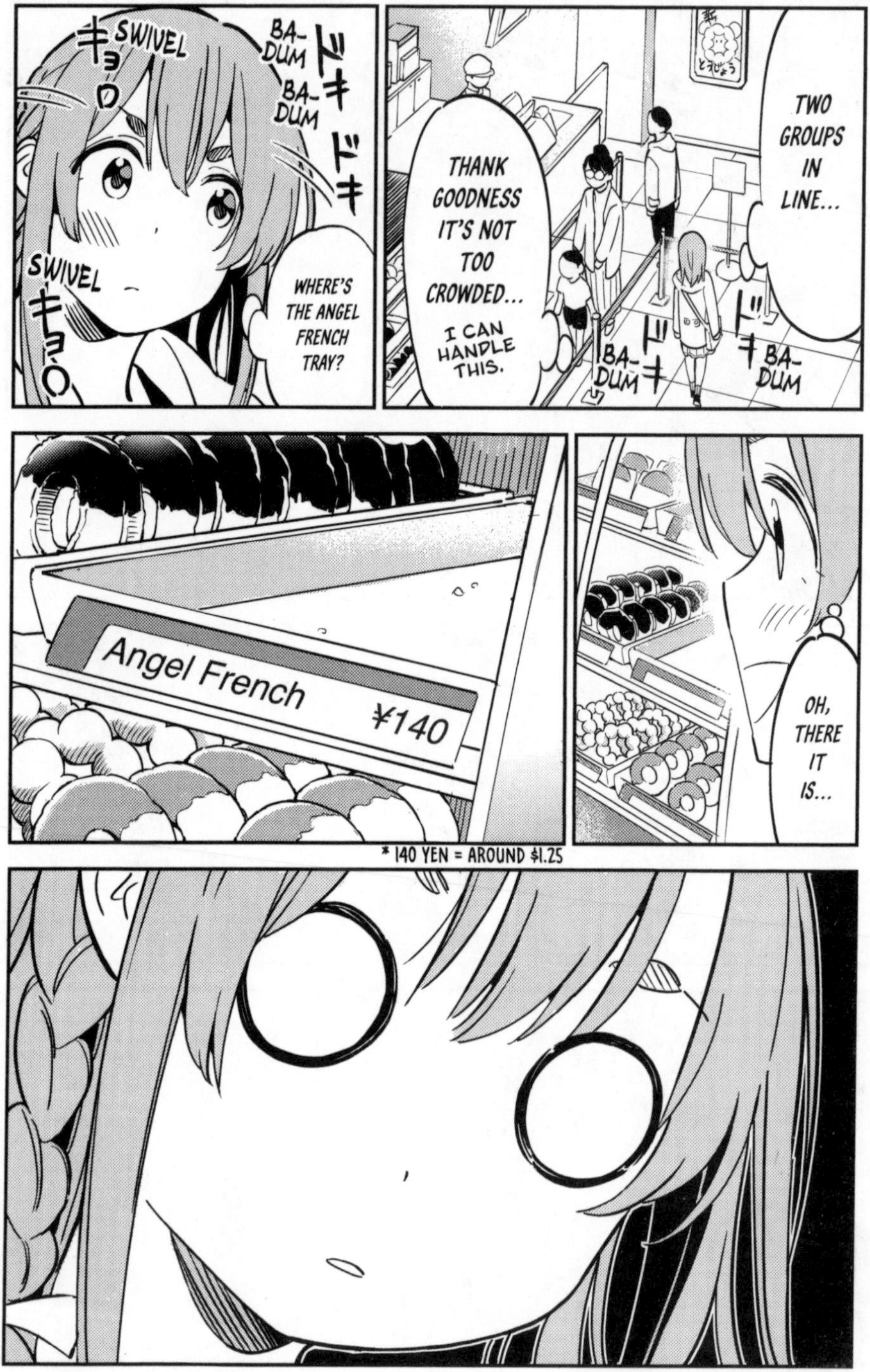
TWO GROUPS IN LINE...
THANK GOODNESS IT'S NOT TOO CROWDED...
I CAN HANDLE THIS.
ドキ BA-DUM
ドキ BA-DUM
キョロ SWIVEL
ドキ BA-DUM
ドキ BA-DUM
キョロ SWIVEL
WHERE'S THE ANGEL FRENCH TRAY?
OH, THERE IT IS...
Angel French ¥140
* 140 YEN = AROUND $1.25

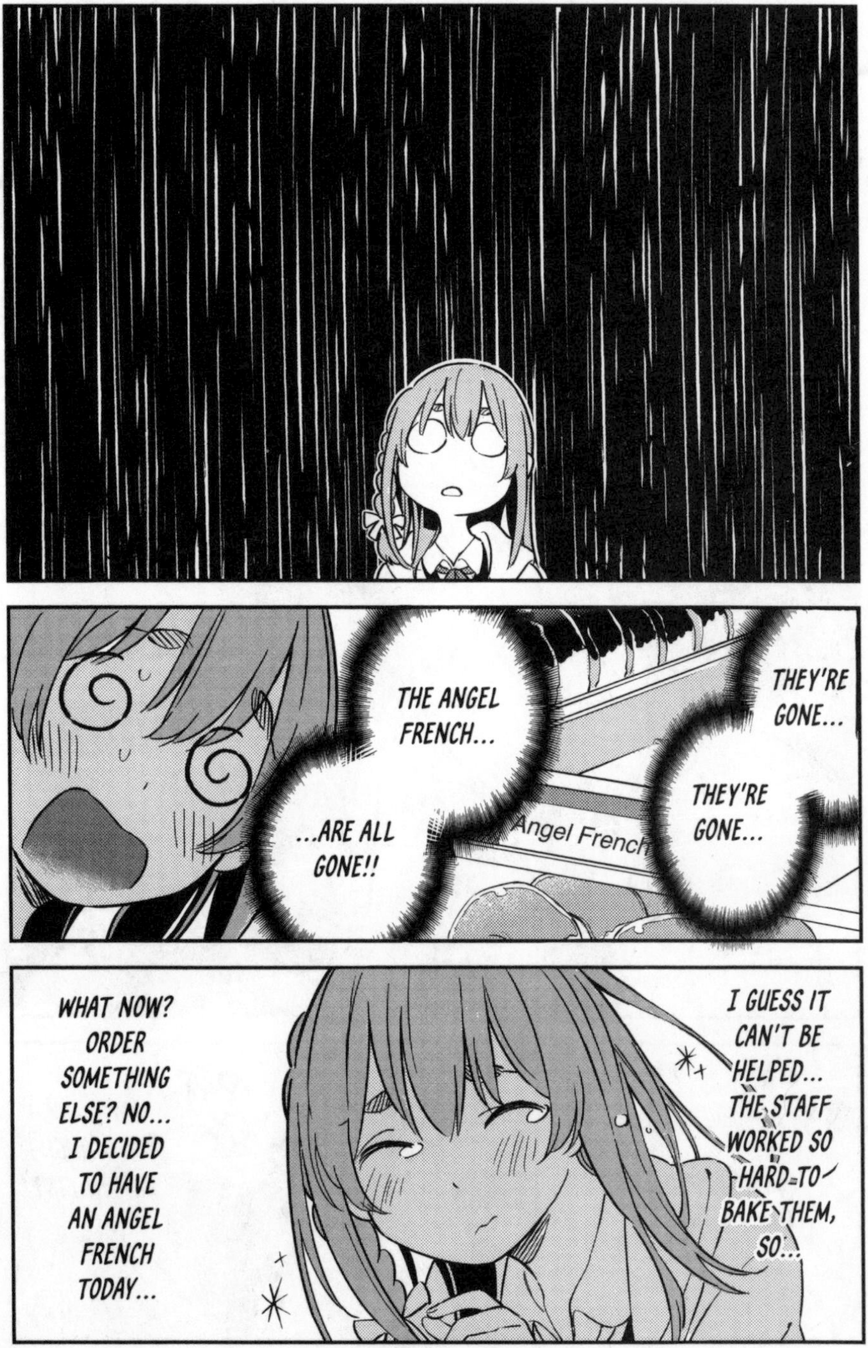

THEY'RE GONE...
THE ANGEL FRENCH...
THEY'RE GONE...
...ARE ALL GONE!!
Angel French
I GUESS IT CAN'T BE HELPED... THE STAFF WORKED SO HARD TO BAKE THEM, SO...
WHAT NOW? ORDER SOMETHING ELSE? NO... I DECIDED TO HAVE AN ANGEL FRENCH TODAY...

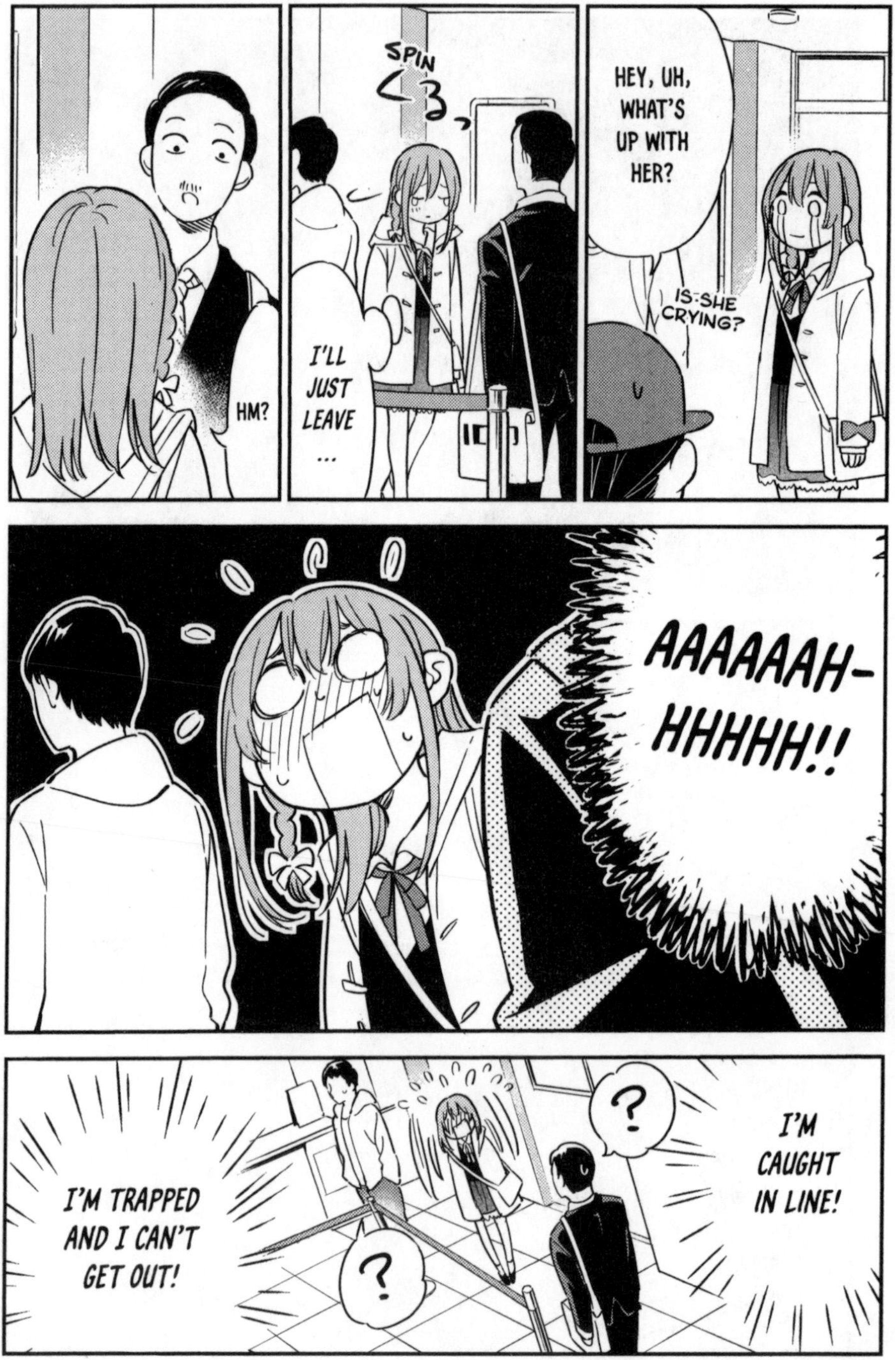
HEY, UH, WHAT'S UP WITH HER?
IS SHE CRYING?
SPIN
くる
I'LL JUST LEAVE ...
HM?
AAAAAAH-HHHHH!!
I'M CAUGHT IN LINE!
?
?
I'M TRAPPED AND I CAN'T GET OUT!

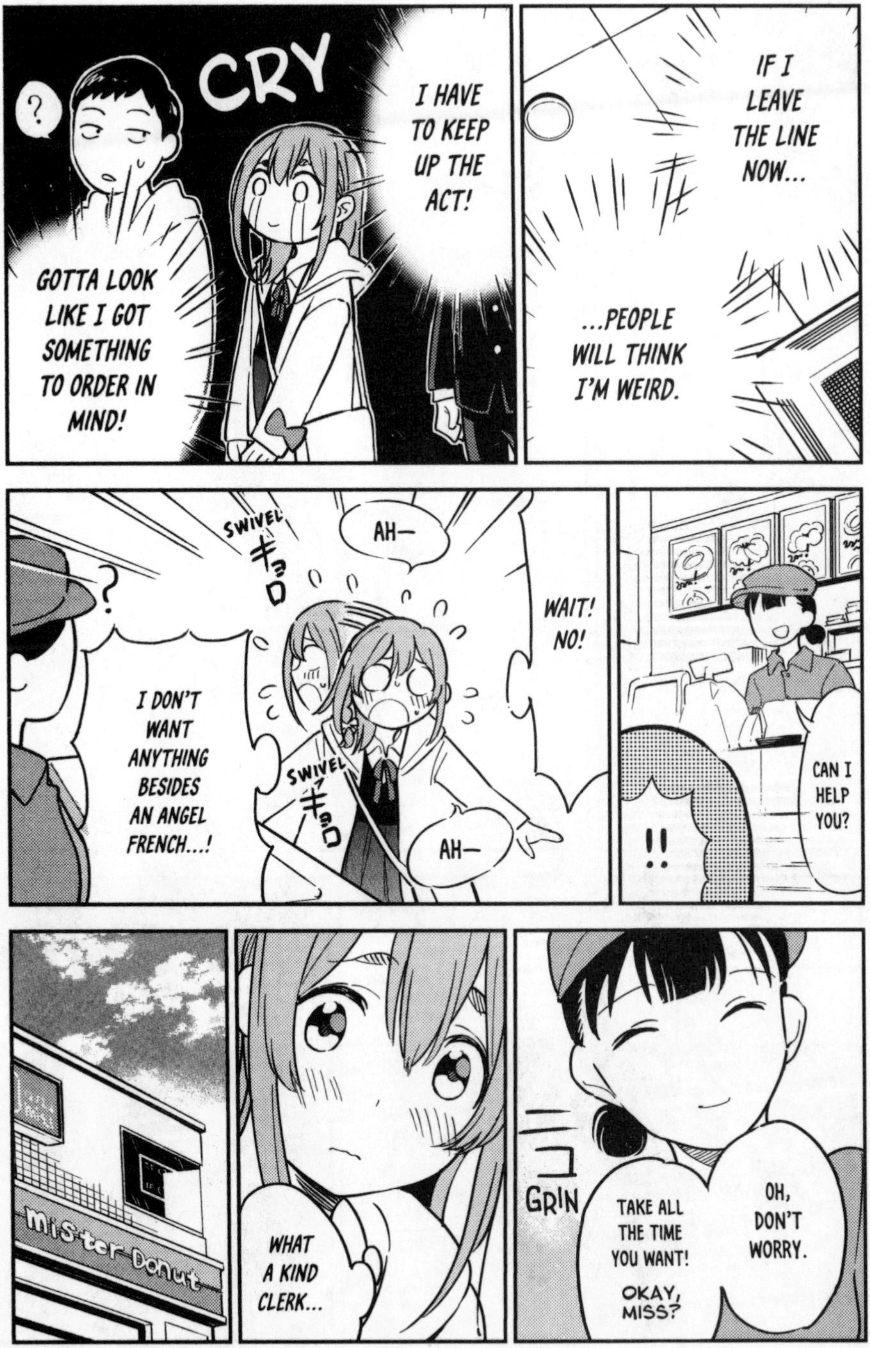
IF I LEAVE THE LINE NOW...
...PEOPLE WILL THINK I'M WEIRD.
CRY
I HAVE TO KEEP UP THE ACT!
?
GOTTA LOOK LIKE I GOT SOMETHING TO ORDER IN MIND!
CAN I HELP YOU?
!!
WAIT! NO!
AH—
SWIVEL
?
I DON'T WANT ANYTHING BESIDES AN ANGEL FRENCH...!
SWIVEL
AH—
OH, DON'T WORRY.
TAKE ALL THE TIME YOU WANT!
OKAY, MISS?
GRIN
WHAT A KIND CLERK...
mister Donut

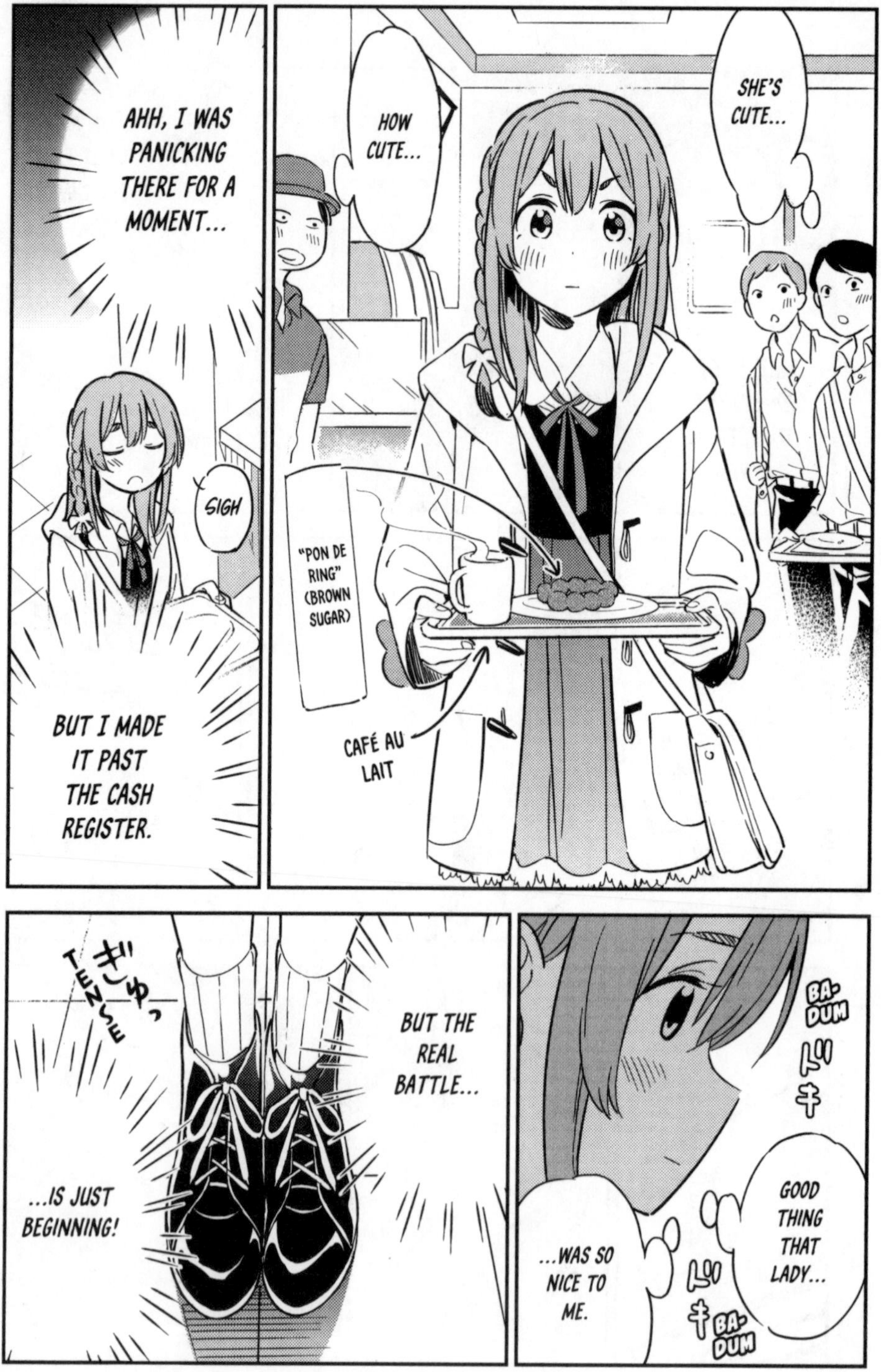
SHE'S CUTE...
HOW CUTE...
"PON DE RING" (BROWN SUGAR)
CAFÉ AU LAIT
AHH, I WAS PANICKING THERE FOR A MOMENT...
SIGH
BUT I MADE IT PAST THE CASH REGISTER.
BA-DUM
ドキ
GOOD THING THAT LADY...
...WAS SO NICE TO ME.
ドキ
BA-DUM
BUT THE REAL BATTLE...
ぎゅっ
TENSE
...IS JUST BEGINNING!

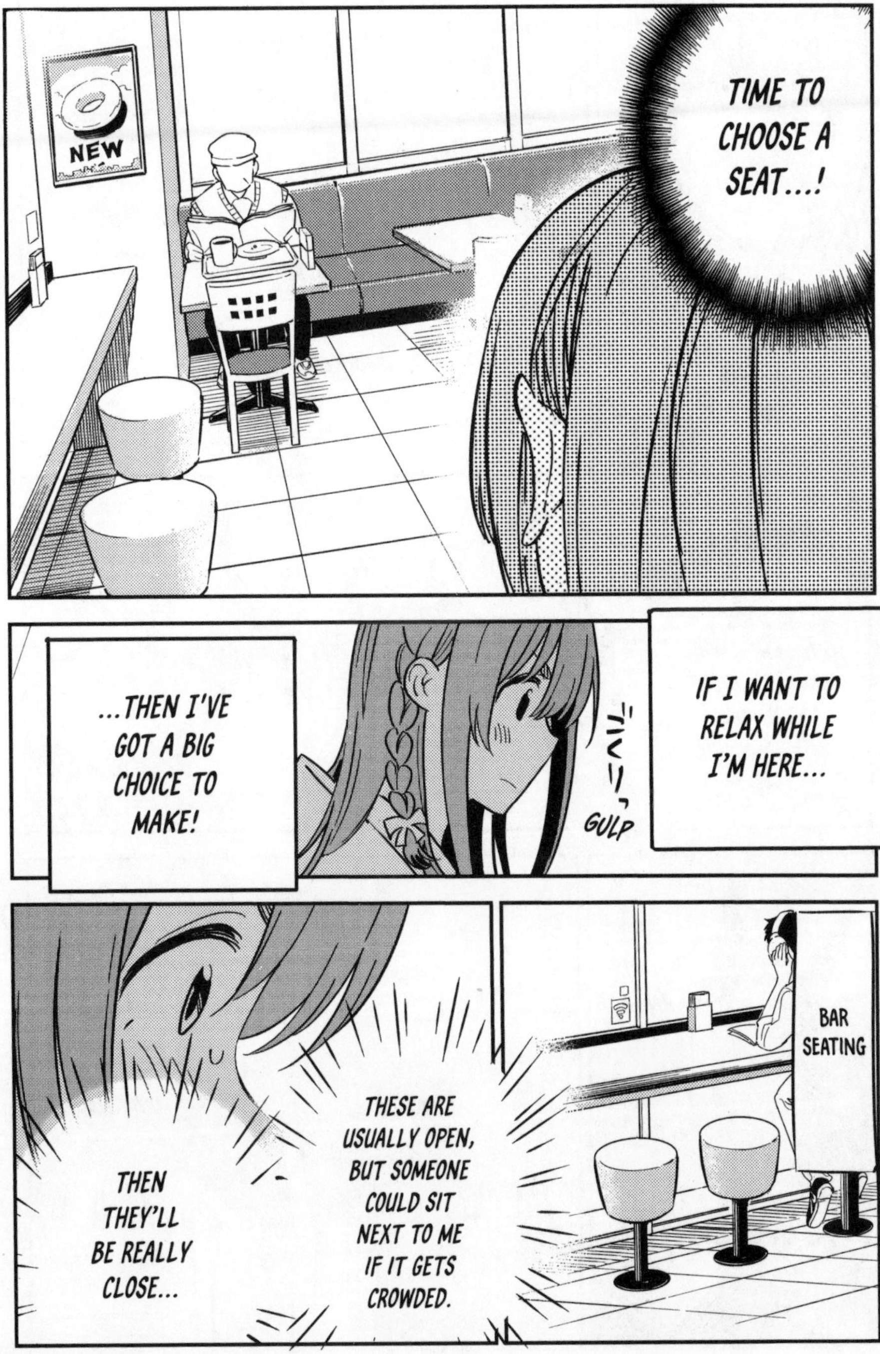
NEW
TIME TO CHOOSE A SEAT...!
IF I WANT TO RELAX WHILE I'M HERE...
GULP
...THEN I'VE GOT A BIG CHOICE TO MAKE!
BAR SEATING
THESE ARE USUALLY OPEN, BUT SOMEONE COULD SIT NEXT TO ME IF IT GETS CROWDED.
THEN THEY'LL BE REALLY CLOSE...

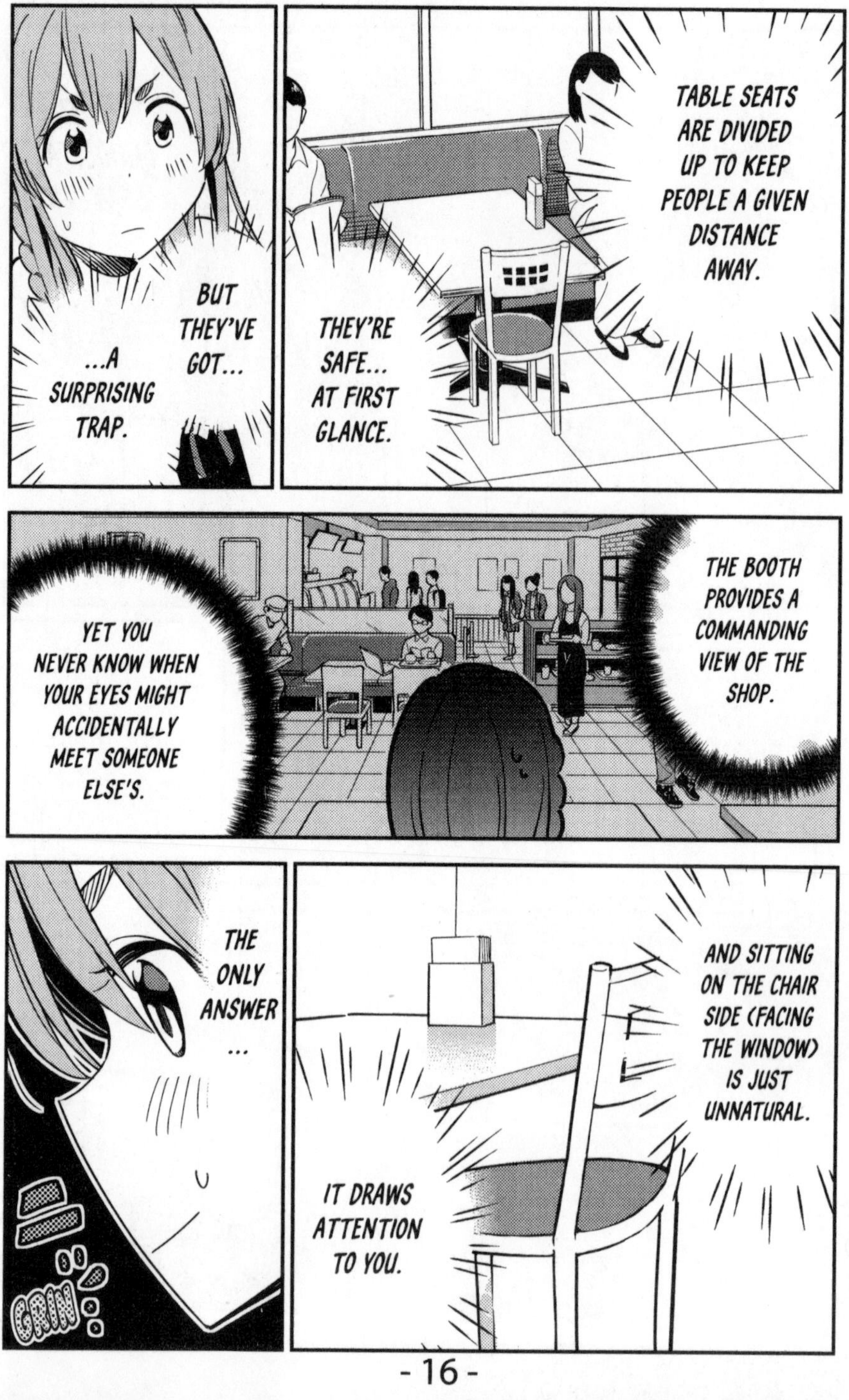
TABLE SEATS ARE DIVIDED UP TO KEEP PEOPLE A GIVEN DISTANCE AWAY.
THEY'RE SAFE... AT FIRST GLANCE.
BUT THEY'VE GOT...
...A SURPRISING TRAP.
THE BOOTH PROVIDES A COMMANDING VIEW OF THE SHOP.
YET YOU NEVER KNOW WHEN YOUR EYES MIGHT ACCIDENTALLY MEET SOMEONE ELSE'S.
AND SITTING ON THE CHAIR SIDE (FACING THE WINDOW) IS JUST UNNATURAL.
IT DRAWS ATTENTION TO YOU.
THE ONLY ANSWER ...
GRIN

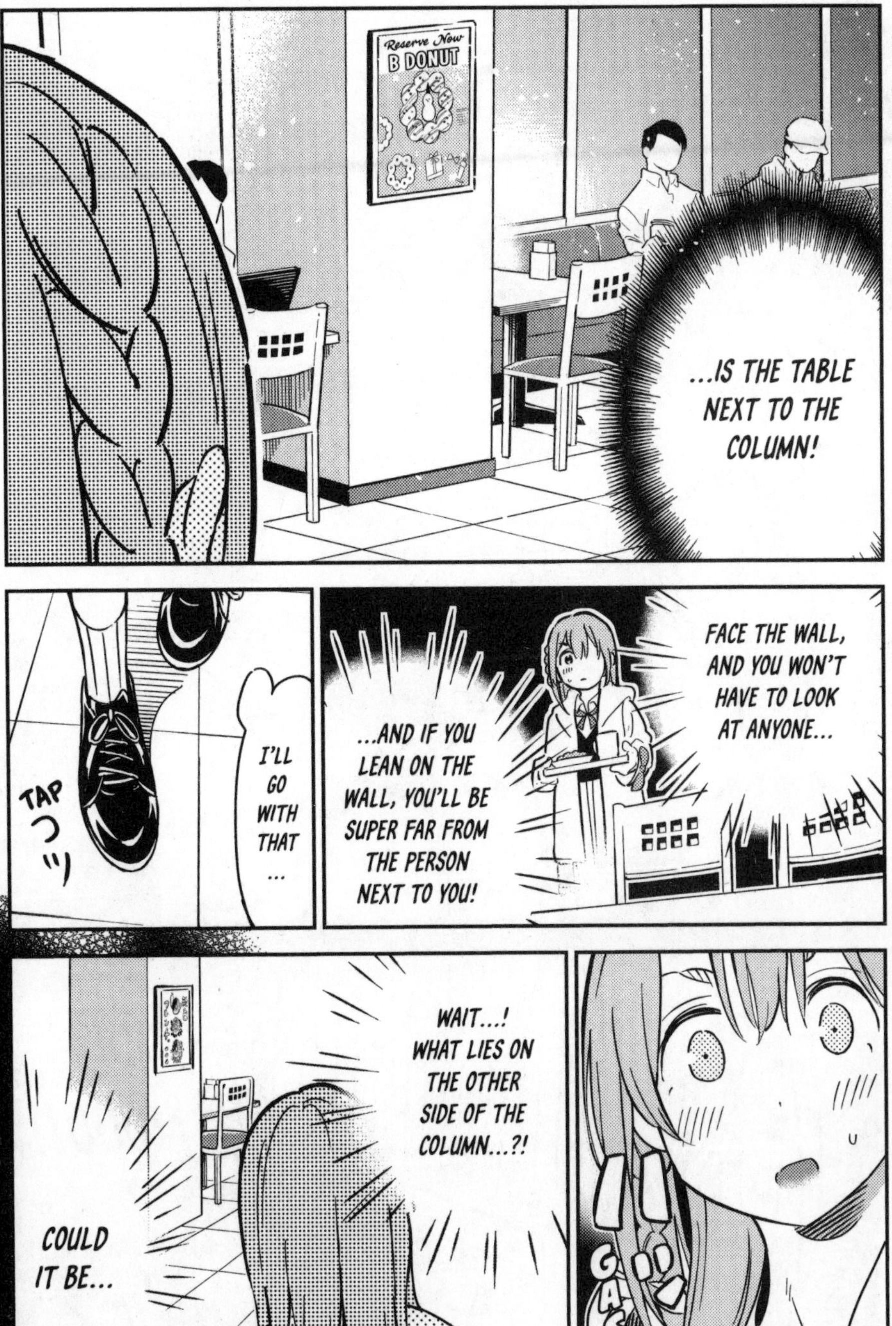
Reserve Now
B DONUT
...IS THE TABLE NEXT TO THE COLUMN!
FACE THE WALL, AND YOU WON'T HAVE TO LOOK AT ANYONE...
...AND IF YOU LEAN ON THE WALL, YOU'LL BE SUPER FAR FROM THE PERSON NEXT TO YOU!
I'LL GO WITH THAT ...
TAP
つッ
GASP
WAIT...! WHAT LIES ON THE OTHER SIDE OF THE COLUMN...?!
COULD IT BE...

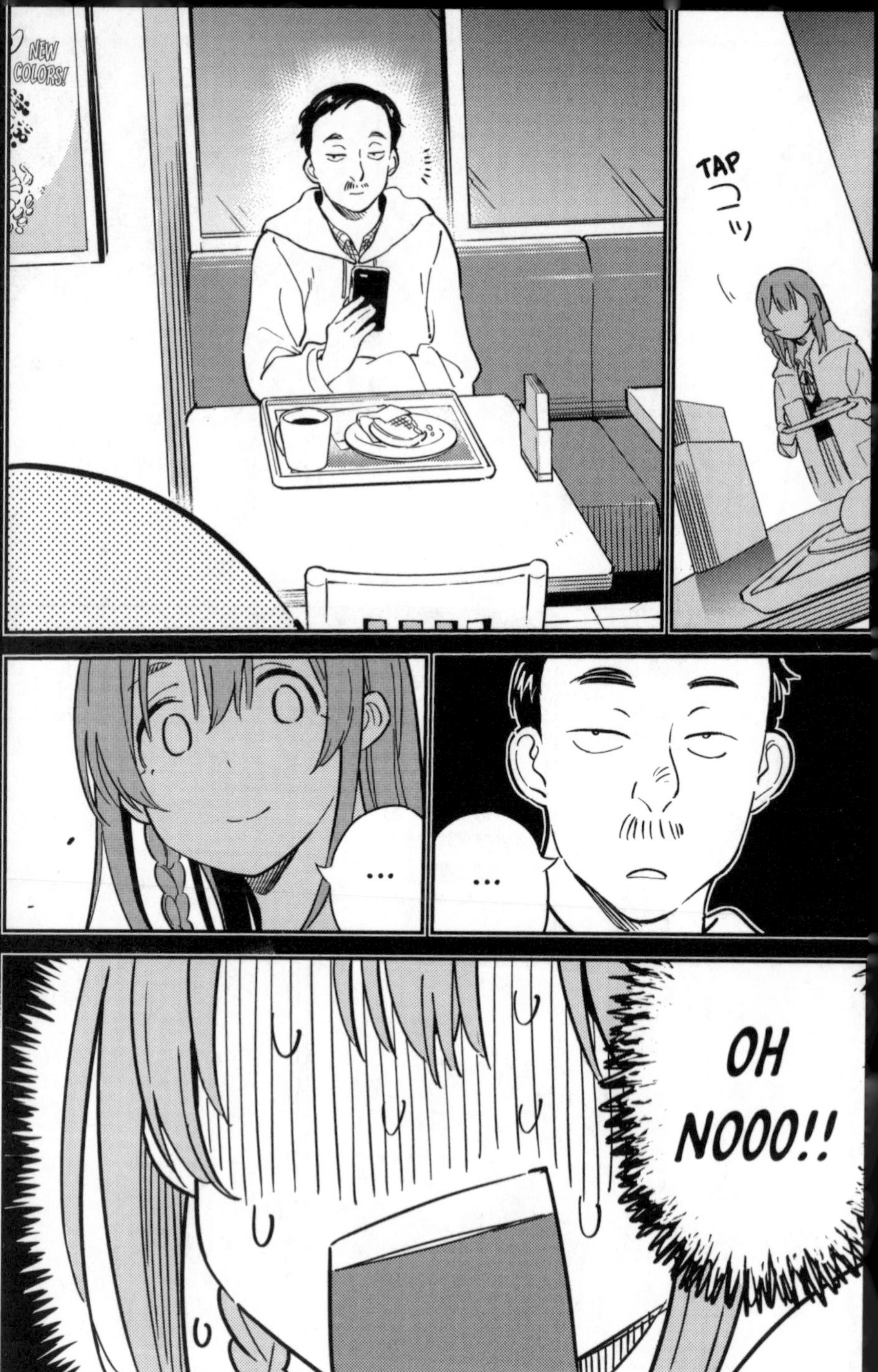
TAP
コッ
NEW COLORS!
...
...
OH NOOO!!

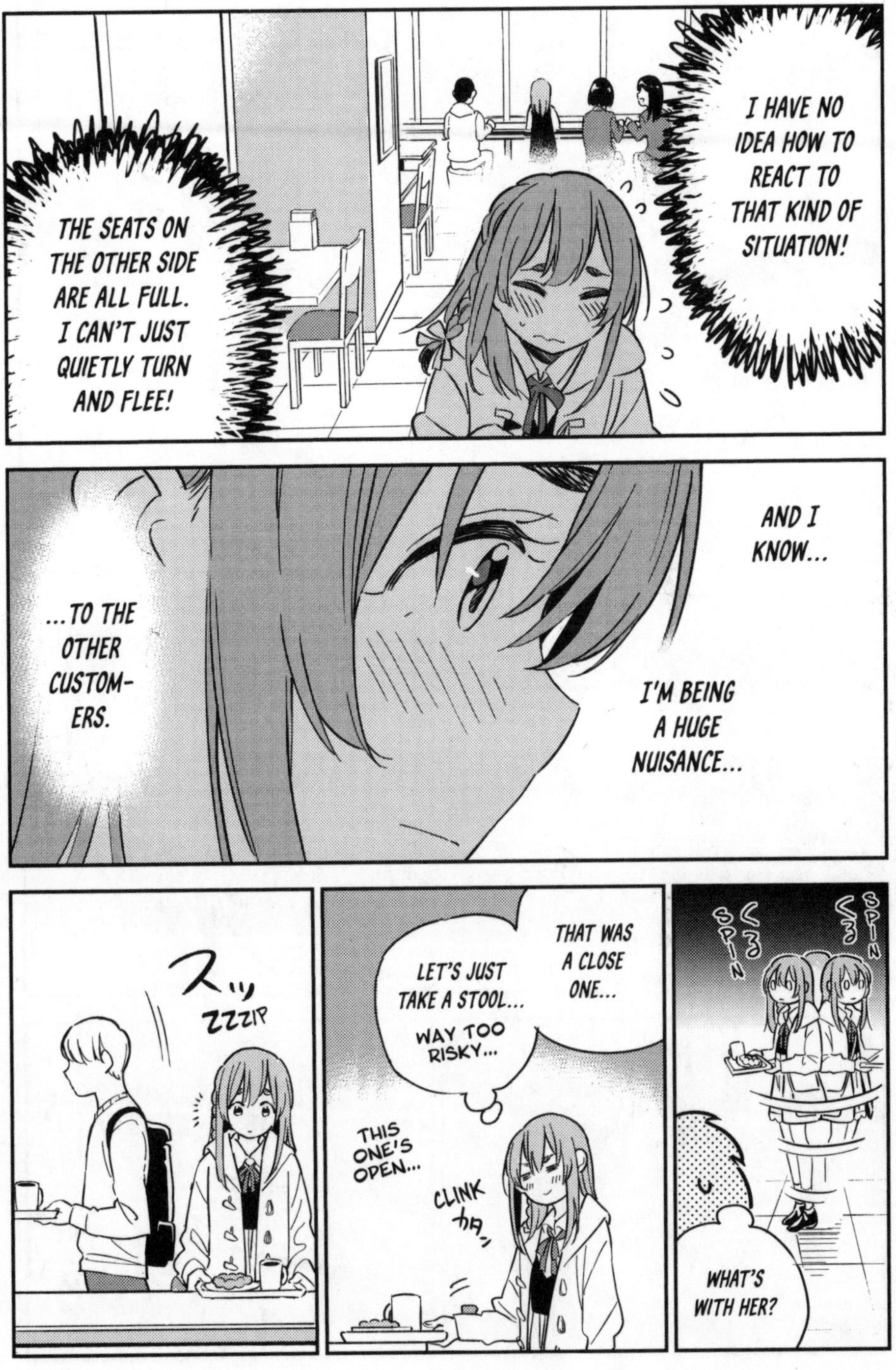
I HAVE NO IDEA HOW TO REACT TO THAT KIND OF SITUATION!
THE SEATS ON THE OTHER SIDE ARE ALL FULL. I CAN'T JUST QUIETLY TURN AND FLEE!
AND I KNOW...
I'M BEING A HUGE NUISANCE...
...TO THE OTHER CUSTOMERS.
くる SPIN
くる SPIN
WHAT'S WITH HER?
THAT WAS A CLOSE ONE...
LET'S JUST TAKE A STOOL... WAY TOO RISKY...
THIS ONE'S OPEN...
CLINK カタッ
スッ ZZZIP

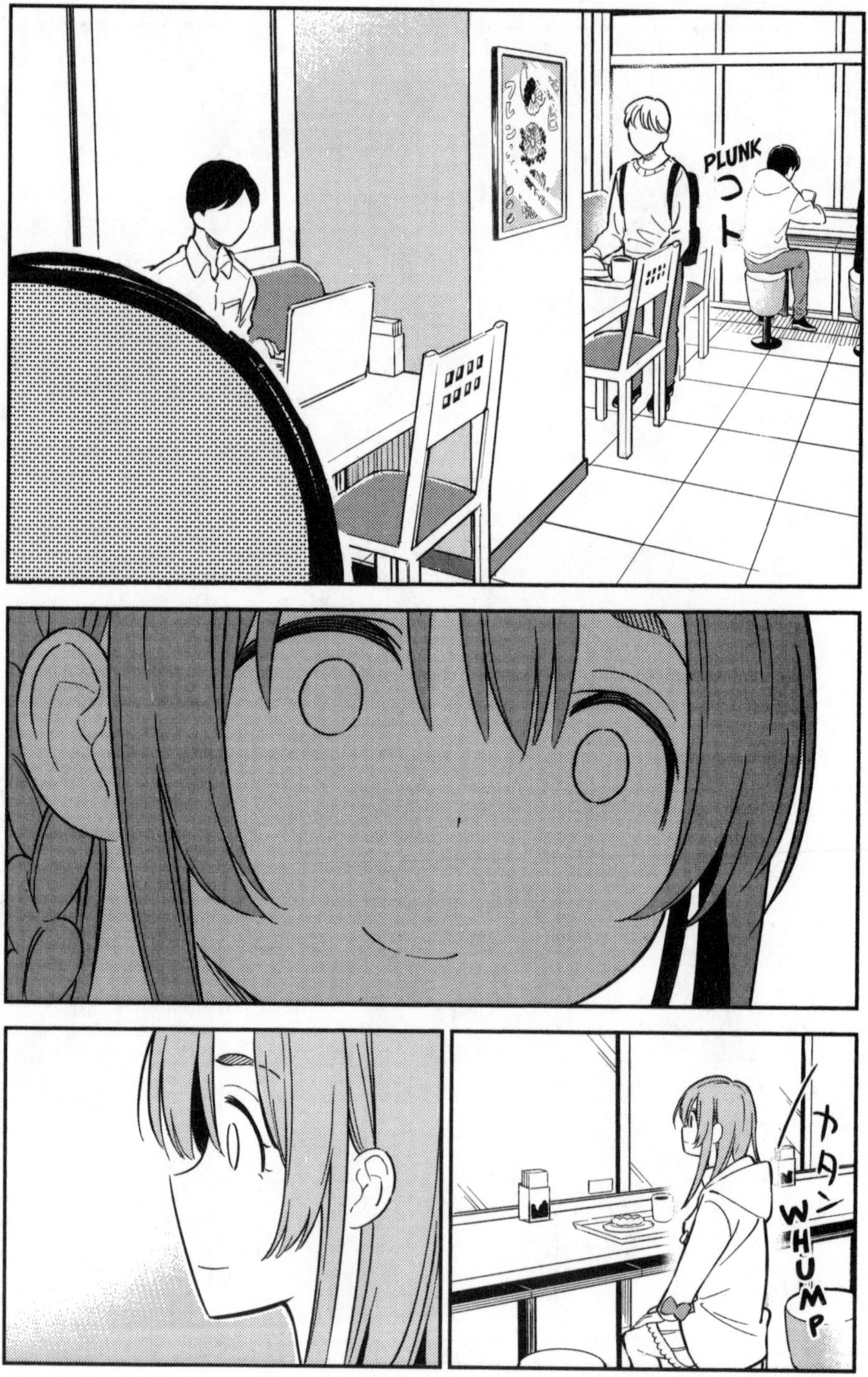
PLUNK
コト
カタン
WHUMP

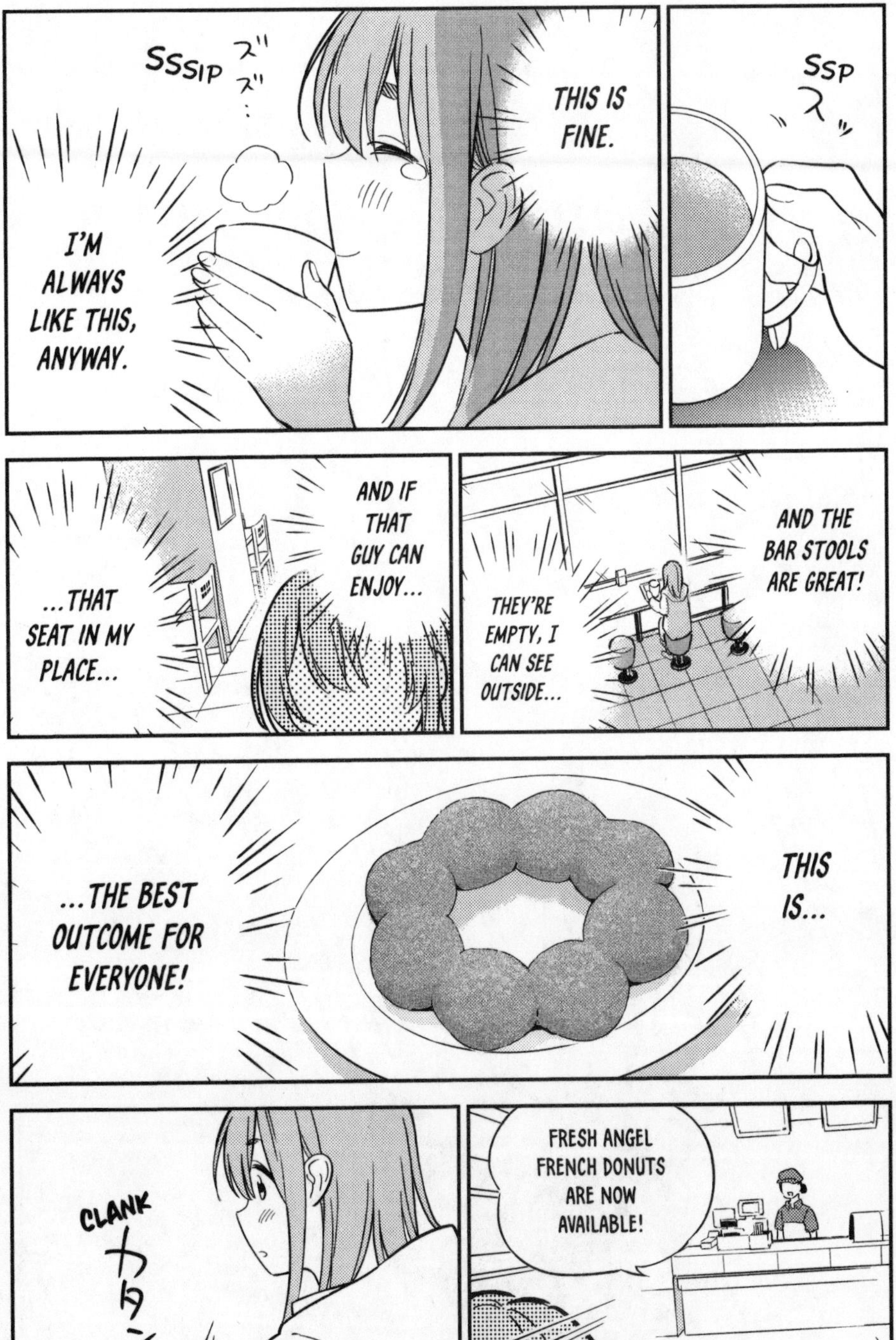
SSP
スッ
THIS IS FINE.
SSSIP
ズズ…
I'M ALWAYS LIKE THIS, ANYWAY.
AND THE BAR STOOLS ARE GREAT!
THEY'RE EMPTY, I CAN SEE OUTSIDE...
AND IF THAT GUY CAN ENJOY...
...THAT SEAT IN MY PLACE...
THIS IS...
...THE BEST OUTCOME FOR EVERYONE!
FRESH ANGEL FRENCH DONUTS ARE NOW AVAILABLE!
CLANK
カタン

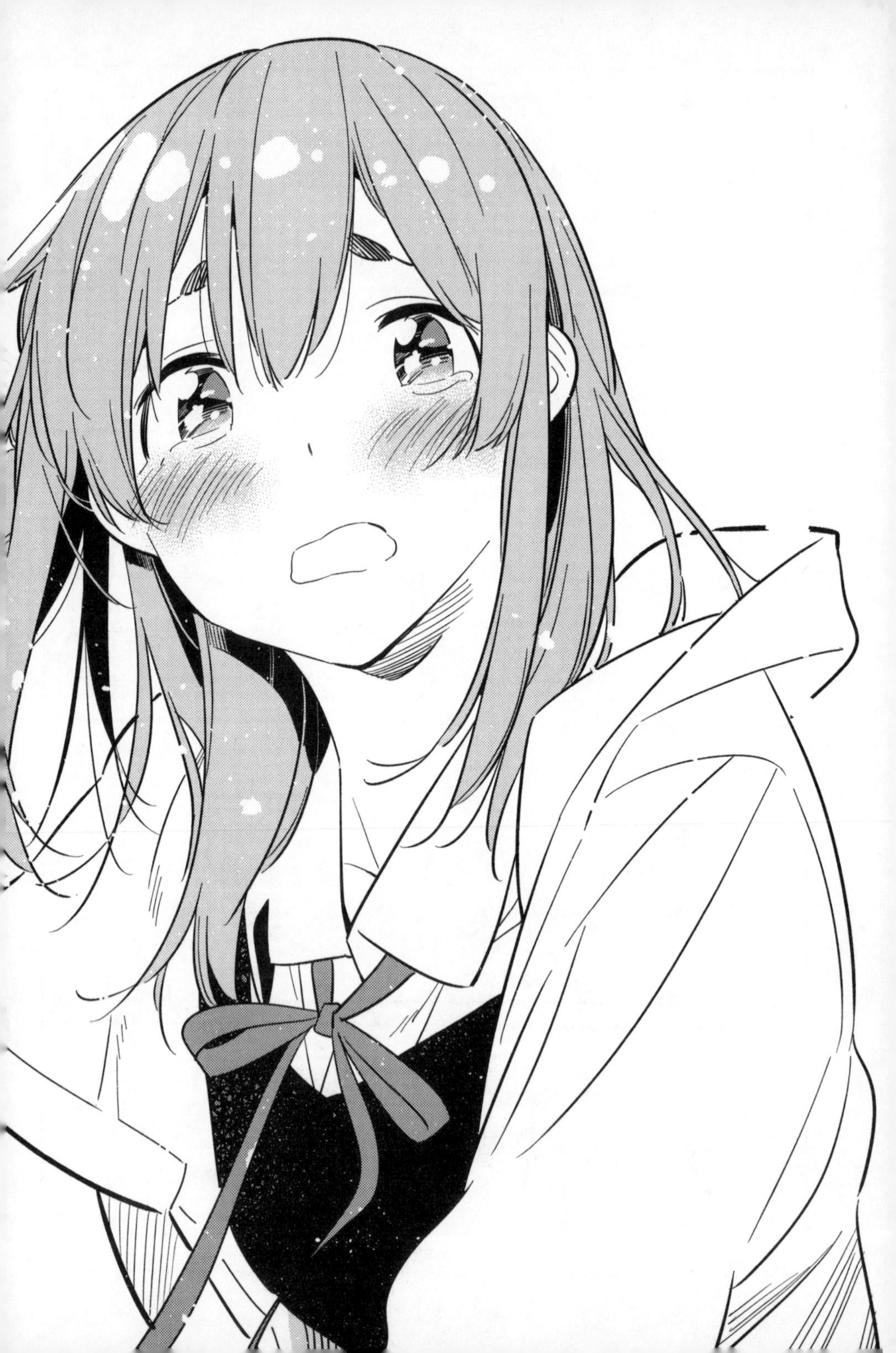

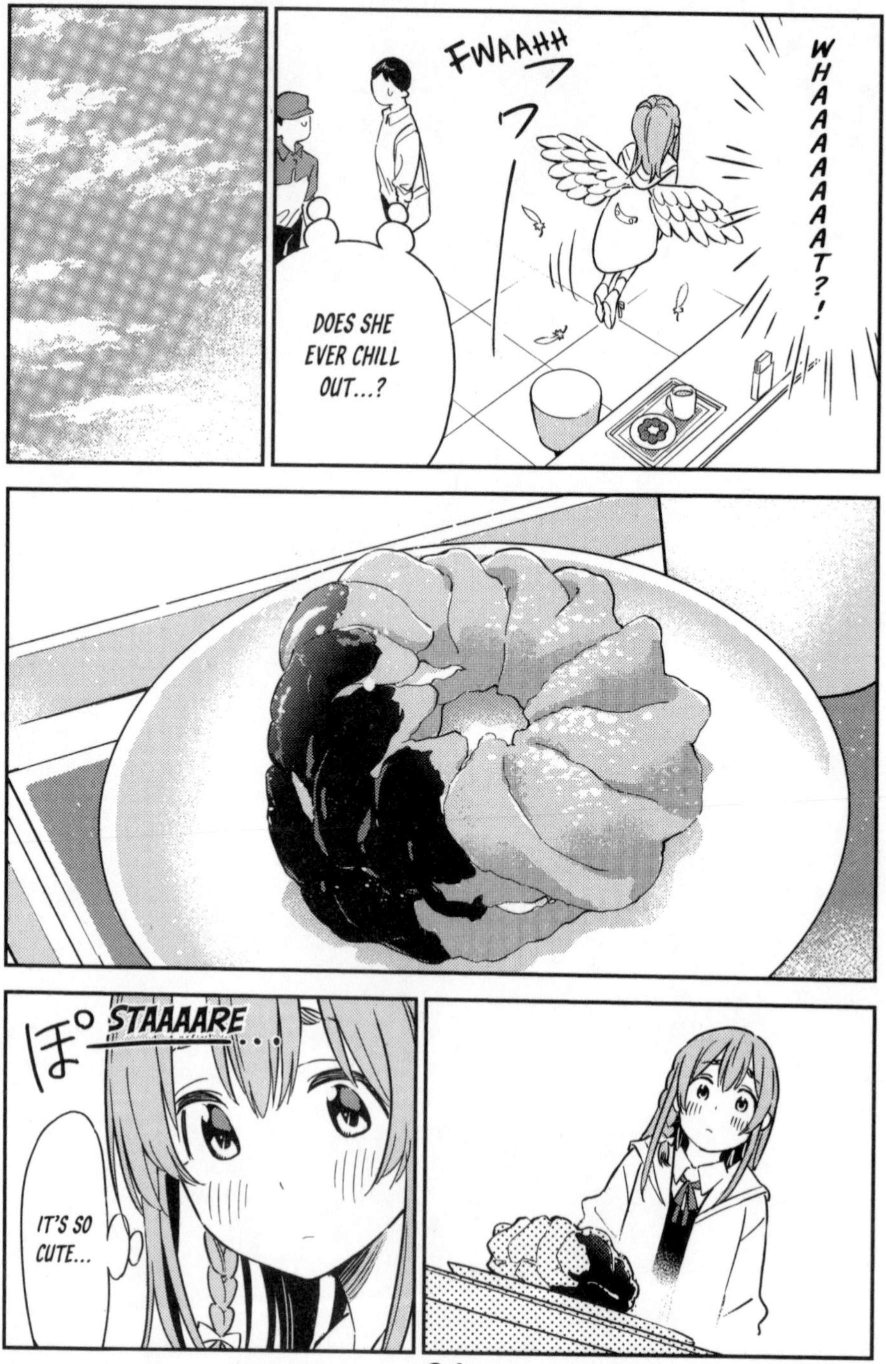
WHAAAAAAAAT?!
FWAAHH
DOES SHE EVER CHILL OUT...?
ぽ
STAAAARE...
IT'S SO CUTE...

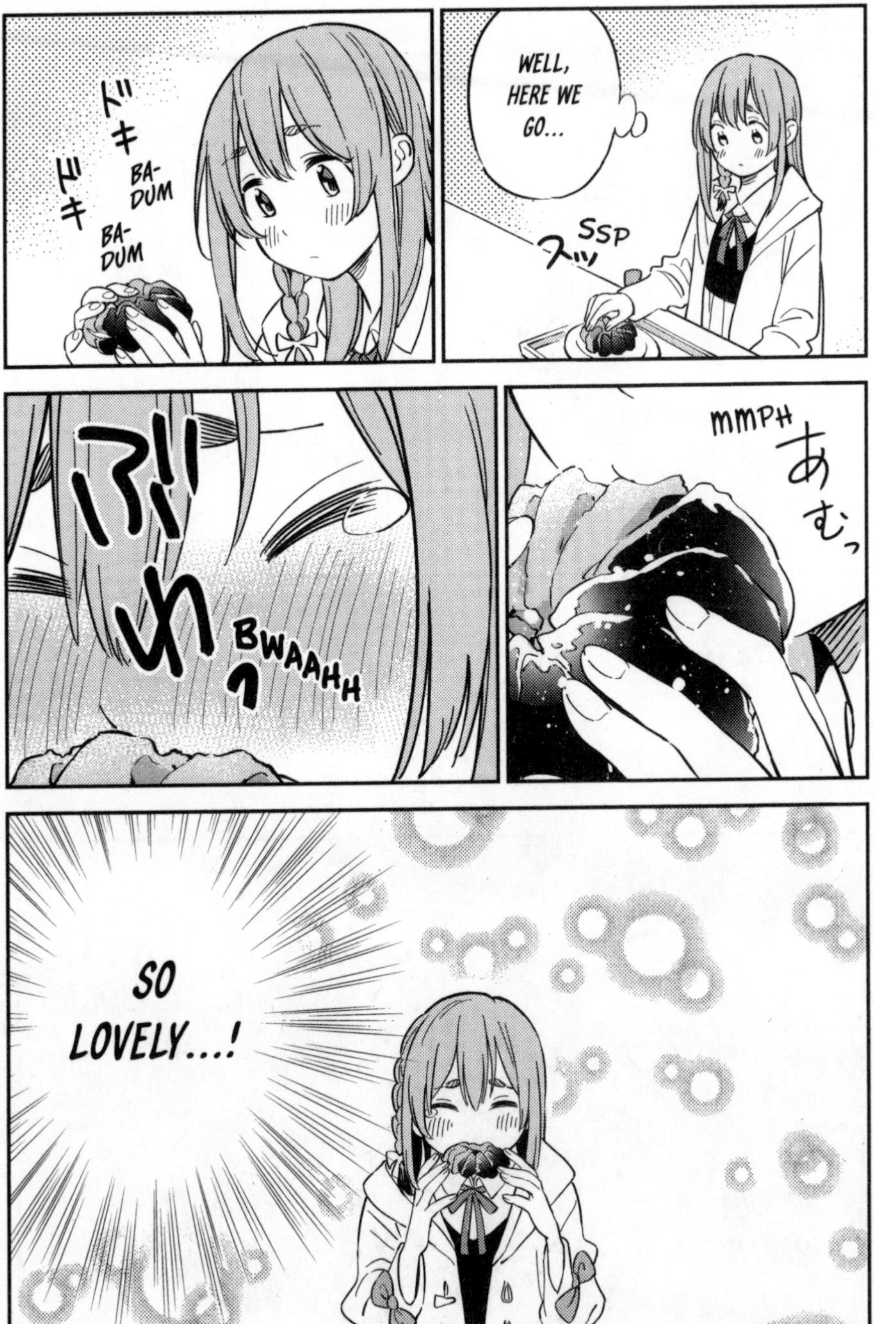

WELL, HERE WE GO...
SSP
スッ
ドキ
ドキ
BA-DUM
BA-DUM
MMPH
あむっ
ぶわっ
BWAAHH
SO LOVELY...!

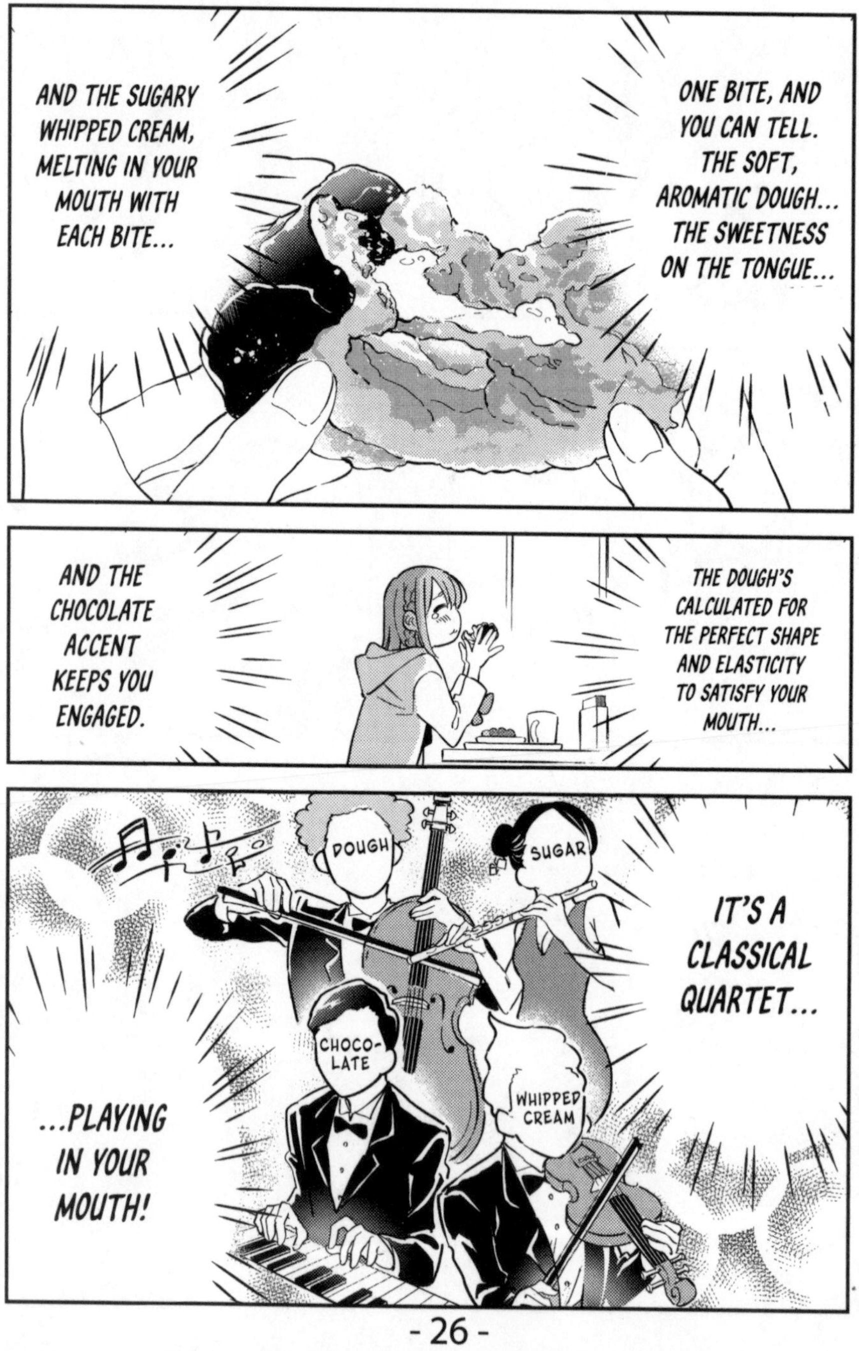
ONE BITE, AND YOU CAN TELL. THE SOFT, AROMATIC DOUGH... THE SWEETNESS ON THE TONGUE...
AND THE SUGARY WHIPPED CREAM, MELTING IN YOUR MOUTH WITH EACH BITE...
THE DOUGH'S CALCULATED FOR THE PERFECT SHAPE AND ELASTICITY TO SATISFY YOUR MOUTH...
AND THE CHOCOLATE ACCENT KEEPS YOU ENGAGED.
IT'S A CLASSICAL QUARTET...
SUGAR
DOUGH
CHOCO-LATE
WHIPPED CREAM
...PLAYING IN YOUR MOUTH!

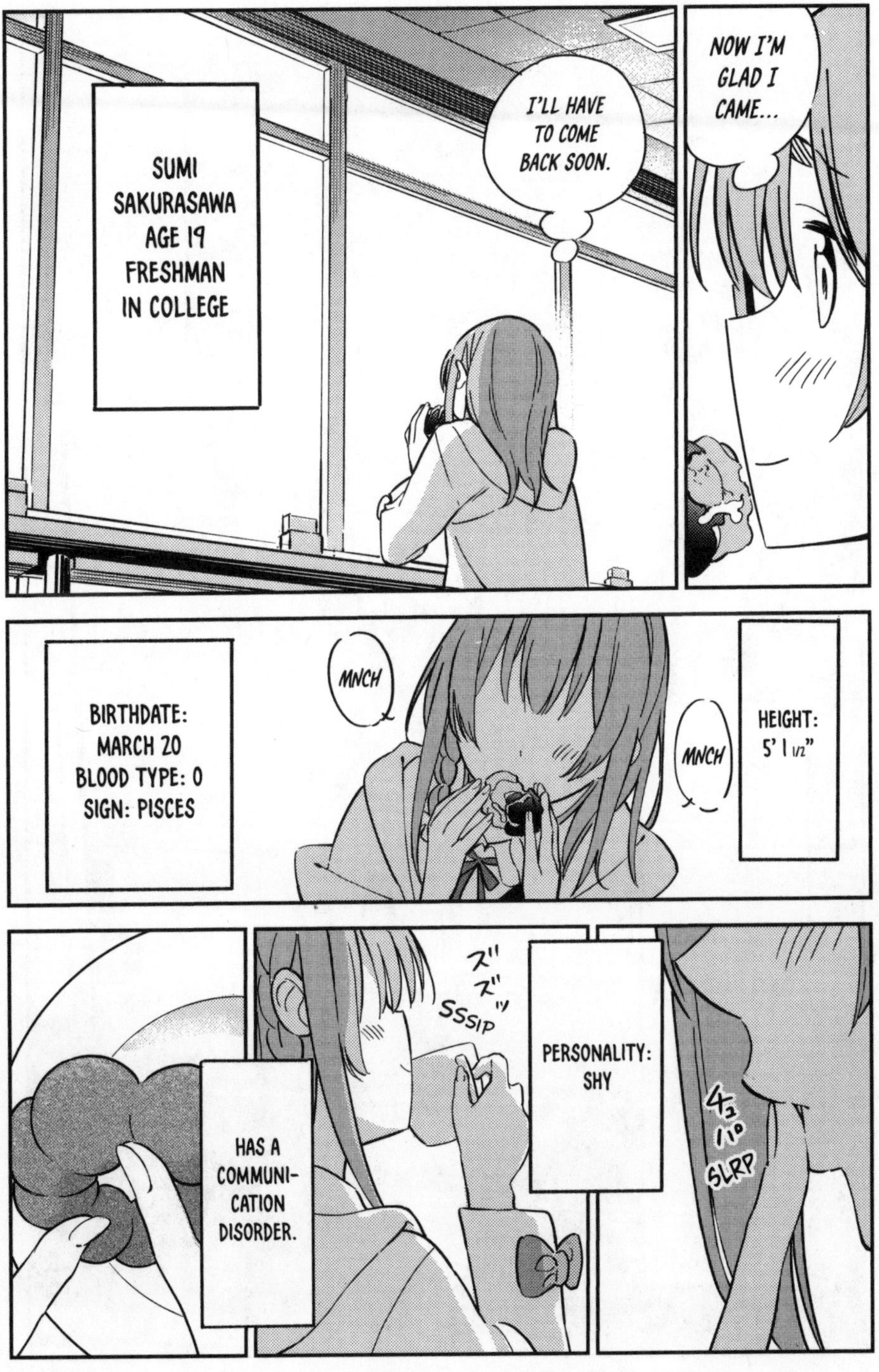
NOW I'M GLAD I CAME...
I'LL HAVE TO COME BACK SOON.
SUMI SAKURASAWA AGE 19 FRESHMAN IN COLLEGE
HEIGHT: 5' 1 1/2"
MNCH
MNCH
BIRTHDATE: MARCH 20 BLOOD TYPE: O SIGN: PISCES
PERSONALITY: SHY
チュパ
SLRP
ズズッ
SSSIP
HAS A COMMUNI-CATION DISORDER.

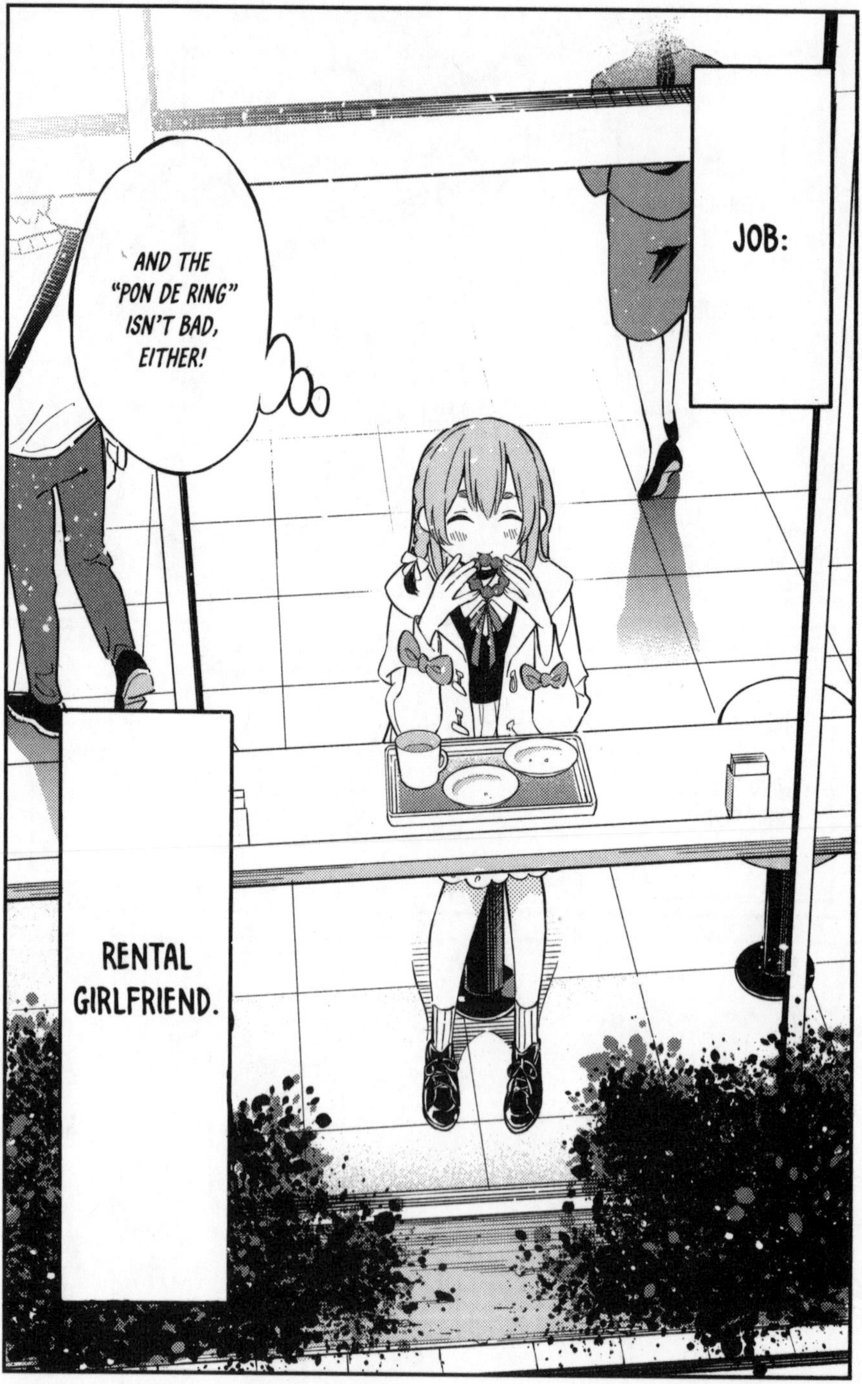
JOB:
AND THE "PON DE RING" ISN'T BAD, EITHER!
RENTAL GIRLFRIEND.

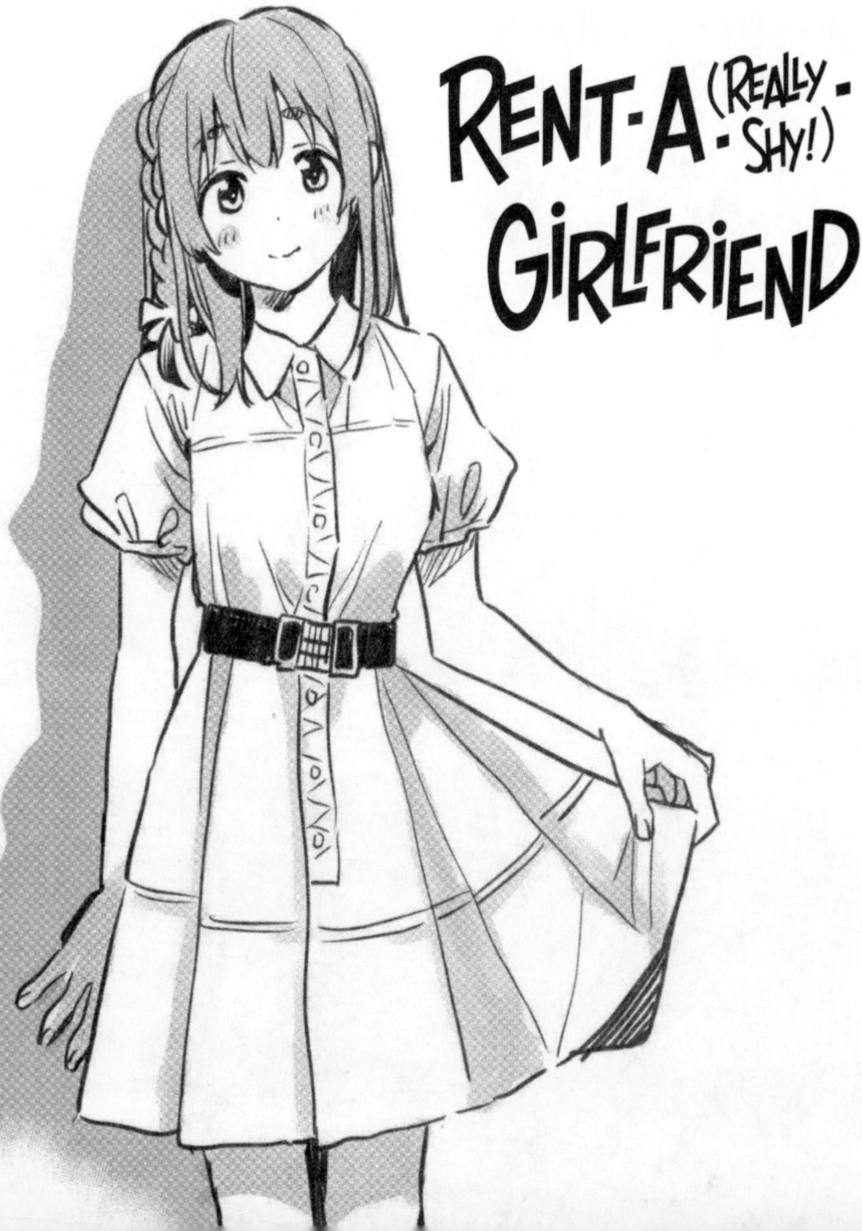
RENT-A-(REALLY-SHY!)-GIRLFRIEND

RENT-A-(REALLY-SHY!)-GIRLFRIEND

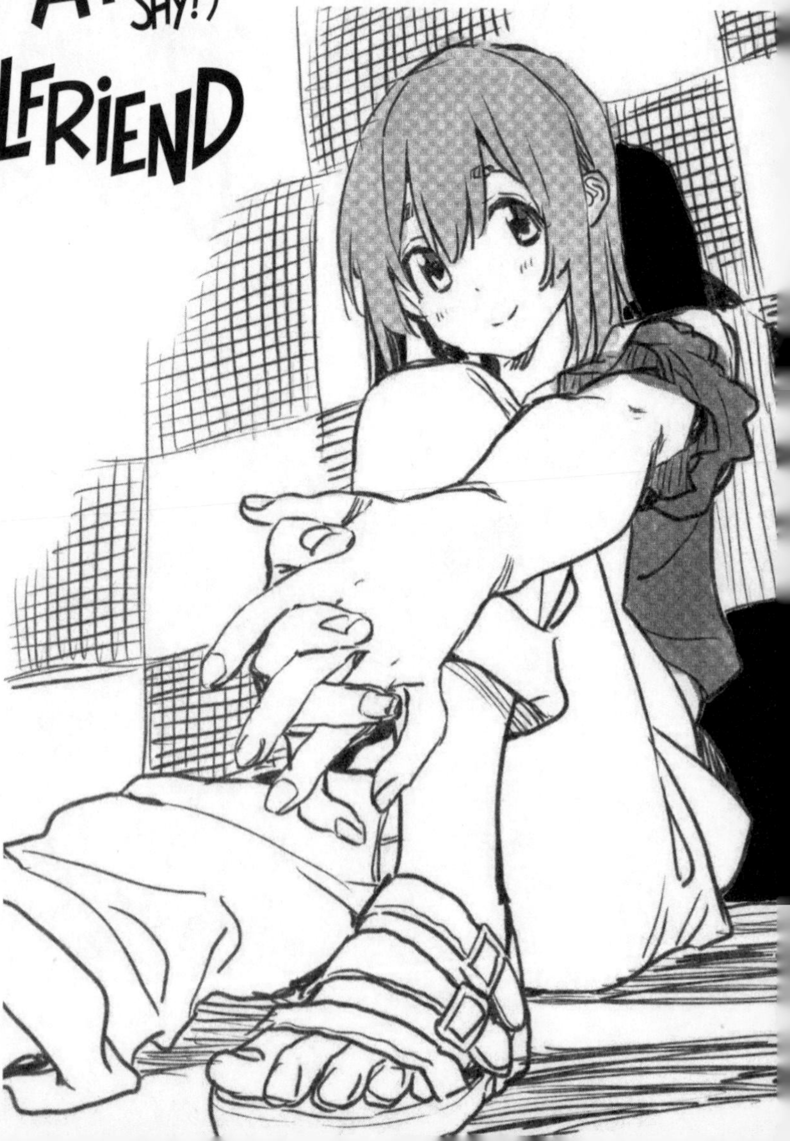

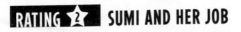

RATING 2 SUMI AND HER JOB

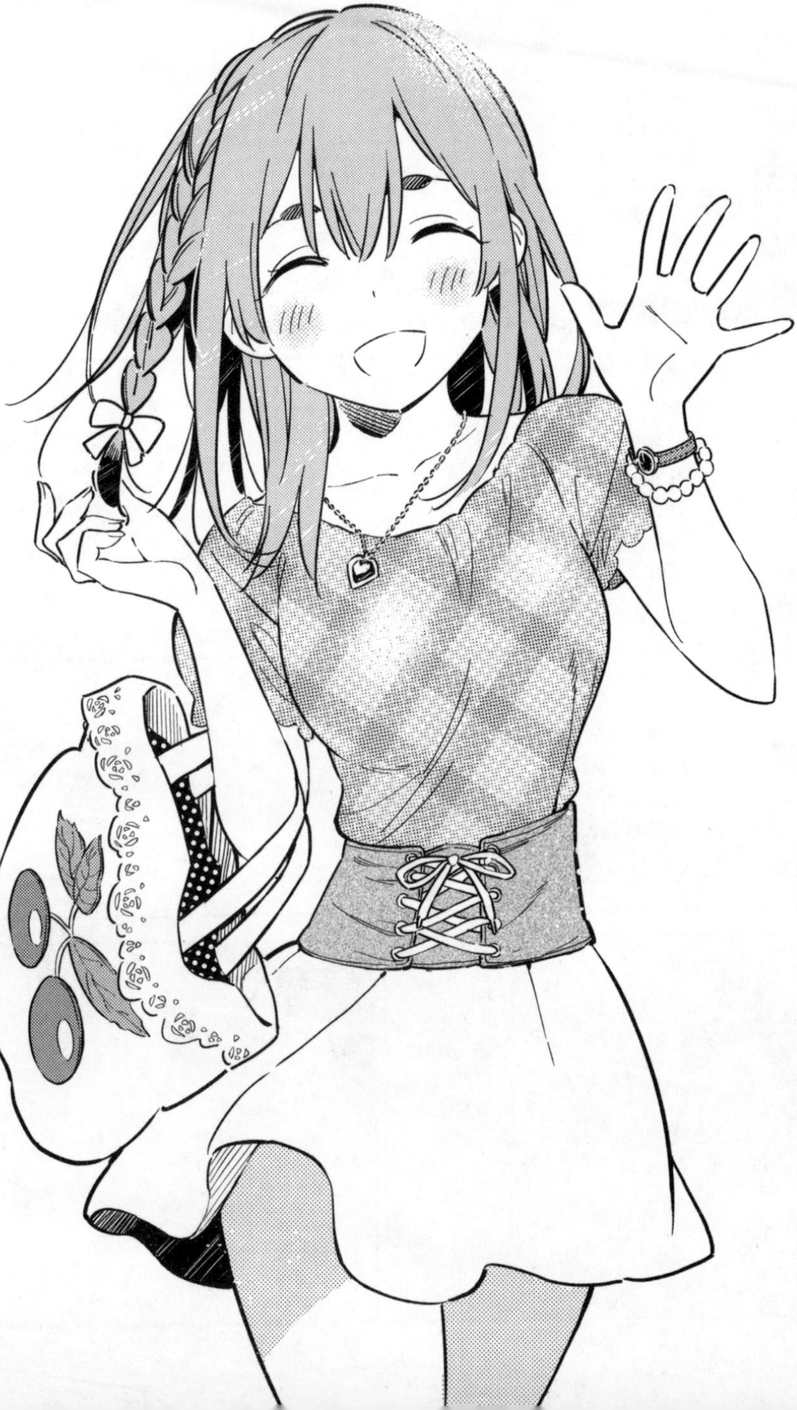

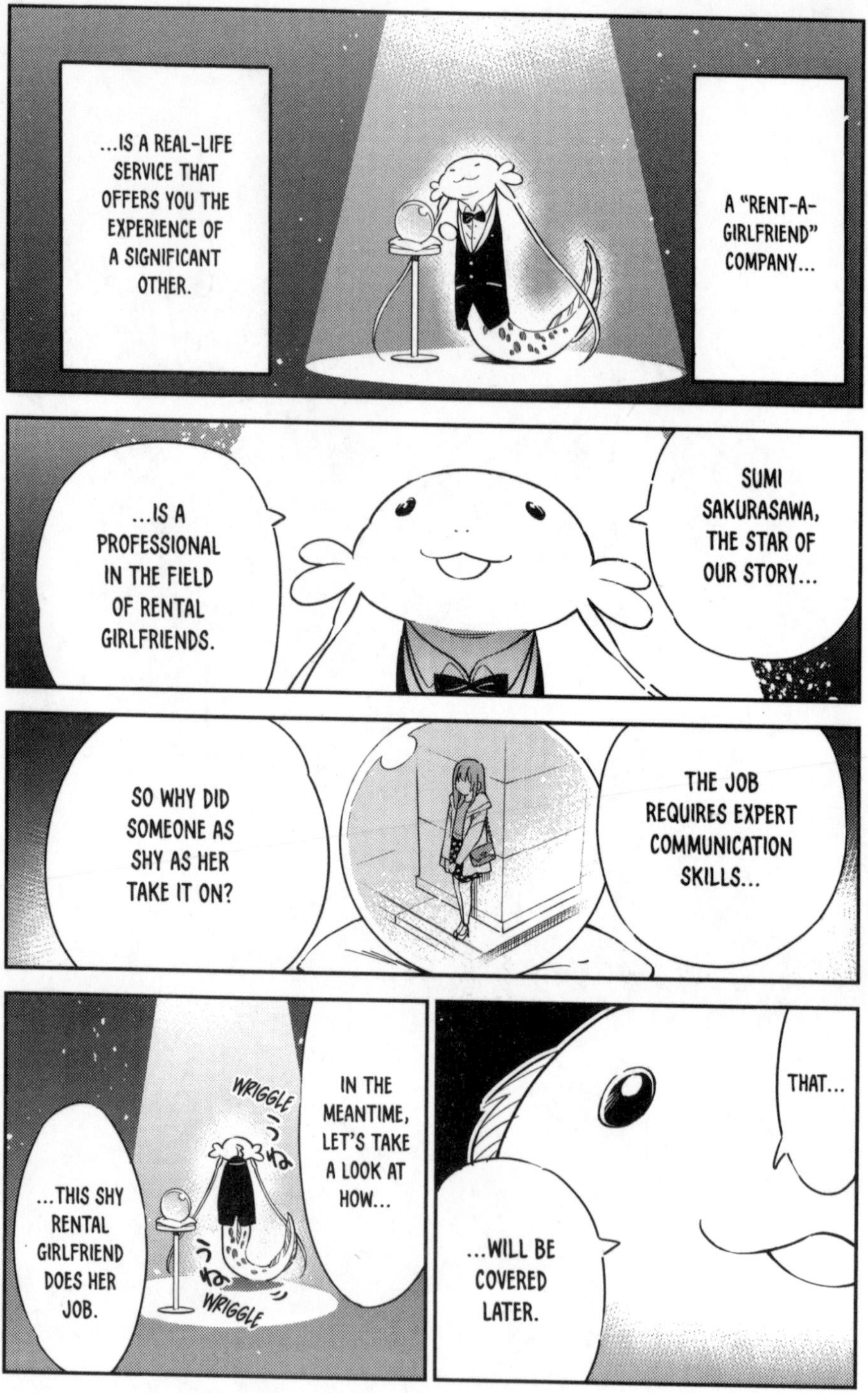
A "RENT-A-GIRLFRIEND" COMPANY...
...IS A REAL-LIFE SERVICE THAT OFFERS YOU THE EXPERIENCE OF A SIGNIFICANT OTHER.
SUMI SAKURASAWA, THE STAR OF OUR STORY...
...IS A PROFESSIONAL IN THE FIELD OF RENTAL GIRLFRIENDS.
THE JOB REQUIRES EXPERT COMMUNICATION SKILLS...
SO WHY DID SOMEONE AS SHY AS HER TAKE IT ON?
THAT...
...WILL BE COVERED LATER.
IN THE MEANTIME, LET'S TAKE A LOOK AT HOW...
...THIS SHY RENTAL GIRLFRIEND DOES HER JOB.
WRIGGLE うね
うね WRIGGLE

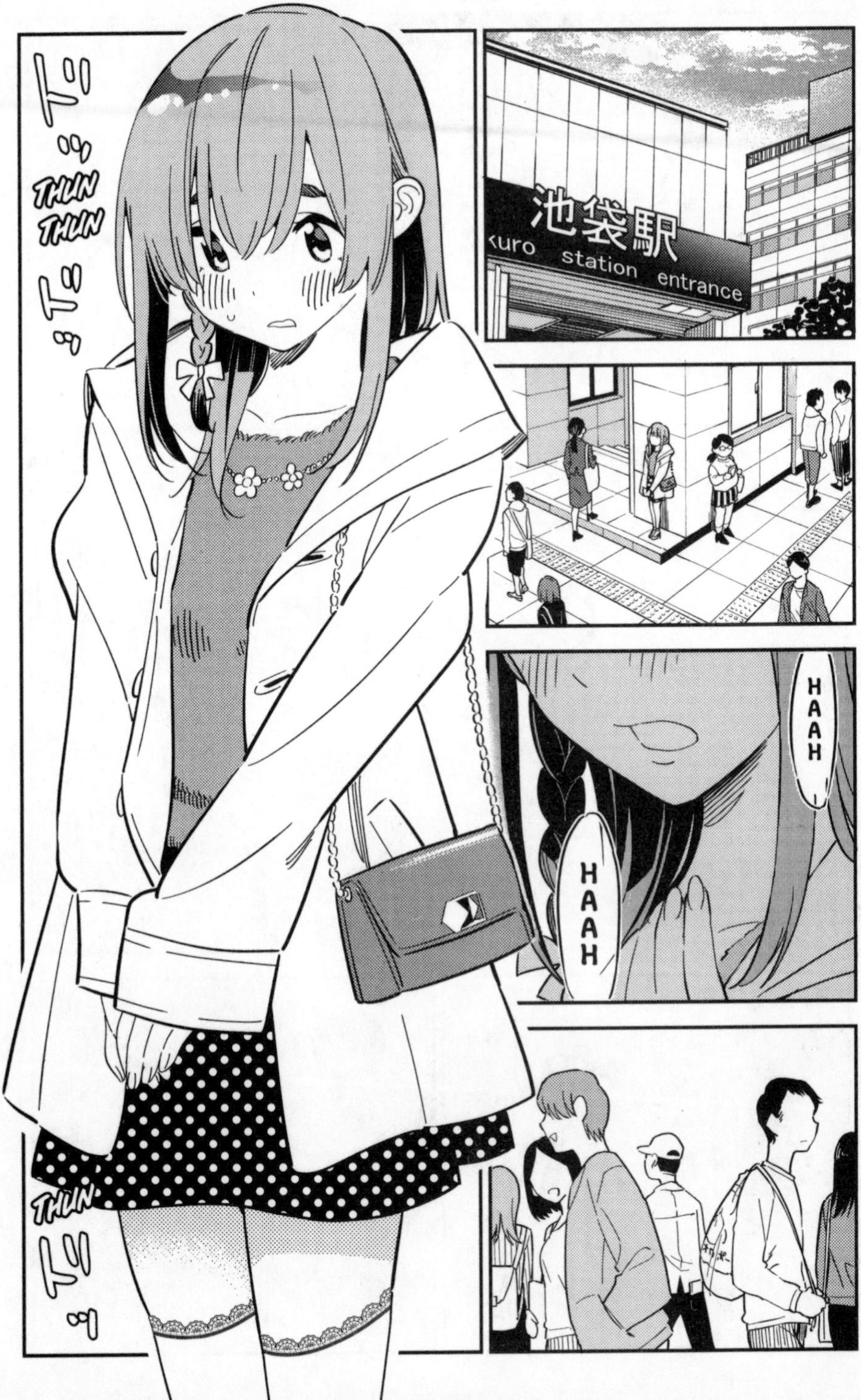
池袋駅
kuro station entrance
HAAH
HAAH
ドッ
THUN THUN
ドッ
THUN
ドッ

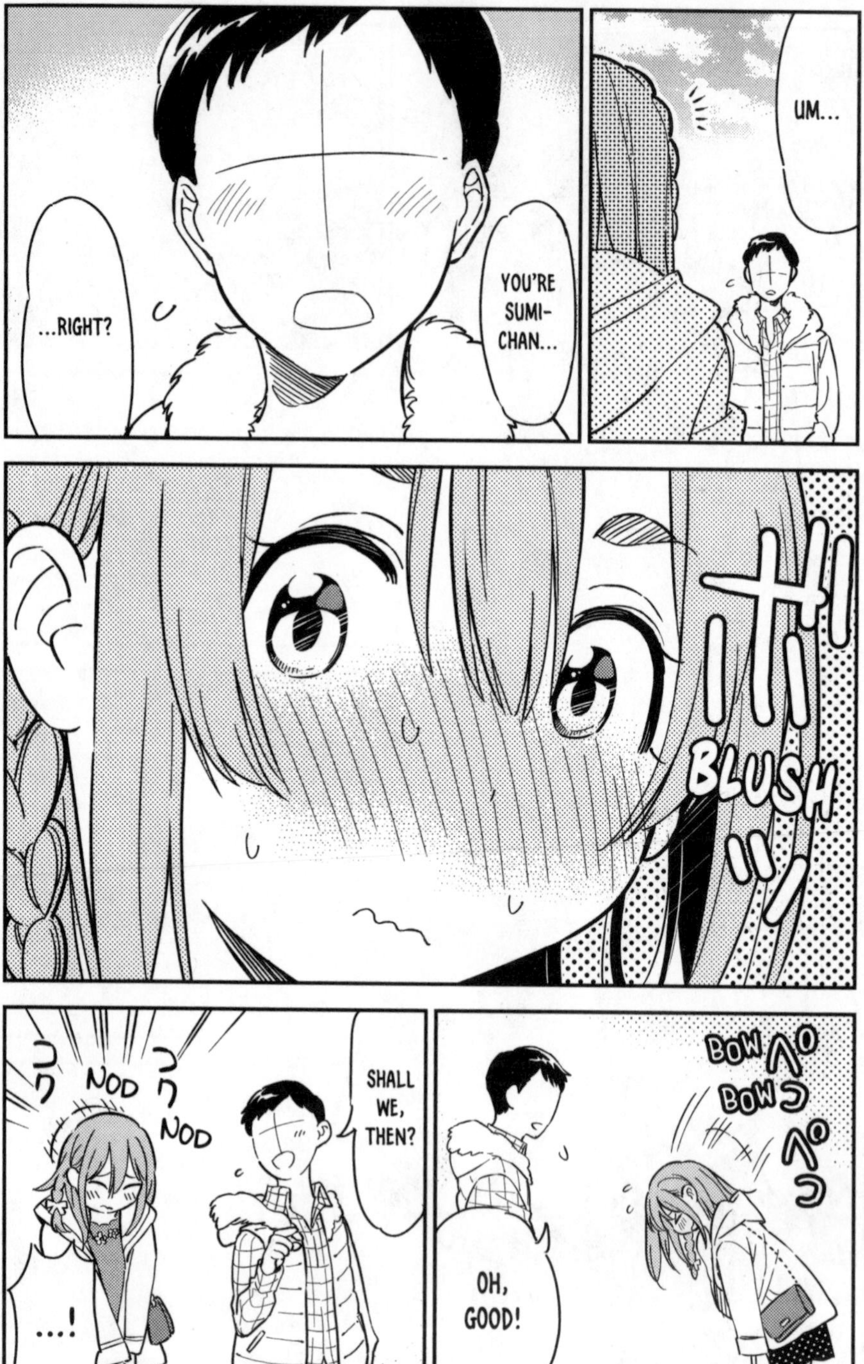
UM...
YOU'RE SUMI-CHAN...
...RIGHT?
BLUSH
BOW BOW
OH, GOOD!
SHALL WE, THEN?
NOD NOD
...!

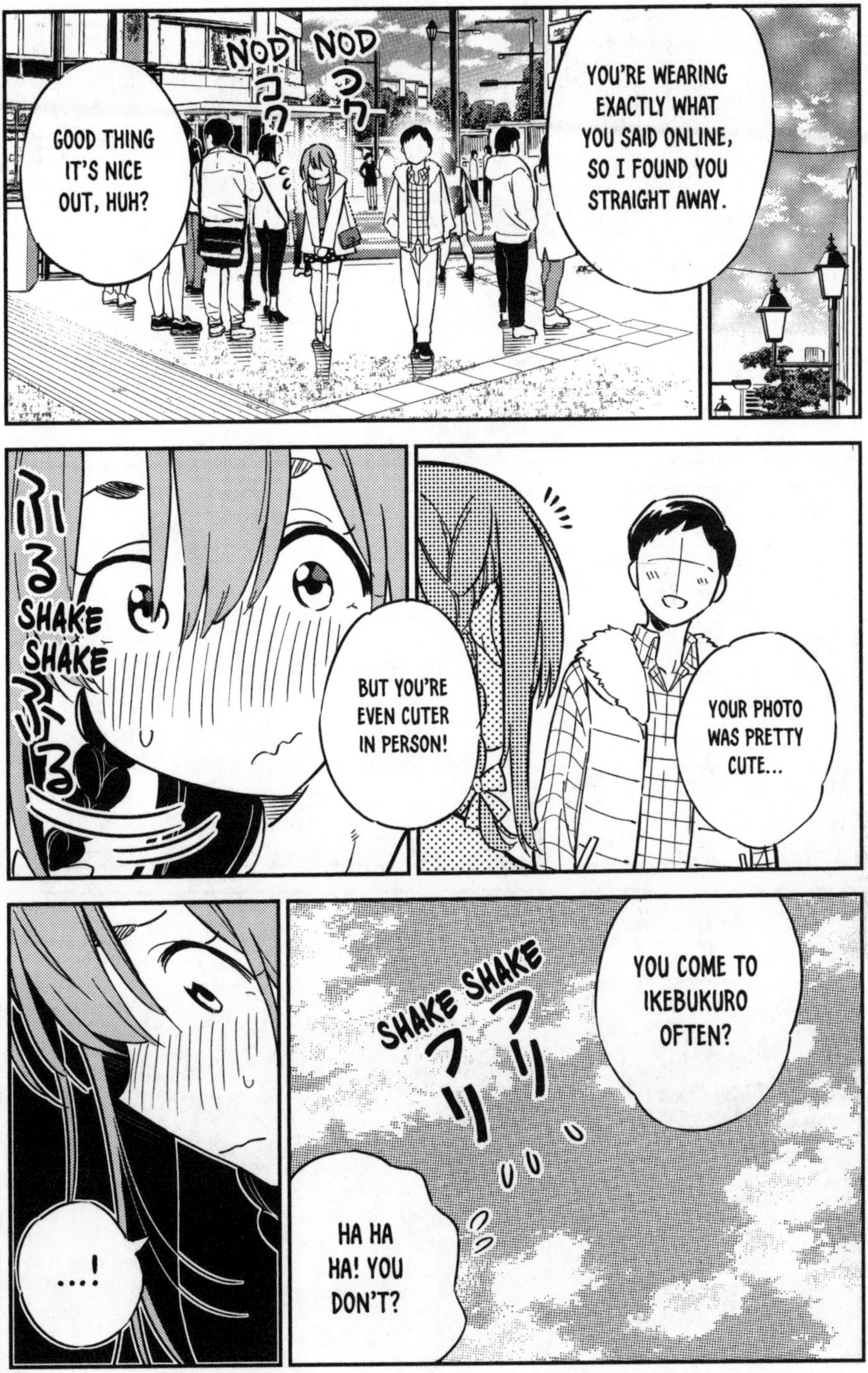
YOU'RE WEARING EXACTLY WHAT YOU SAID ONLINE, SO I FOUND YOU STRAIGHT AWAY.
NOD NOD
コク コク
GOOD THING IT'S NICE OUT, HUH?
YOUR PHOTO WAS PRETTY CUTE...
BUT YOU'RE EVEN CUTER IN PERSON!
ふる ふる
SHAKE SHAKE
YOU COME TO IKEBUKURO OFTEN?
SHAKE SHAKE
フリ フリ
HA HA HA! YOU DON'T?
...!

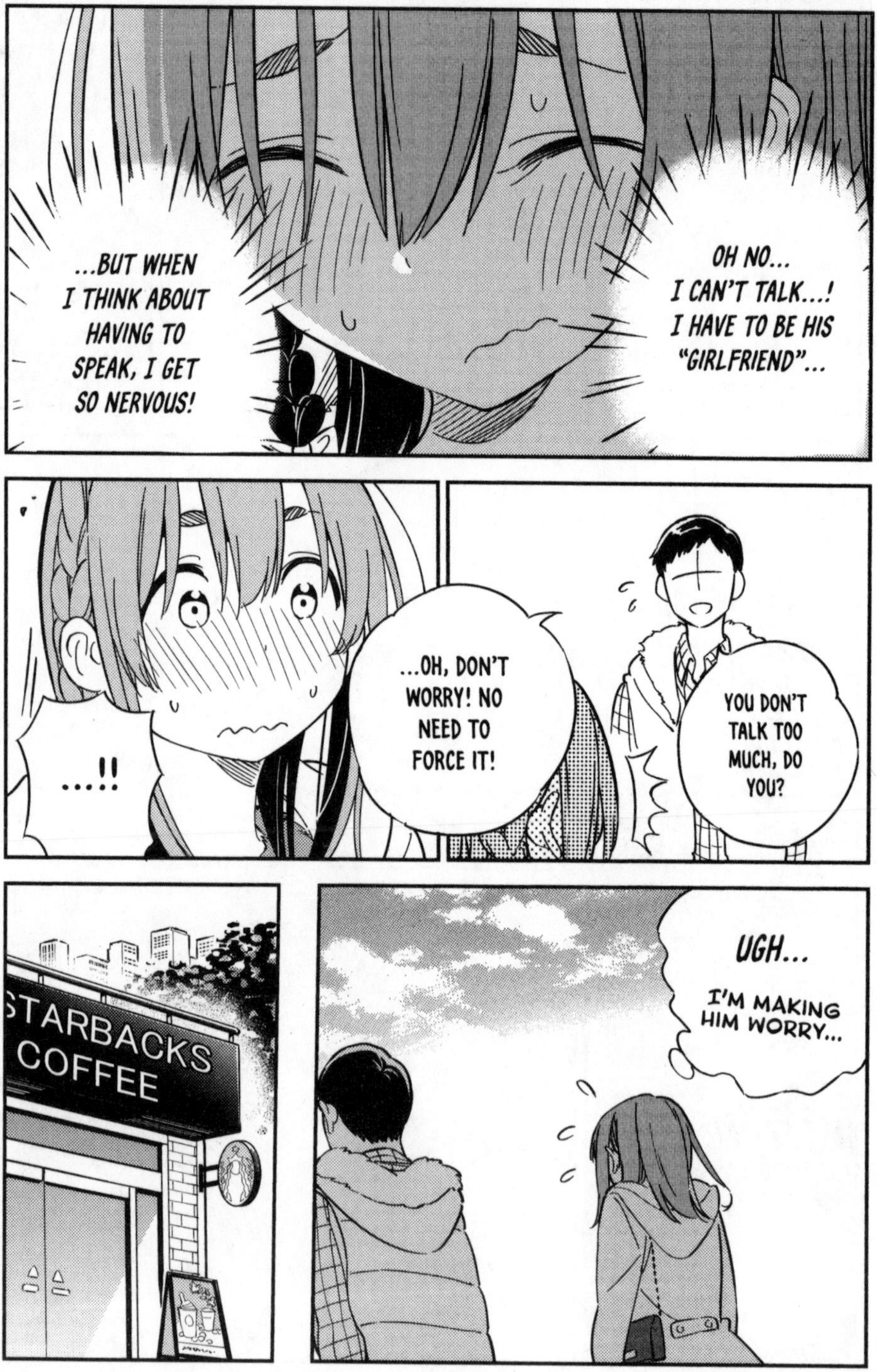
OH NO... I CAN'T TALK...! I HAVE TO BE HIS "GIRLFRIEND"...
...BUT WHEN I THINK ABOUT HAVING TO SPEAK, I GET SO NERVOUS!
YOU DON'T TALK TOO MUCH, DO YOU?
...OH, DON'T WORRY! NO NEED TO FORCE IT!
...!!
UGH...
I'M MAKING HIM WORRY...
STARBACKS COFFEE

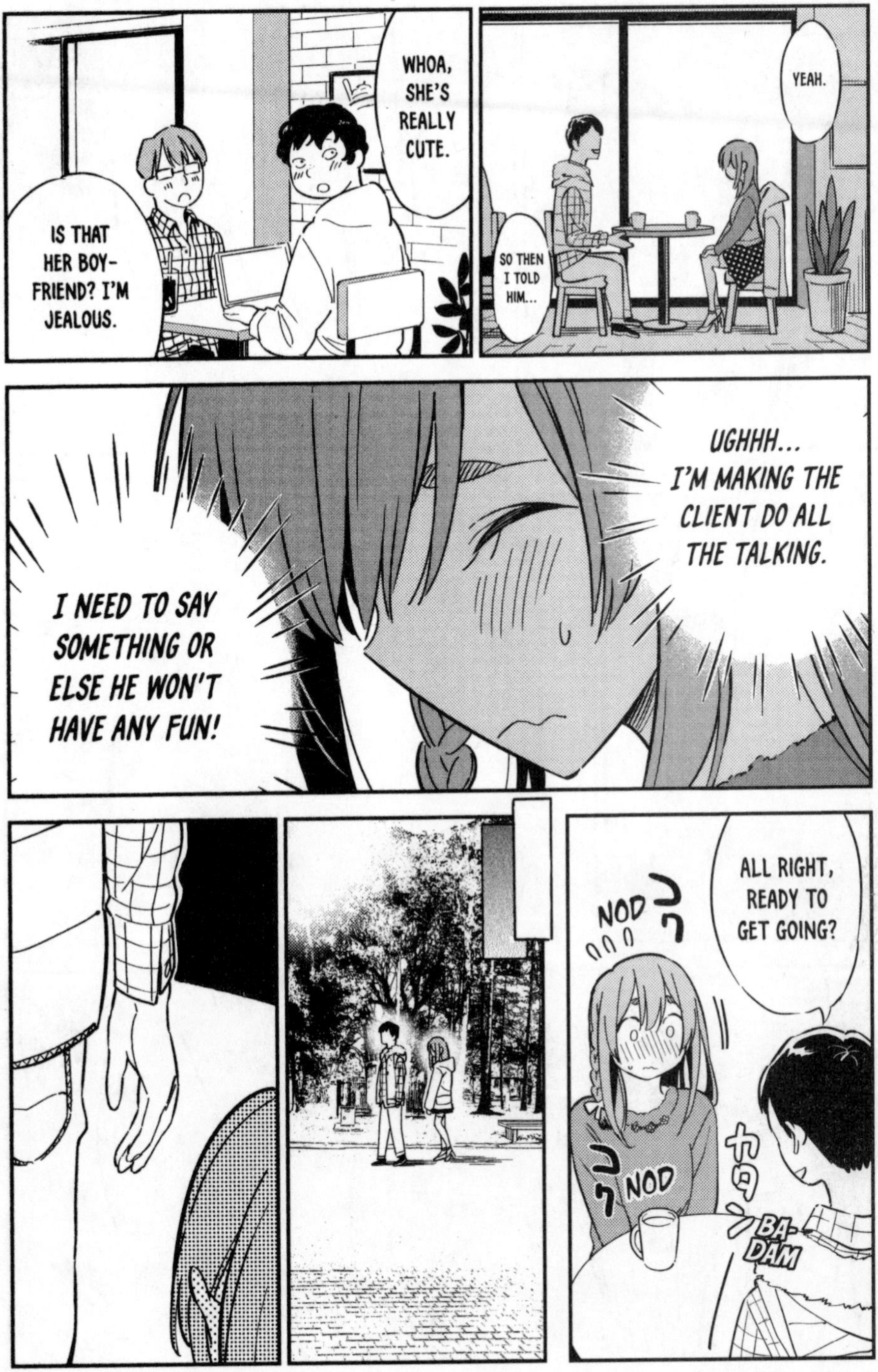
YEAH.
SO THEN I TOLD HIM...
WHOA, SHE'S REALLY CUTE.
IS THAT HER BOY-FRIEND? I'M JEALOUS.
UGHHH... I'M MAKING THE CLIENT DO ALL THE TALKING.
I NEED TO SAY SOMETHING OR ELSE HE WON'T HAVE ANY FUN!
ALL RIGHT, READY TO GET GOING?
NOD
NOD
BA-DAM

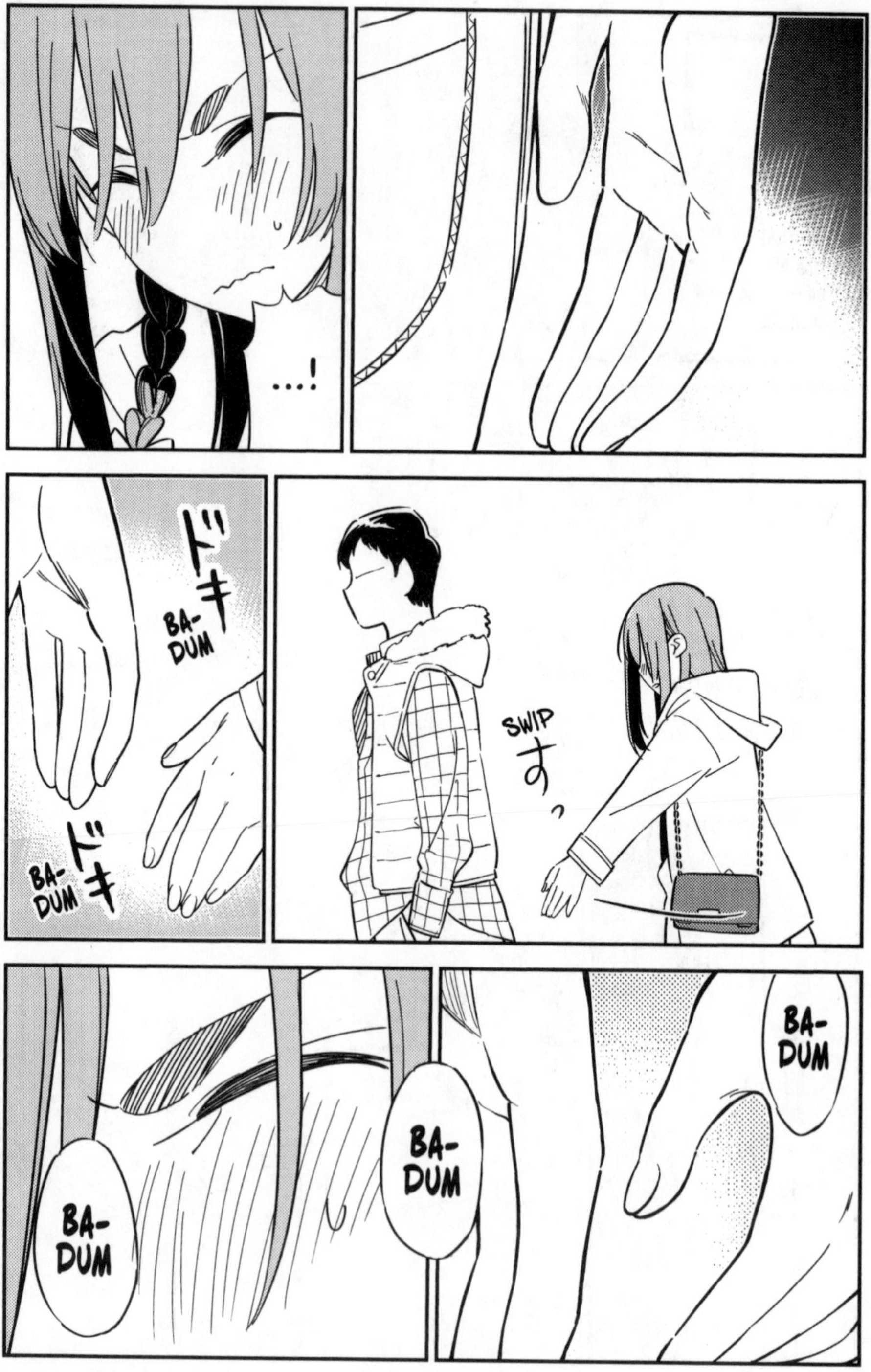
...!
SWIP
すっ
ドキ
BA-DUM
ドキ
BA-DUM
BA-DUM
BA-DUM
BA-DUM

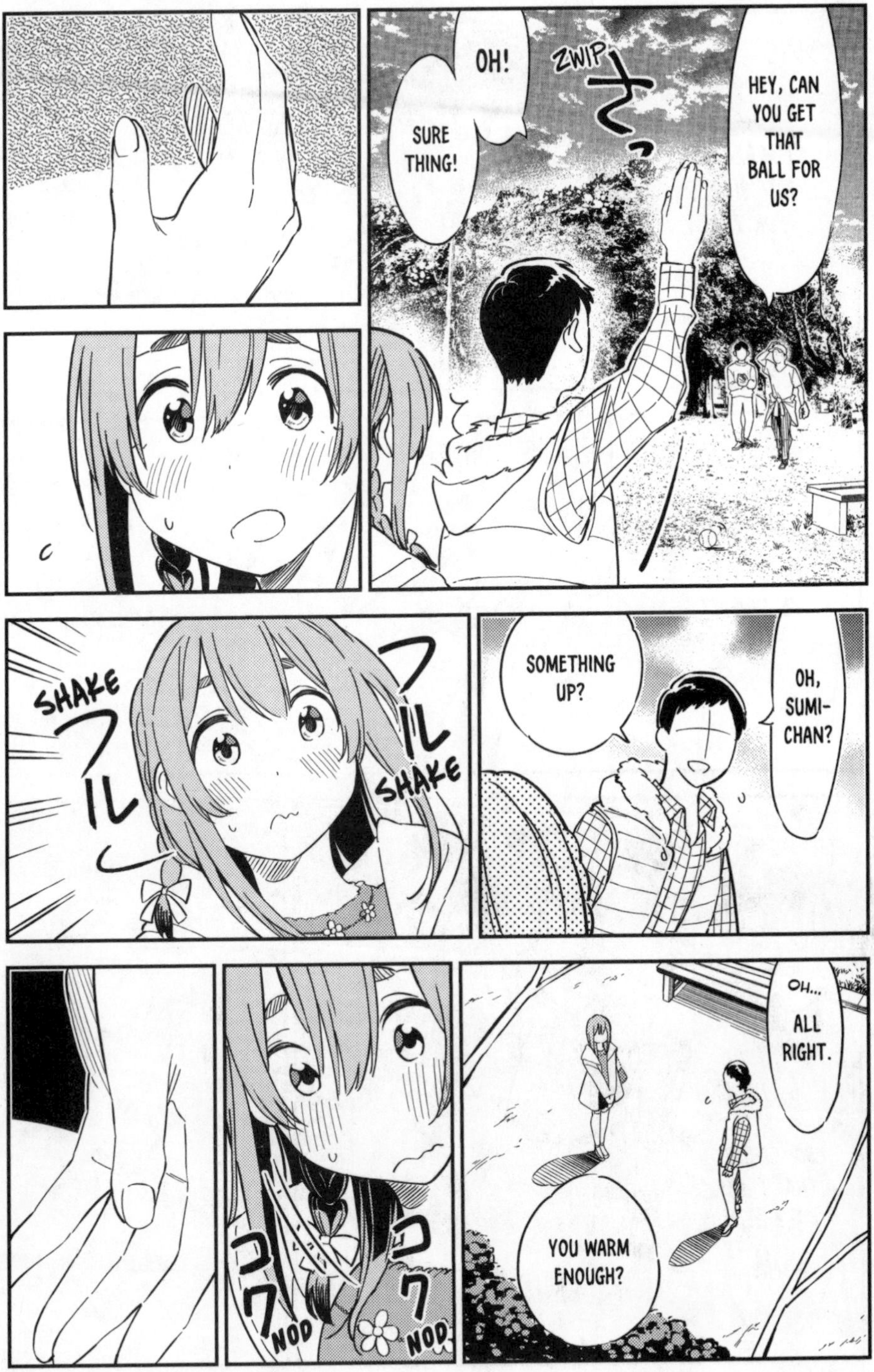
HEY, CAN YOU GET THAT BALL FOR US?
ZWIP
OH!
SURE THING!
OH, SUMI-CHAN?
SOMETHING UP?
SHAKE
SHAKE
OH... ALL RIGHT.
YOU WARM ENOUGH?
NOD
NOD

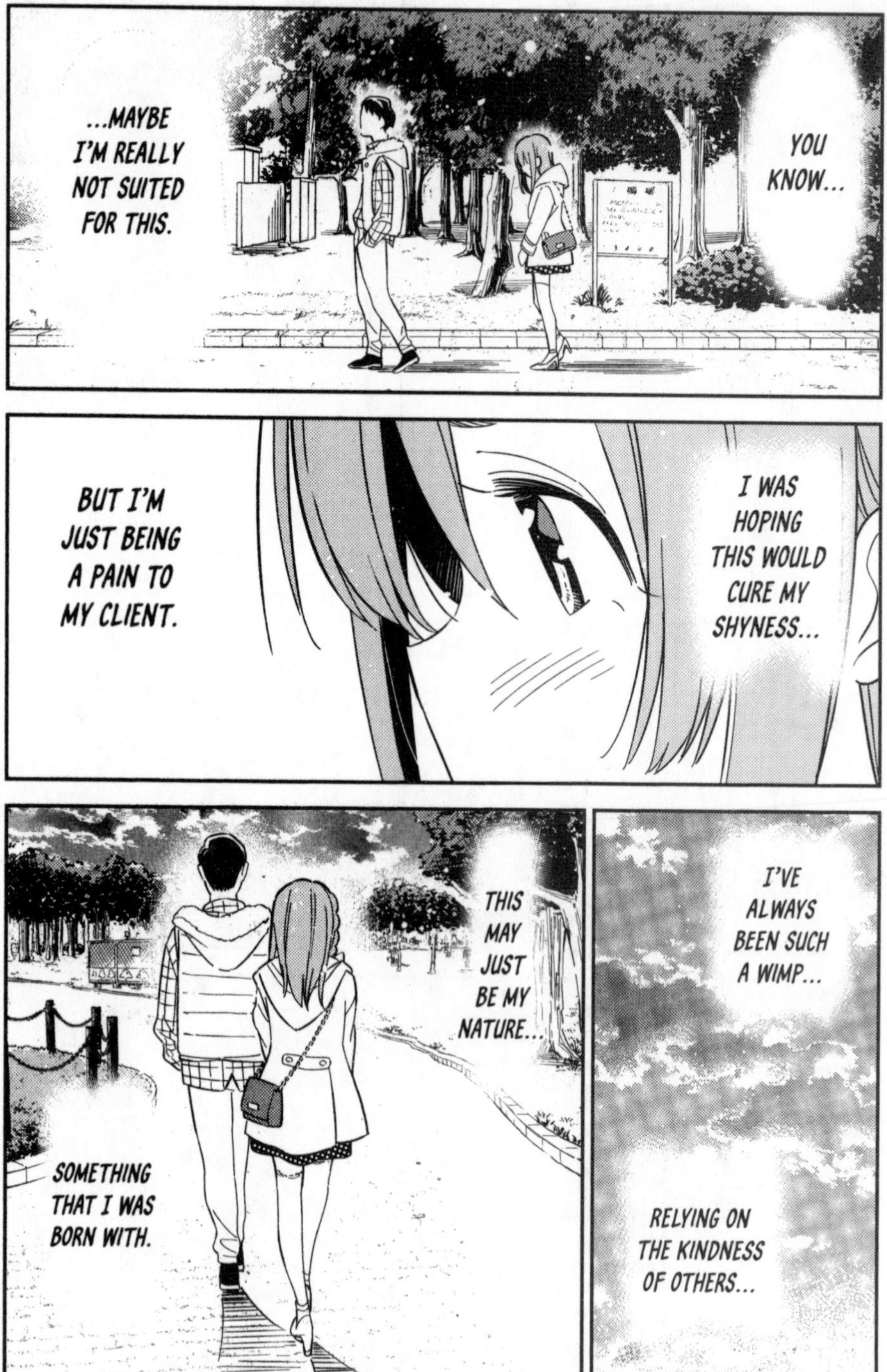
YOU KNOW...
...MAYBE I'M REALLY NOT SUITED FOR THIS.
I WAS HOPING THIS WOULD CURE MY SHYNESS...
BUT I'M JUST BEING A PAIN TO MY CLIENT.
I'VE ALWAYS BEEN SUCH A WIMP...
RELYING ON THE KINDNESS OF OTHERS...
THIS MAY JUST BE MY NATURE...
SOMETHING THAT I WAS BORN WITH.

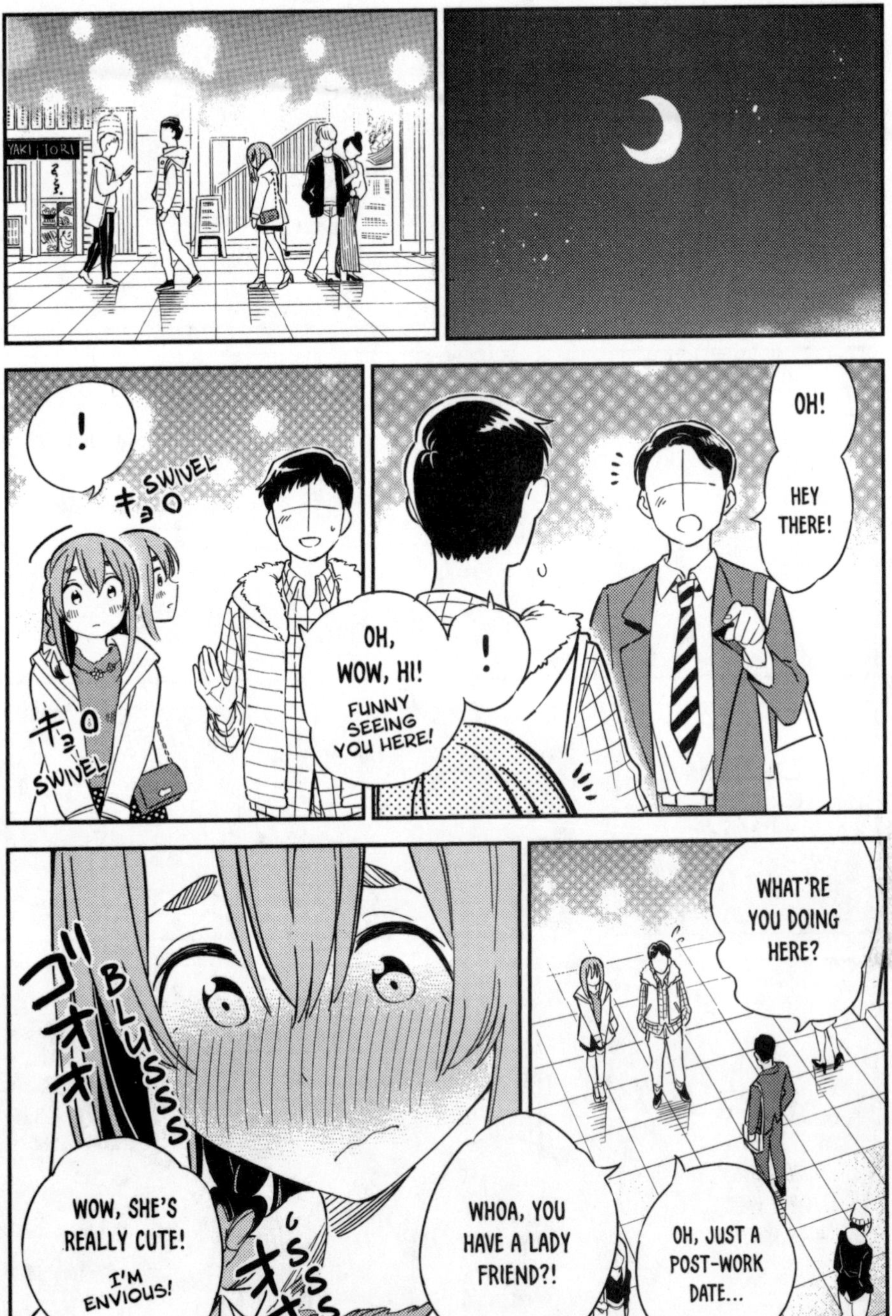
YAKI TORI
OH!
HEY THERE!
!
OH, WOW, HI! FUNNY SEEING YOU HERE!
!
キョロ SWIVEL
キョロ SWIVEL
WHAT'RE YOU DOING HERE?
OH, JUST A POST-WORK DATE...
WHOA, YOU HAVE A LADY FRIEND?!
WOW, SHE'S REALLY CUTE! I'M ENVIOUS!
ゴオオ BLUSSSS
オオ SSSHHH

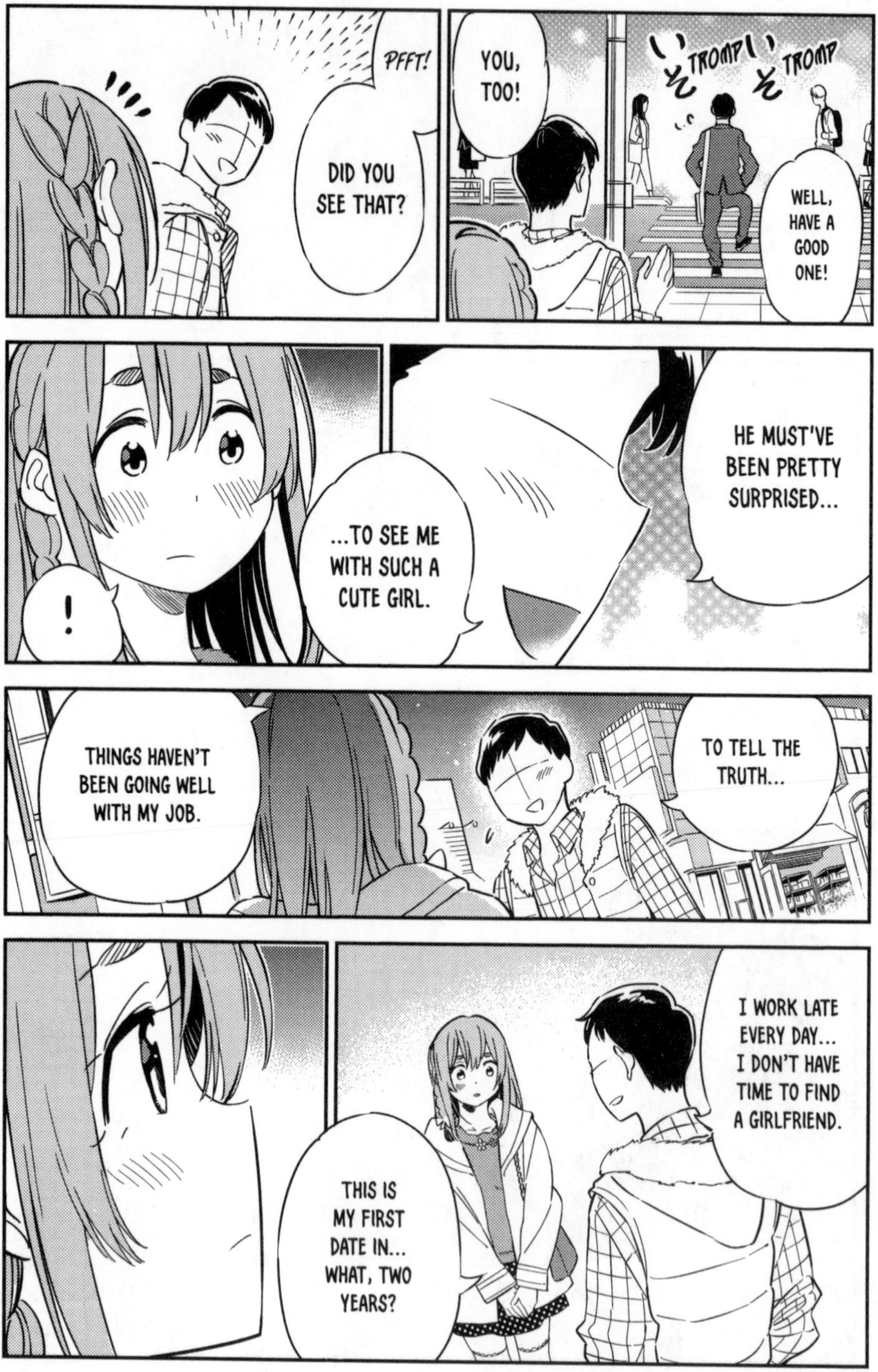
いそ TROMP いそ TROMP
WELL, HAVE A GOOD ONE!
YOU, TOO!
PFFT!
DID YOU SEE THAT?
HE MUST'VE BEEN PRETTY SURPRISED...
...TO SEE ME WITH SUCH A CUTE GIRL.
!
TO TELL THE TRUTH...
THINGS HAVEN'T BEEN GOING WELL WITH MY JOB.
I WORK LATE EVERY DAY... I DON'T HAVE TIME TO FIND A GIRLFRIEND.
THIS IS MY FIRST DATE IN... WHAT, TWO YEARS?

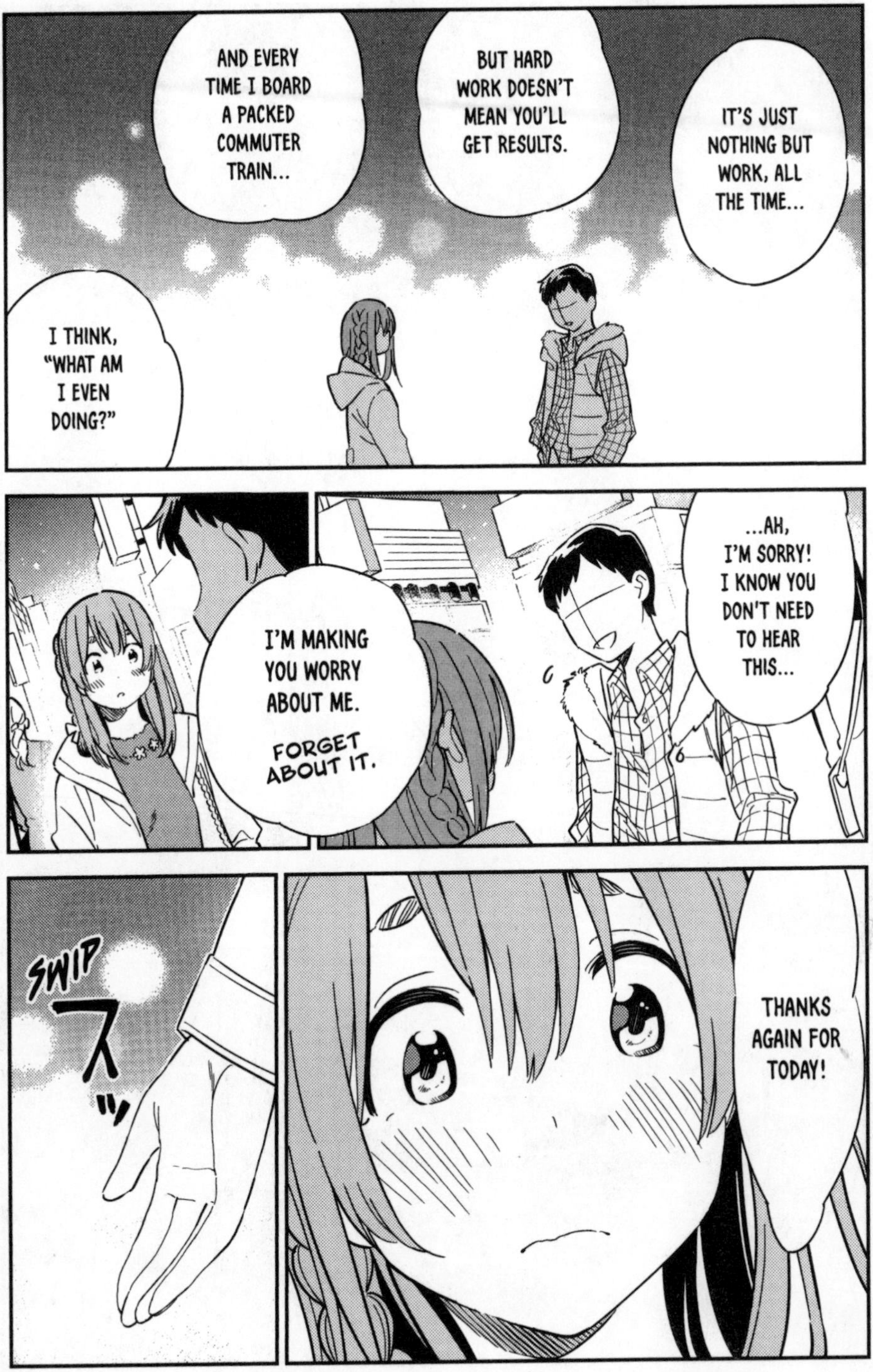
IT'S JUST NOTHING BUT WORK, ALL THE TIME...
BUT HARD WORK DOESN'T MEAN YOU'LL GET RESULTS.
AND EVERY TIME I BOARD A PACKED COMMUTER TRAIN...
I THINK, "WHAT AM I EVEN DOING?"
...AH, I'M SORRY! I KNOW YOU DON'T NEED TO HEAR THIS...
I'M MAKING YOU WORRY ABOUT ME.
FORGET ABOUT IT.
THANKS AGAIN FOR TODAY!
SWIP

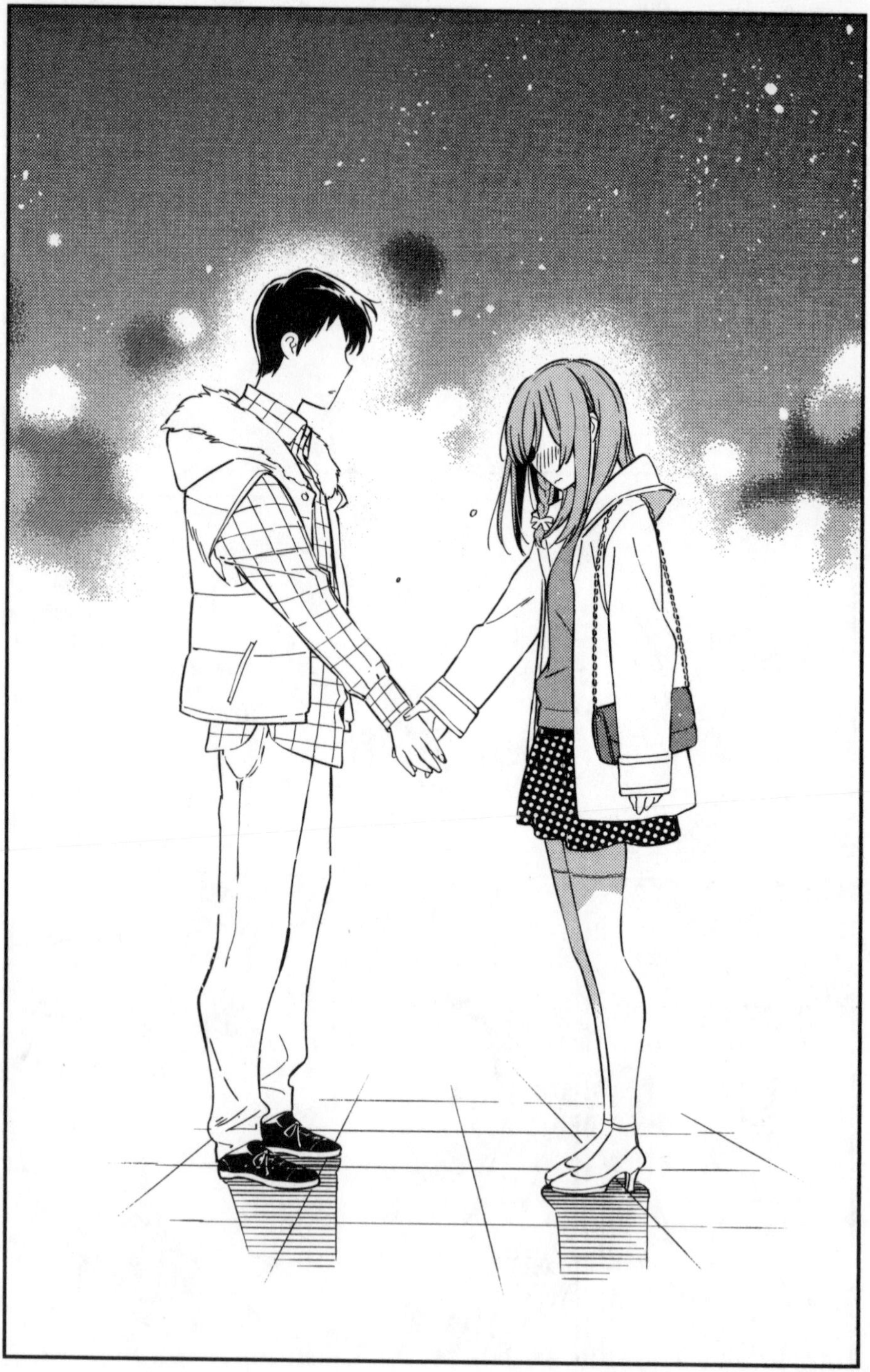

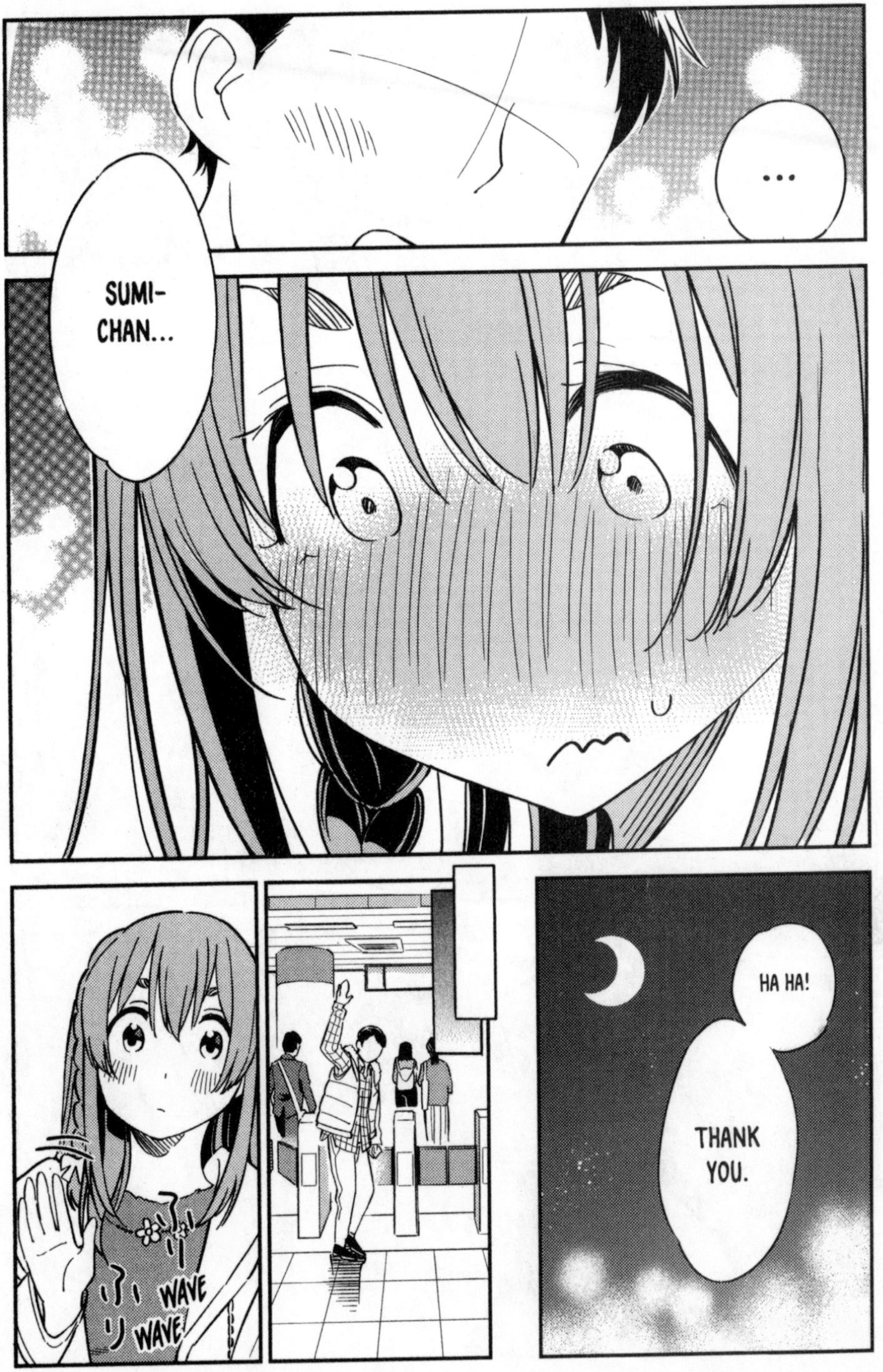
...
SUMI-CHAN...
HA HA!
THANK YOU.
WAVE
WAVE

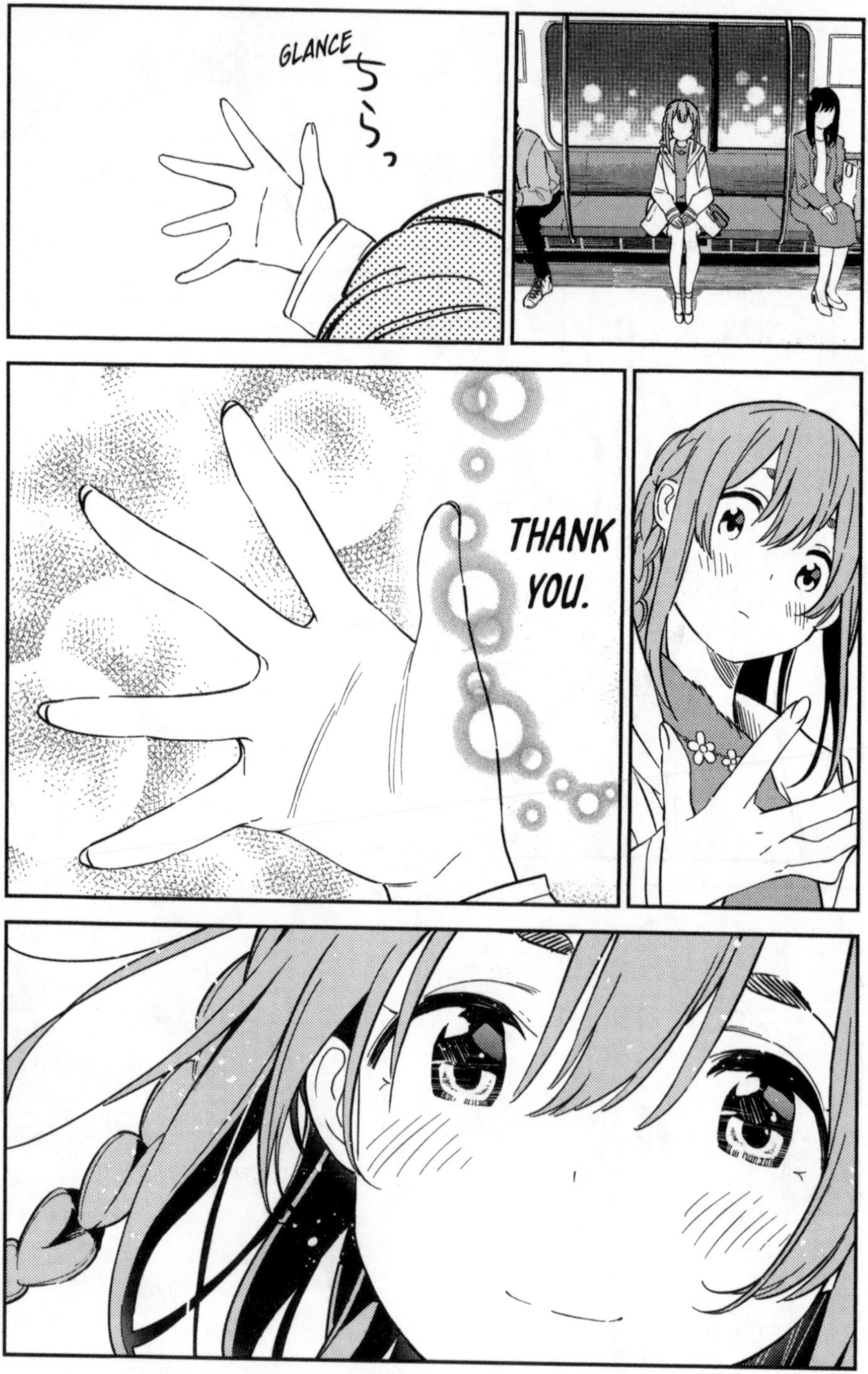
GLANCE
ちらっ
THANK YOU.

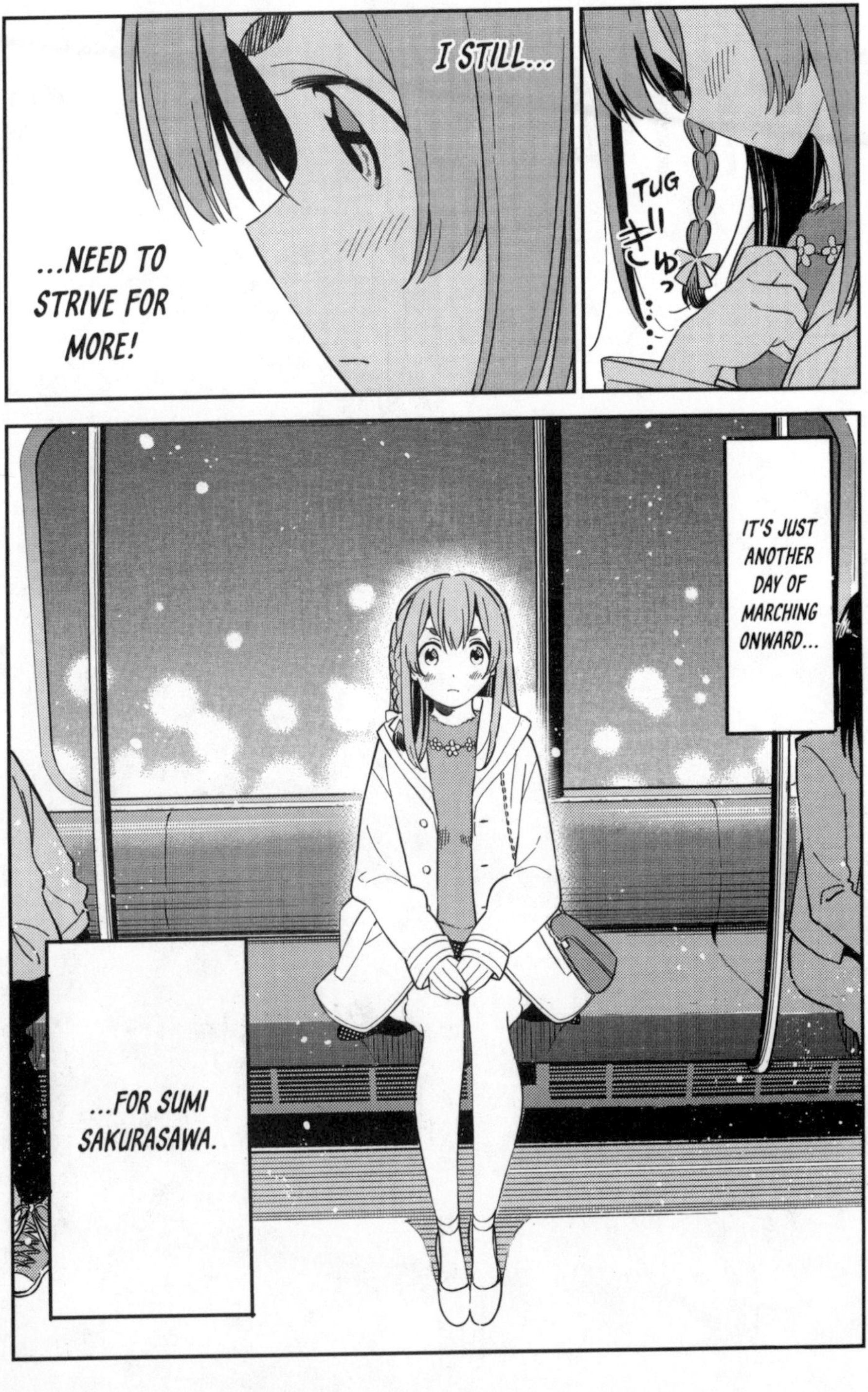
TUG
ぎゅっ
I STILL...
...NEED TO STRIVE FOR MORE!
IT'S JUST ANOTHER DAY OF MARCHING ONWARD...
...FOR SUMI SAKURASAWA.

RENT-A-(REALLY-SHY!)-GIRLFRIEND

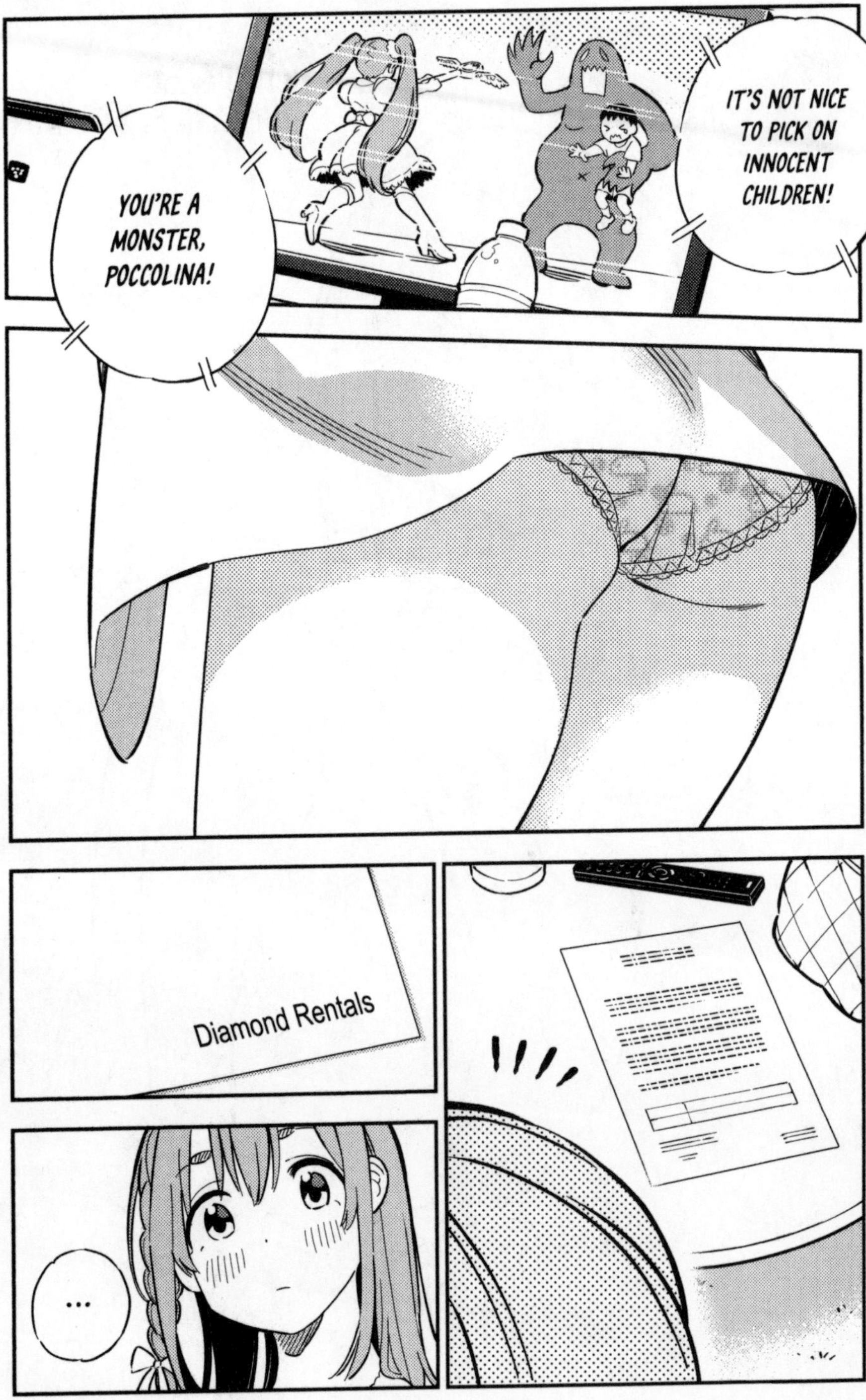
IT'S NOT NICE TO PICK ON INNOCENT CHILDREN!
YOU'RE A MONSTER, POCCOLINA!
Diamond Rentals
...

RATING 3
SUMI AND HER CO-WORKER

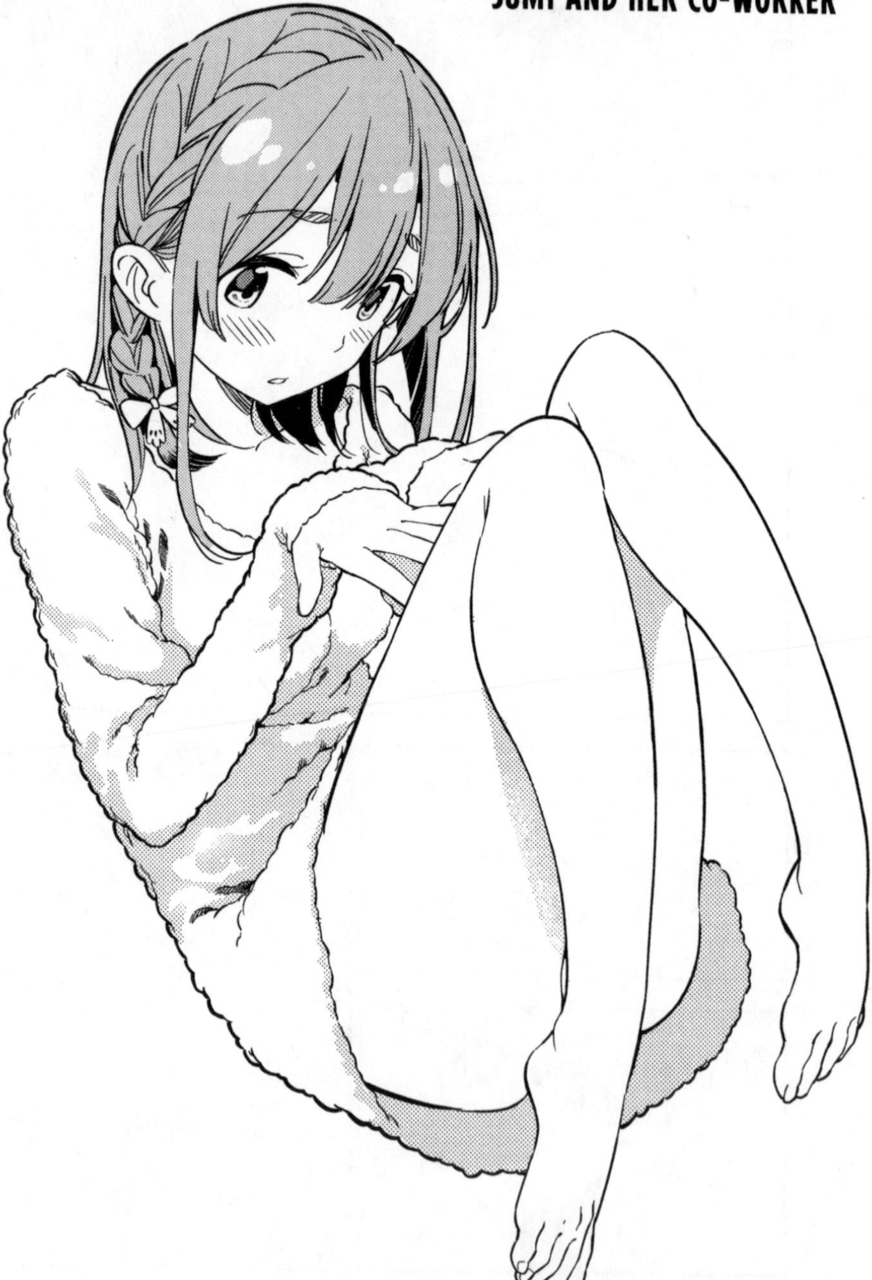

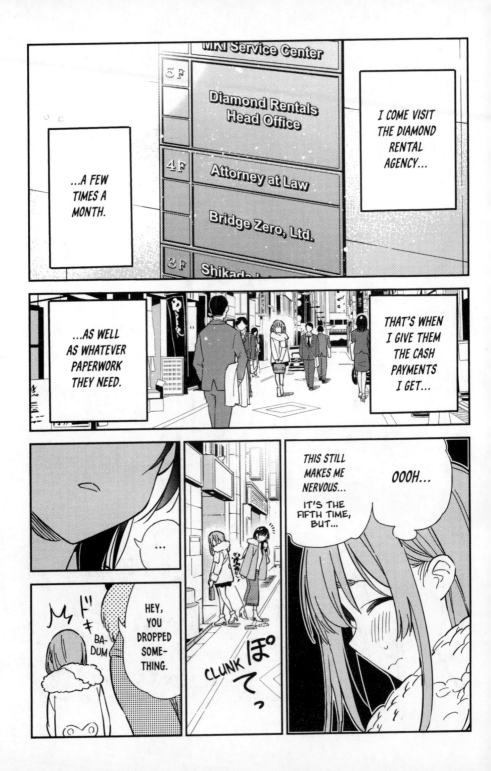

I COME VISIT THE DIAMOND RENTAL AGENCY...
MKI Service Center
5F
Diamond Rentals Head Office
4F
Attorney at Law
Bridge Zero, Ltd.
3F
...A FEW TIMES A MONTH.
THAT'S WHEN I GIVE THEM THE CASH PAYMENTS I GET...
...AS WELL AS WHATEVER PAPERWORK THEY NEED.
OOOH...
THIS STILL MAKES ME NERVOUS...
IT'S THE FIFTH TIME, BUT...
ぽてっ
CLUNK
...
HEY, YOU DROPPED SOMETHING.
ドキ
BA-DUM

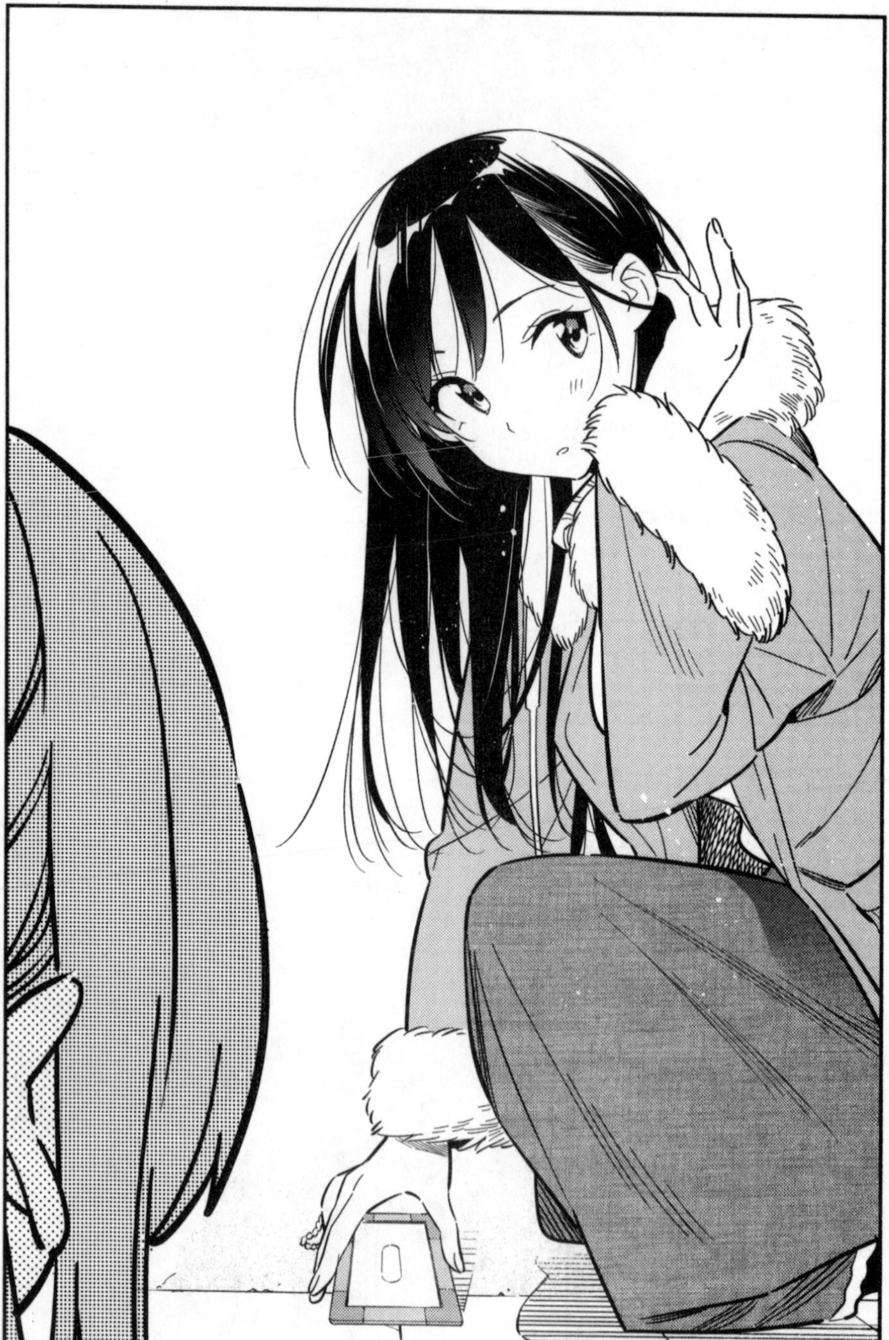

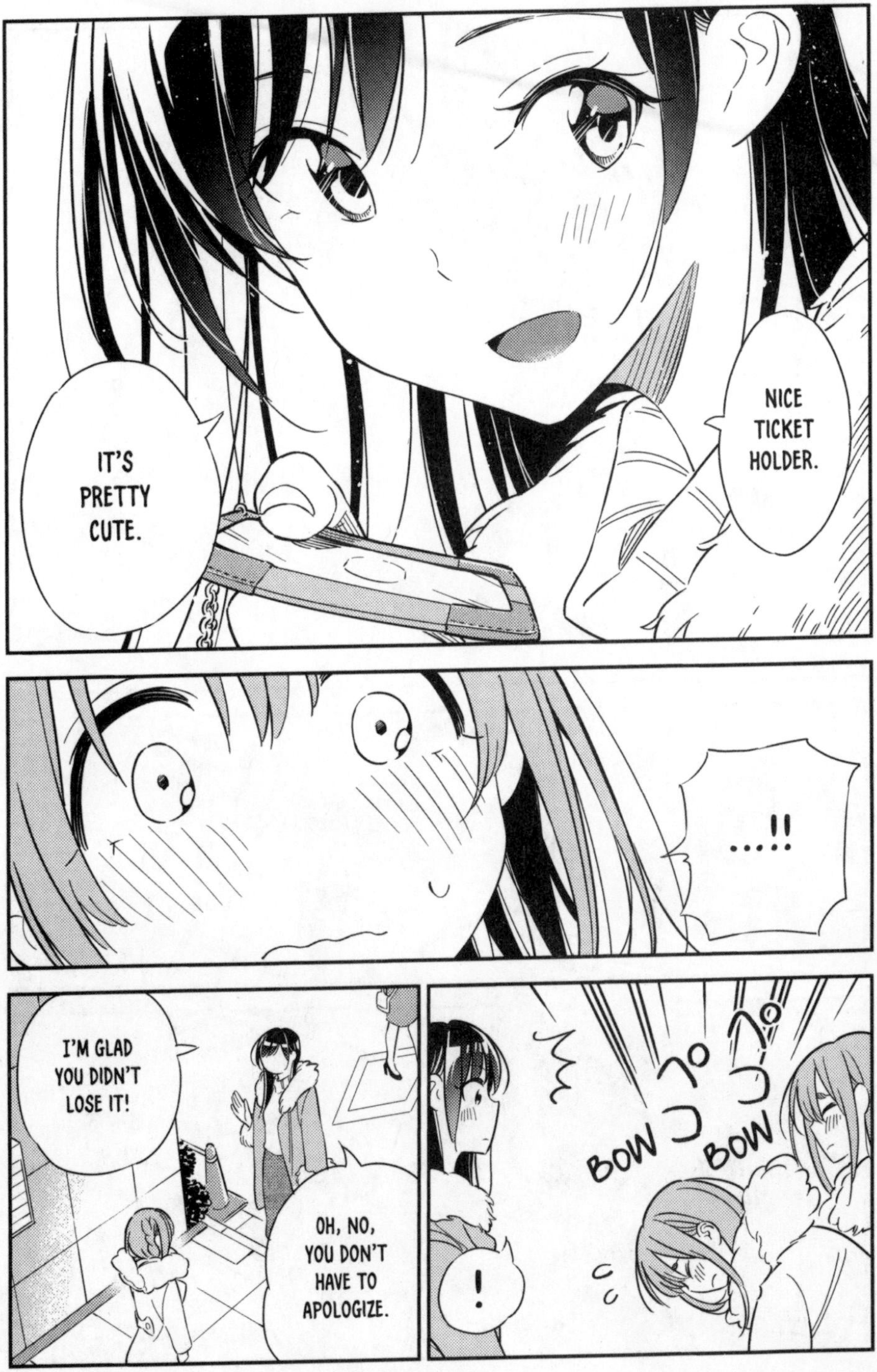
NICE TICKET HOLDER.
IT'S PRETTY CUTE.
...!!
BOW BOW
!
OH, NO, YOU DON'T HAVE TO APOLOGIZE.
I'M GLAD YOU DIDN'T LOSE IT!

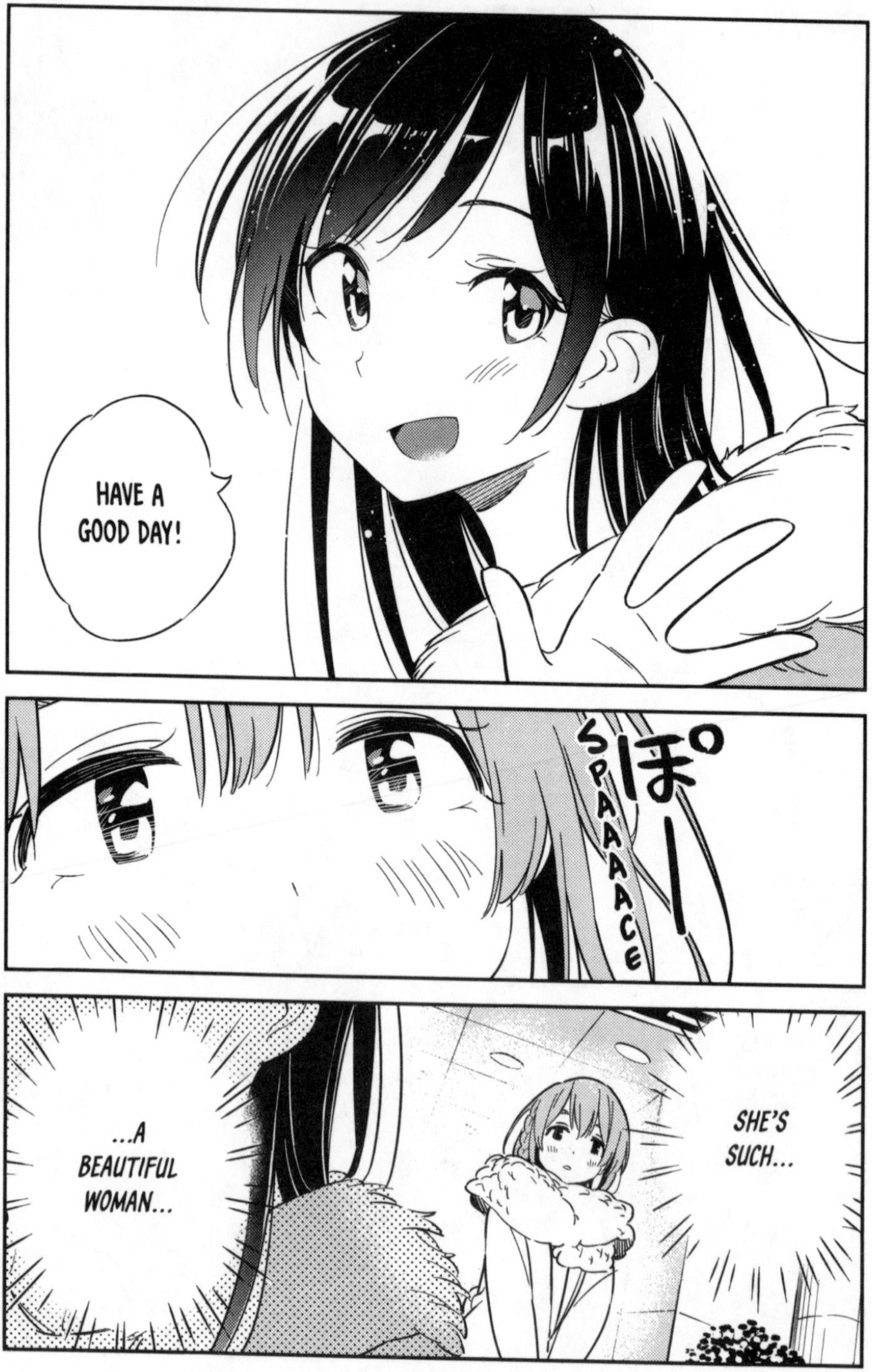
HAVE A GOOD DAY!
ぽー
SPAAAAACE
SHE'S SUCH...
...A BEAUTIFUL WOMAN...

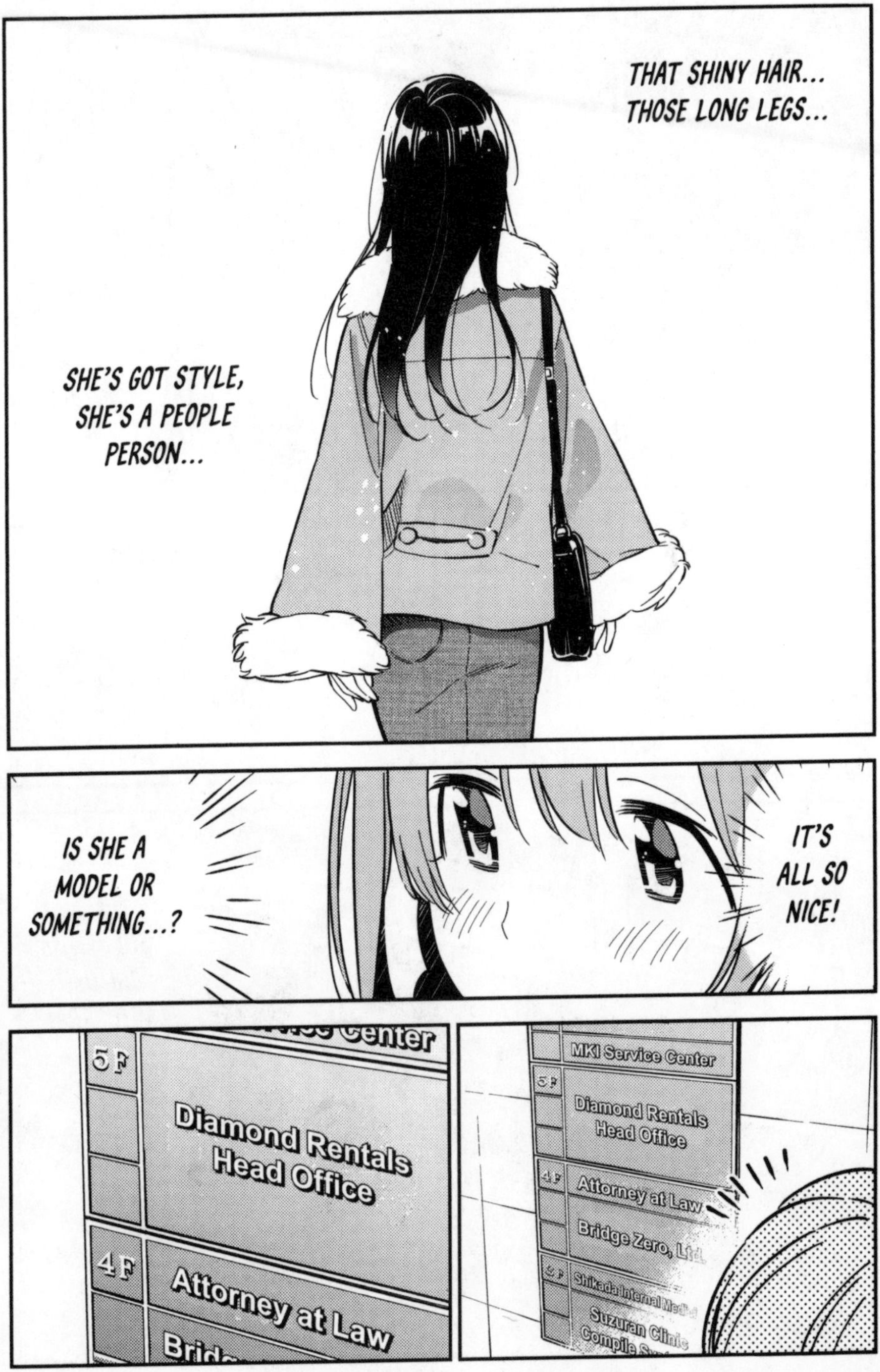
THAT SHINY HAIR... THOSE LONG LEGS...
SHE'S GOT STYLE, SHE'S A PEOPLE PERSON...
IT'S ALL SO NICE!
IS SHE A MODEL OR SOMETHING...?
MKI Service Center
5F
Diamond Rentals Head Office
4F
Attorney at Law
Bridge Zero, Ltd.
Suzuran Clinic
5F
Diamond Rentals Head Office
4F
Attorney at Law

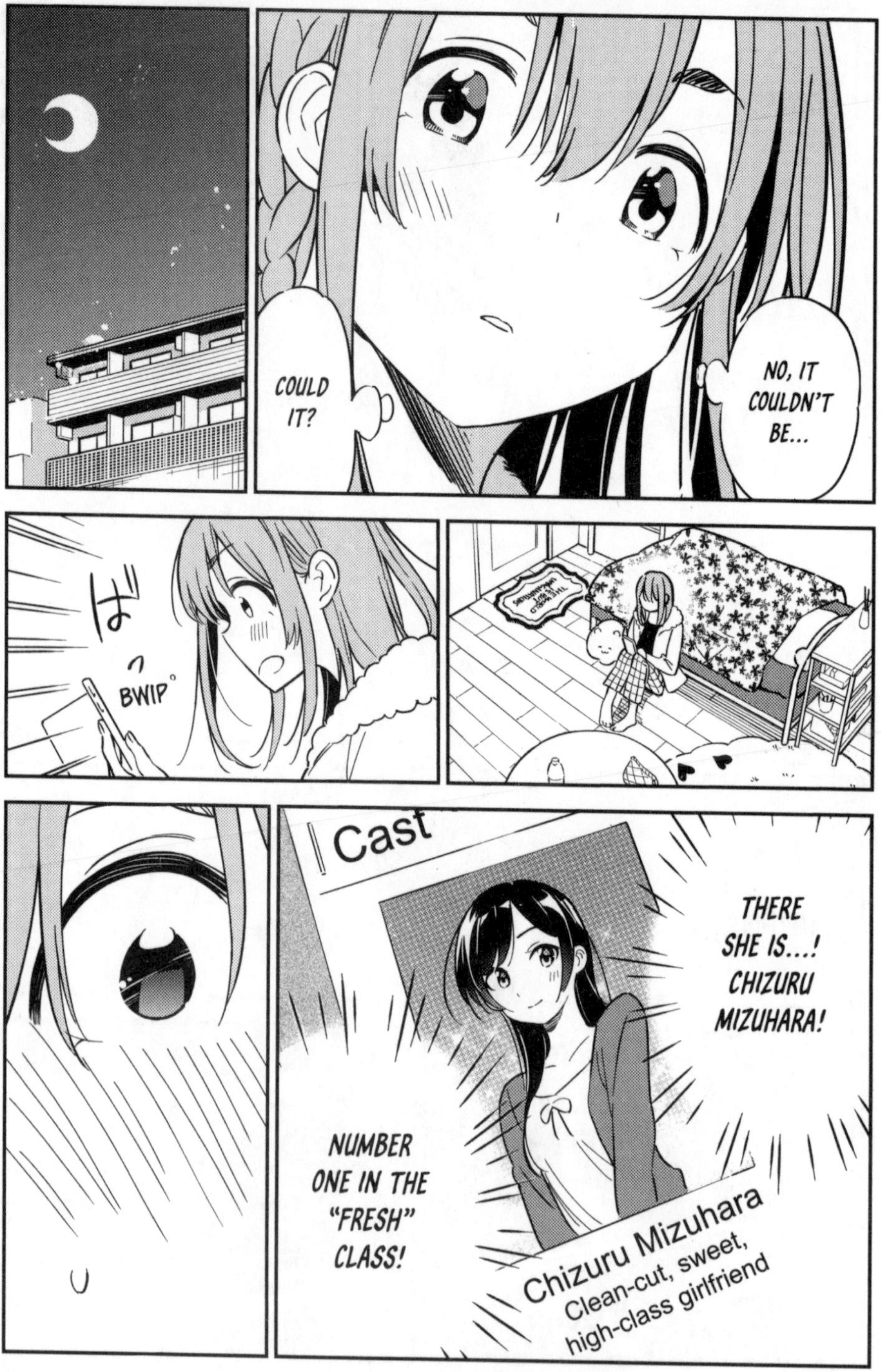
COULD IT?
NO, IT COULDN'T BE...
ぱっ
BWIP
Cast
THERE SHE IS...! CHIZURU MIZUHARA!
NUMBER ONE IN THE "FRESH" CLASS!
Chizuru Mizuhara
Clean-cut, sweet, high-class girlfriend

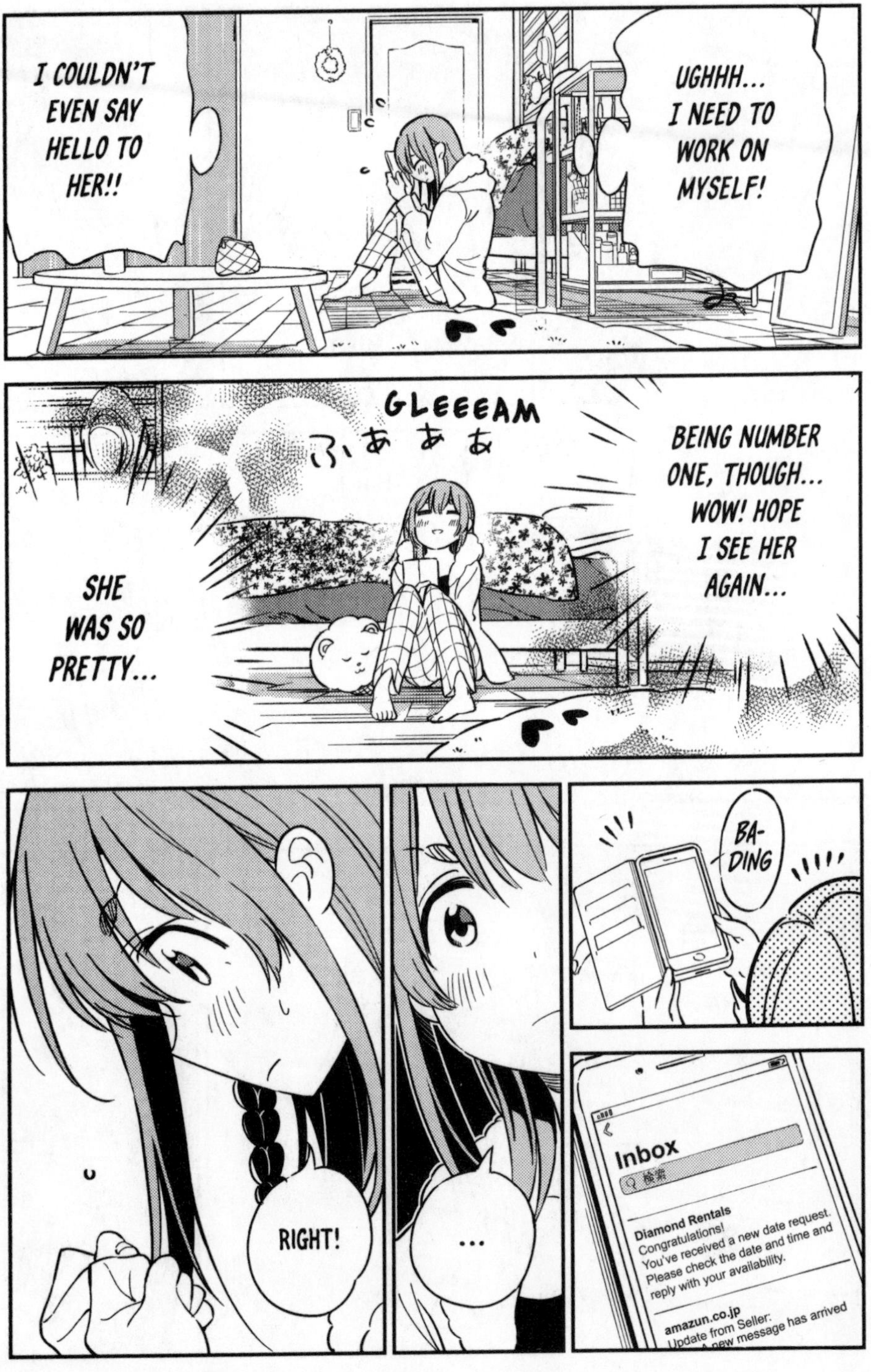
UGHHH... I NEED TO WORK ON MYSELF!
I COULDN'T EVEN SAY HELLO TO HER!!
BEING NUMBER ONE, THOUGH... WOW! HOPE I SEE HER AGAIN...
GLEEEAM
ふあああ
SHE WAS SO PRETTY...
BA-DING
Inbox
検索
Diamond Rentals
Congratulations! You've received a new date request. Please check the date and time and reply with your availability.
amazun.co.jp
Update from Seller:
...
RIGHT!

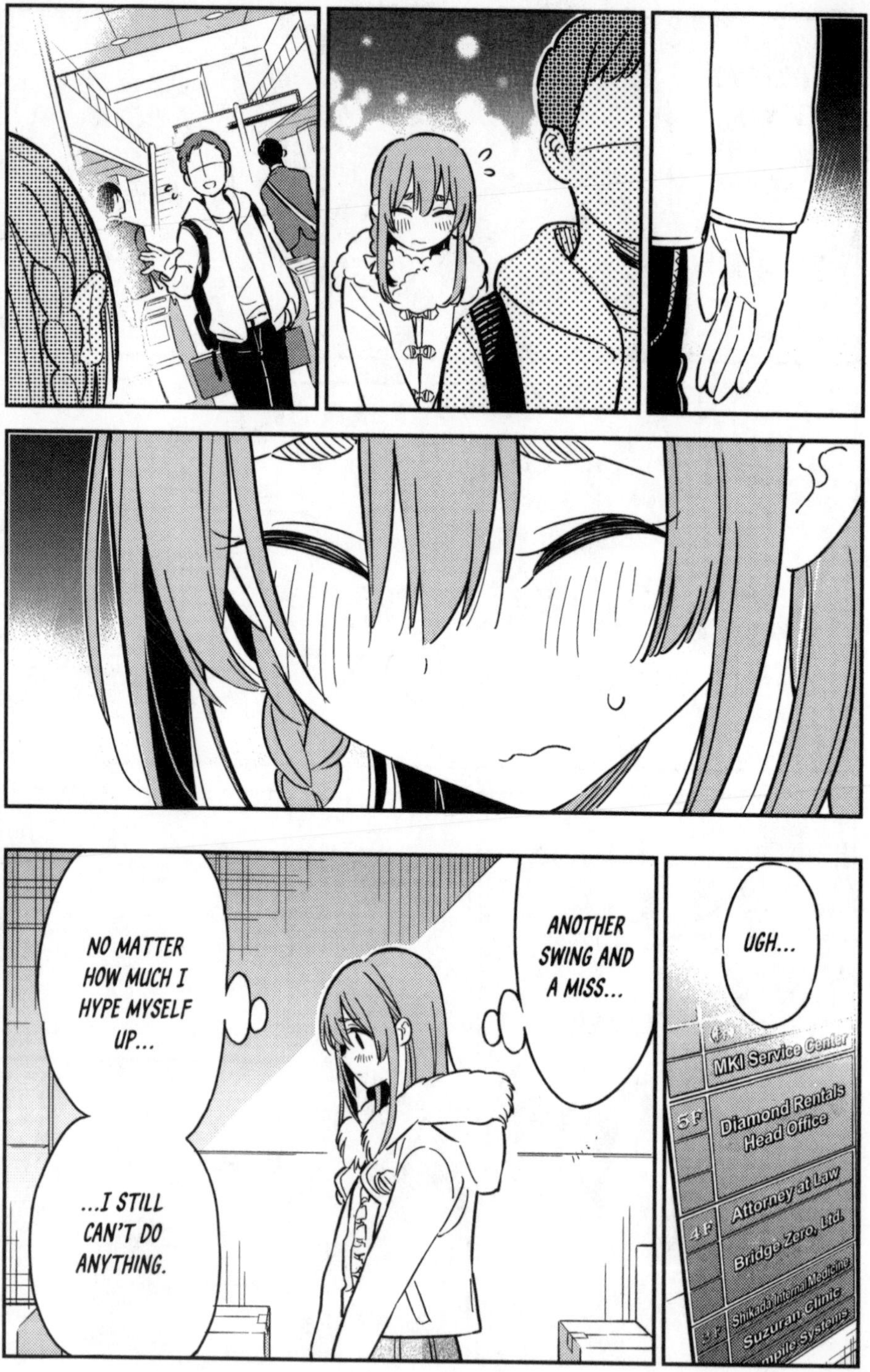
UGH...
MKI Service Center
5 F
Diamond Rentals Head Office
Attorney at Law
4 F
Bridge Zero, Ltd.
Shikada Internal Medicine
Suzuran Clinic
ANOTHER SWING AND A MISS...
NO MATTER HOW MUCH I HYPE MYSELF UP...
...I STILL CAN'T DO ANYTHING.

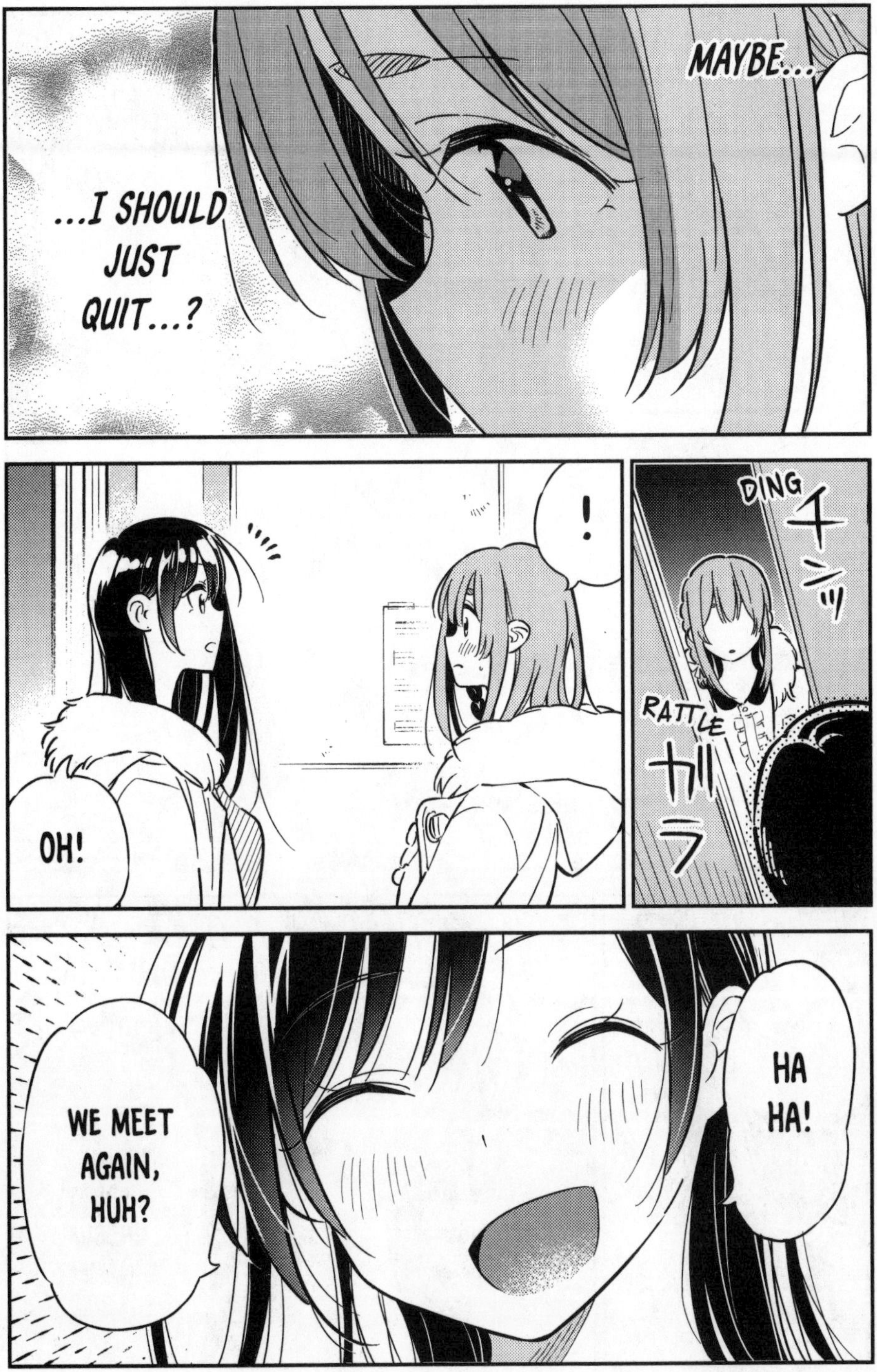
MAYBE...
...I SHOULD JUST QUIT...?
DING
チンッ
RATTLE
ガラ
!
OH!
HA HA!
WE MEET AGAIN, HUH?

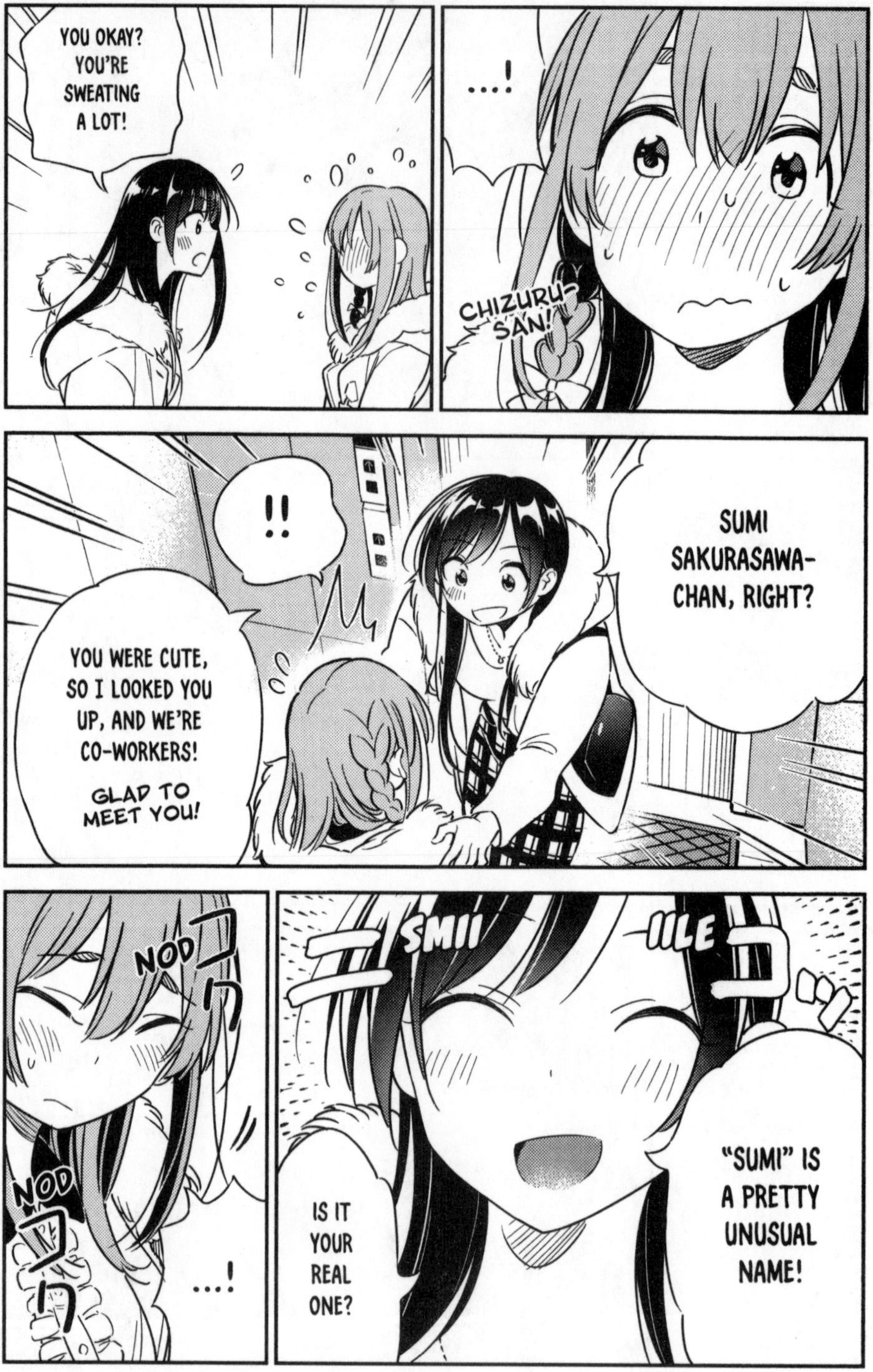
...!
CHIZURU-SAN!
YOU OKAY? YOU'RE SWEATING A LOT!
SUMI SAKURASAWA-CHAN, RIGHT?
!!
YOU WERE CUTE, SO I LOOKED YOU UP, AND WE'RE CO-WORKERS!
GLAD TO MEET YOU!
SMII
ILE
"SUMI" IS A PRETTY UNUSUAL NAME!
IS IT YOUR REAL ONE?
NOD
NOD
...!

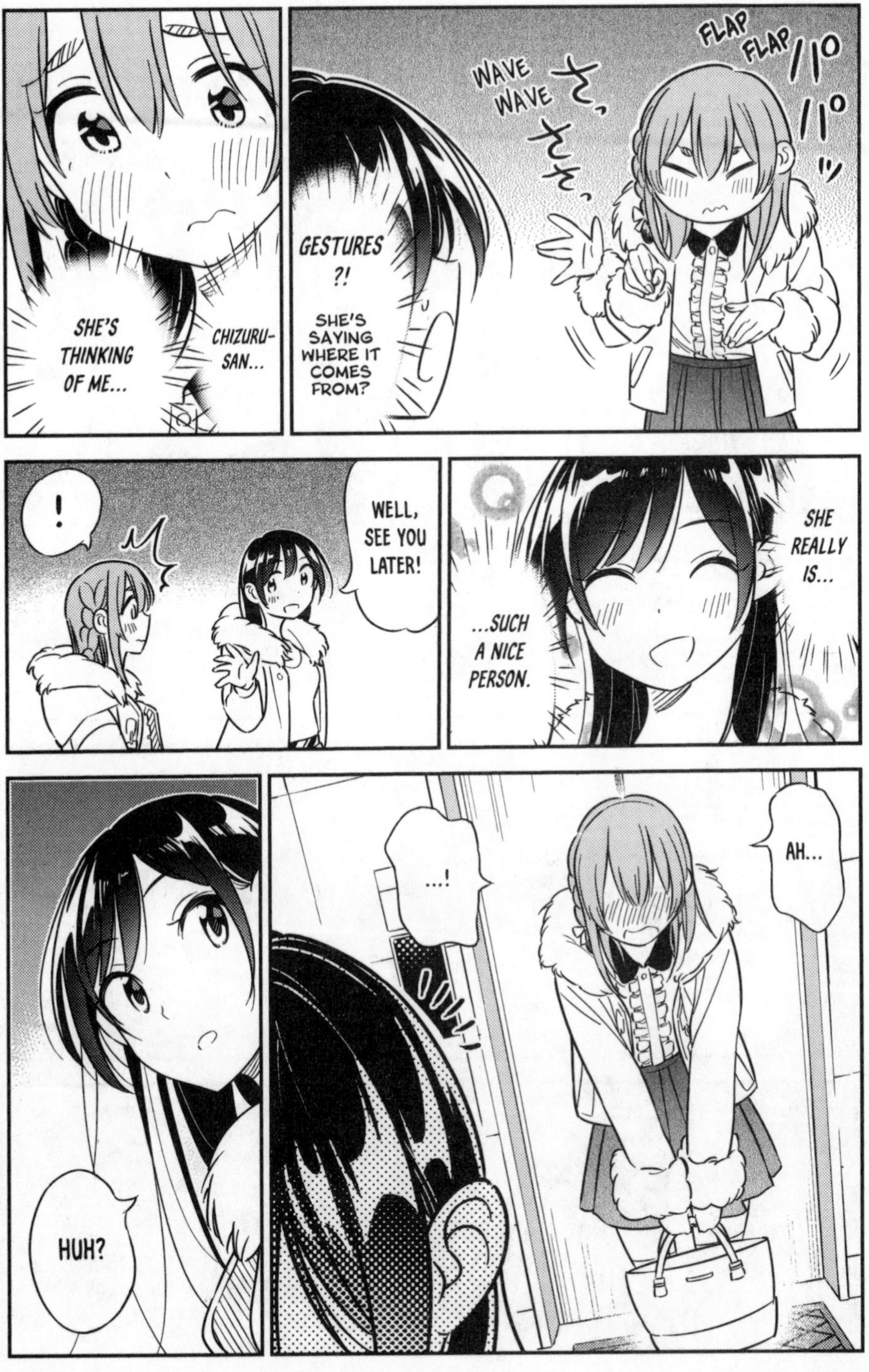
FLAP FLAP
パパッ
WAVE WAVE
さっ ささっ
GESTURES ?!
SHE'S SAYING WHERE IT COMES FROM?
CHIZURU-SAN...
SHE'S THINKING OF ME...
SHE REALLY IS...
...SUCH A NICE PERSON.
WELL, SEE YOU LATER!
!
AH...
...!
HUH?

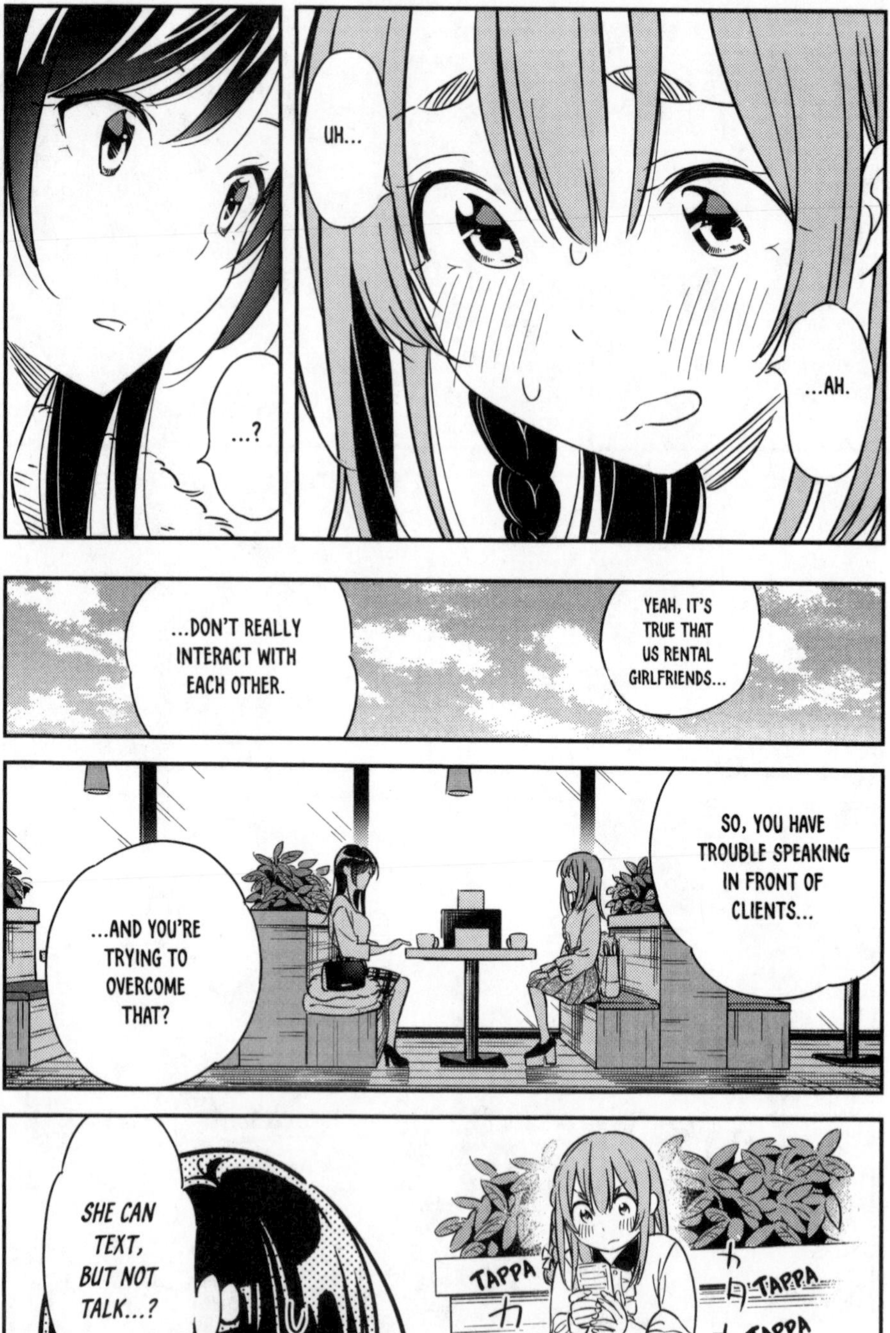
UH...
...AH.
...?
YEAH, IT'S TRUE THAT US RENTAL GIRLFRIENDS...
...DON'T REALLY INTERACT WITH EACH OTHER.
SO, YOU HAVE TROUBLE SPEAKING IN FRONT OF CLIENTS...
...AND YOU'RE TRYING TO OVERCOME THAT?
カタ TAPPA
カタ TAPPA
TAPPA カタ
SHE CAN TEXT, BUT NOT TALK...?

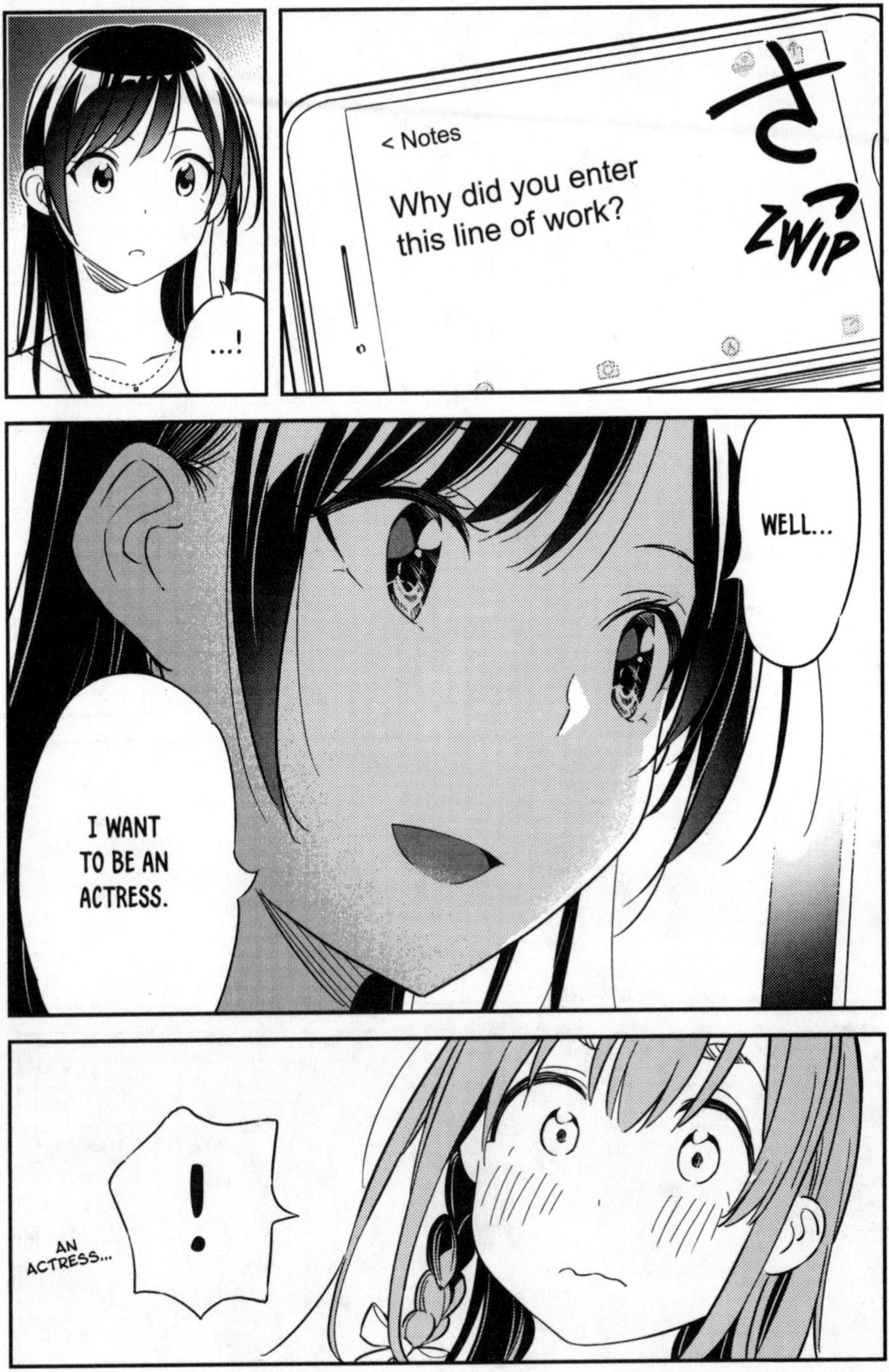
< Notes
Why did you enter this line of work?
さっ
ZWIP
...!
WELL...
I WANT TO BE AN ACTRESS.
!
AN ACTRESS...

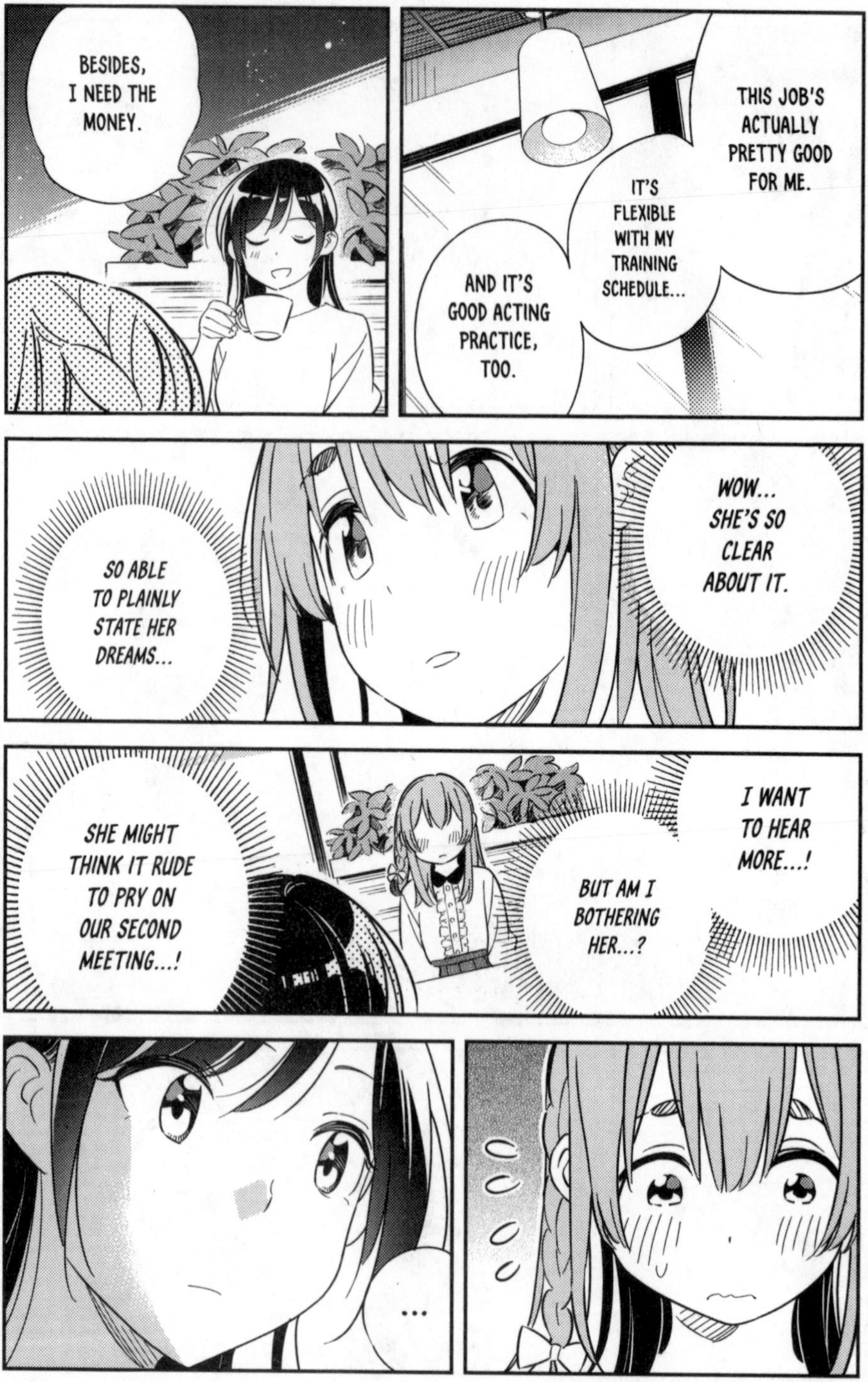
THIS JOB'S ACTUALLY PRETTY GOOD FOR ME.
IT'S FLEXIBLE WITH MY TRAINING SCHEDULE...
AND IT'S GOOD ACTING PRACTICE, TOO.
BESIDES, I NEED THE MONEY.
WOW... SHE'S SO CLEAR ABOUT IT.
SO ABLE TO PLAINLY STATE HER DREAMS...
I WANT TO HEAR MORE...!
BUT AM I BOTHERING HER...?
SHE MIGHT THINK IT RUDE TO PRY ON OUR SECOND MEETING...!
...

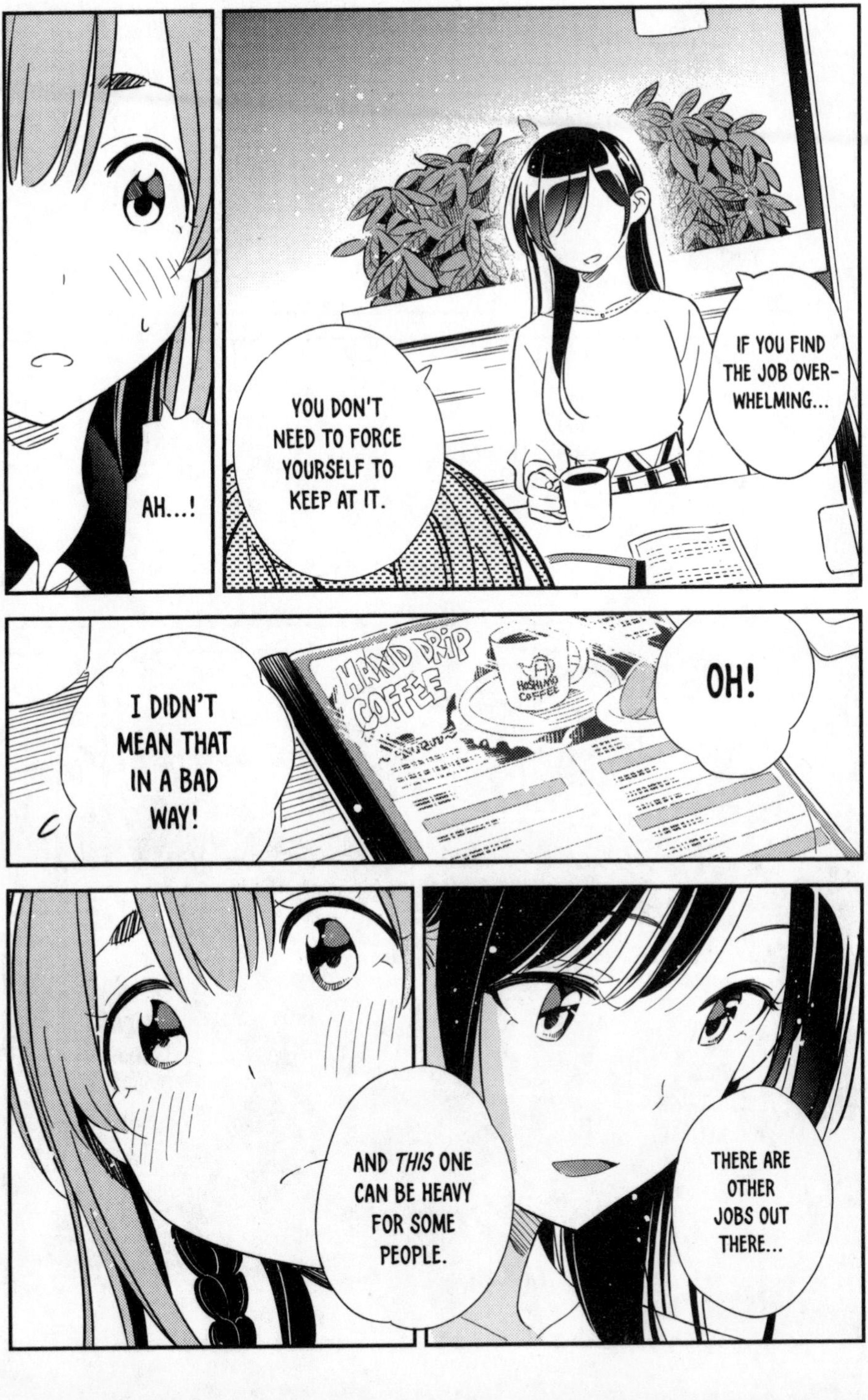
IF YOU FIND THE JOB OVER-WHELMING...
YOU DON'T NEED TO FORCE YOURSELF TO KEEP AT IT.
AH...!
OH!
HAND DRIP COFFEE
HOSHINO COFFEE
I DIDN'T MEAN THAT IN A BAD WAY!
THERE ARE OTHER JOBS OUT THERE...
AND *THIS* ONE CAN BE HEAVY FOR SOME PEOPLE.

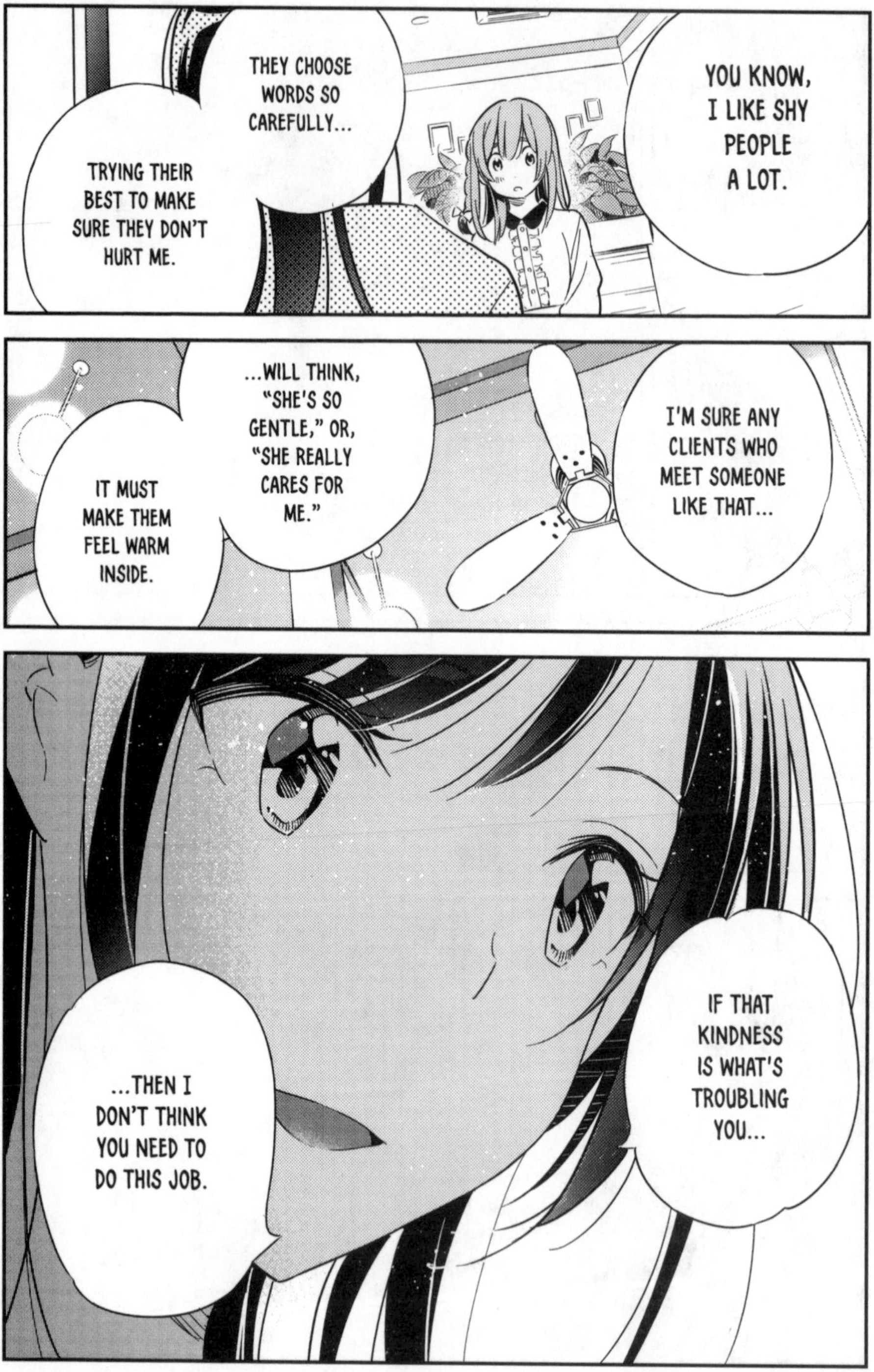
YOU KNOW, I LIKE SHY PEOPLE A LOT.
THEY CHOOSE WORDS SO CAREFULLY...
TRYING THEIR BEST TO MAKE SURE THEY DON'T HURT ME.
I'M SURE ANY CLIENTS WHO MEET SOMEONE LIKE THAT...
...WILL THINK, "SHE'S SO GENTLE," OR, "SHE REALLY CARES FOR ME."
IT MUST MAKE THEM FEEL WARM INSIDE.
IF THAT KINDNESS IS WHAT'S TROUBLING YOU...
...THEN I DON'T THINK YOU NEED TO DO THIS JOB.

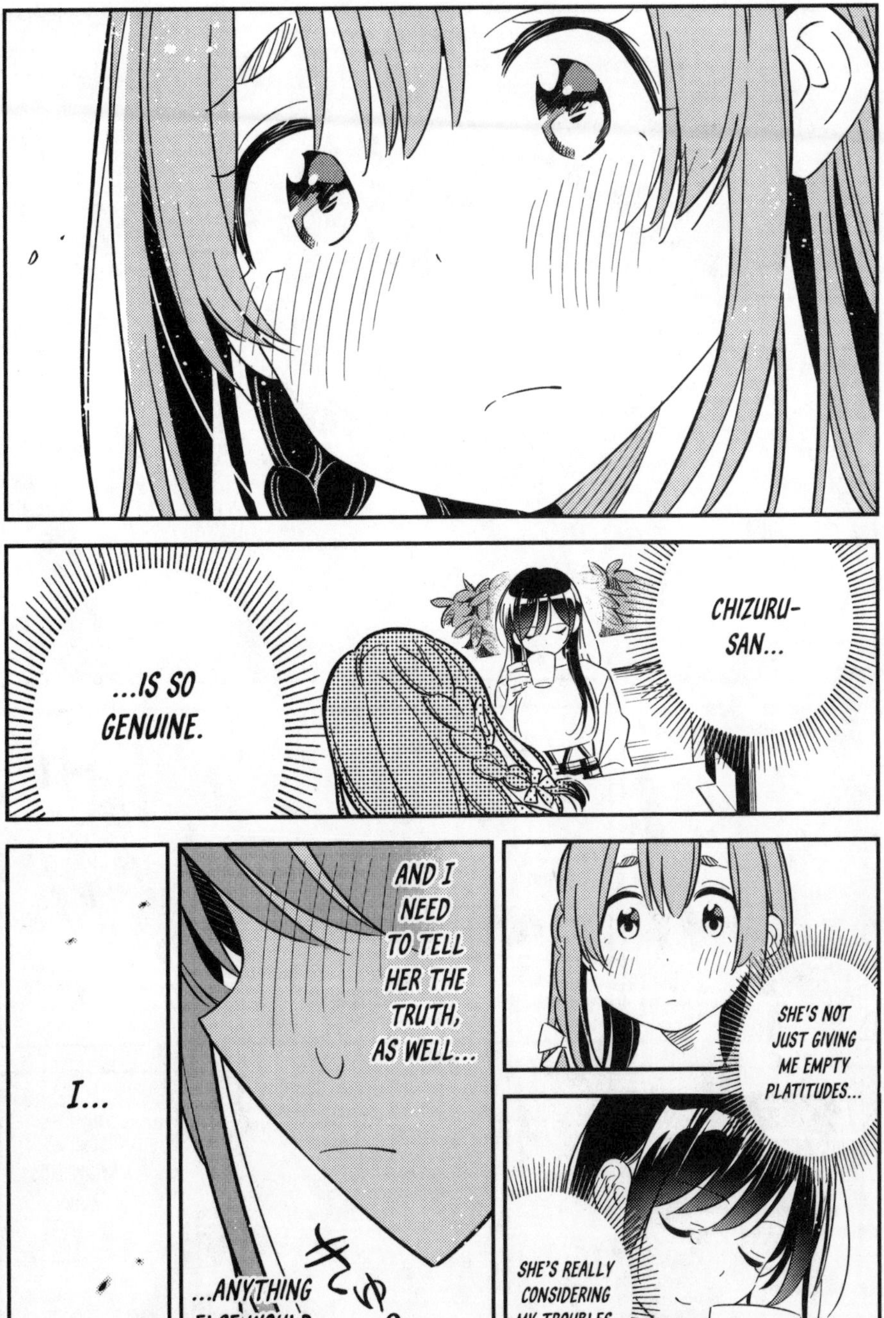
CHIZURU-SAN...
...IS SO GENUINE.
SHE'S NOT JUST GIVING ME EMPTY PLATITUDES...
SHE'S REALLY CONSIDERING MY TROUBLES.
AND I NEED TO TELL HER THE TRUTH, AS WELL...
...ANYTHING ELSE WOULD BE RUDE...
GULP
I...

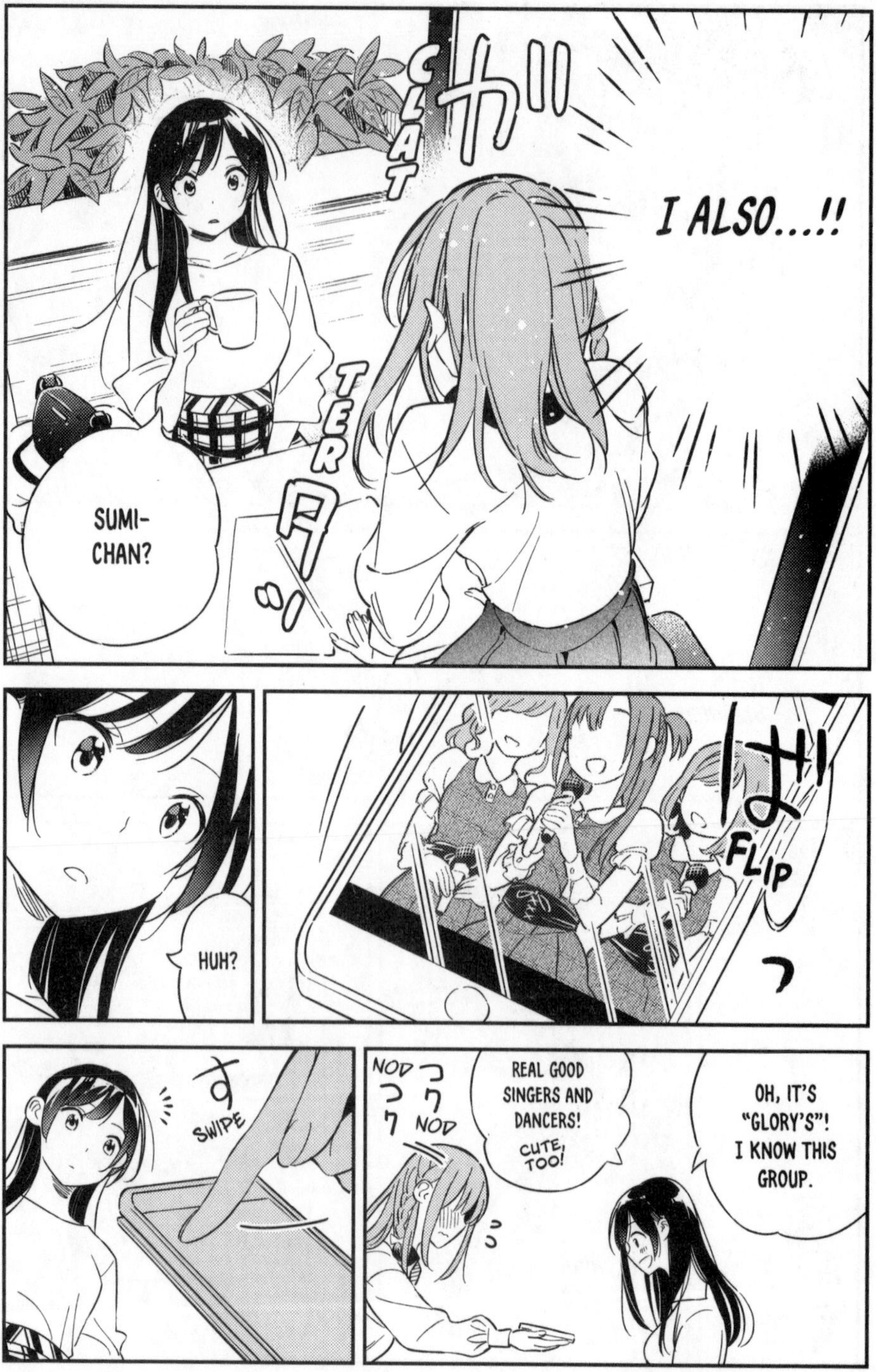
I ALSO...!!
CLAT
TER
SUMI-CHAN?
FLIP
HUH?
OH, IT'S "GLORY'S"! I KNOW THIS GROUP.
REAL GOOD SINGERS AND DANCERS!
CUTE, TOO!
NOD
NOD
SWIPE

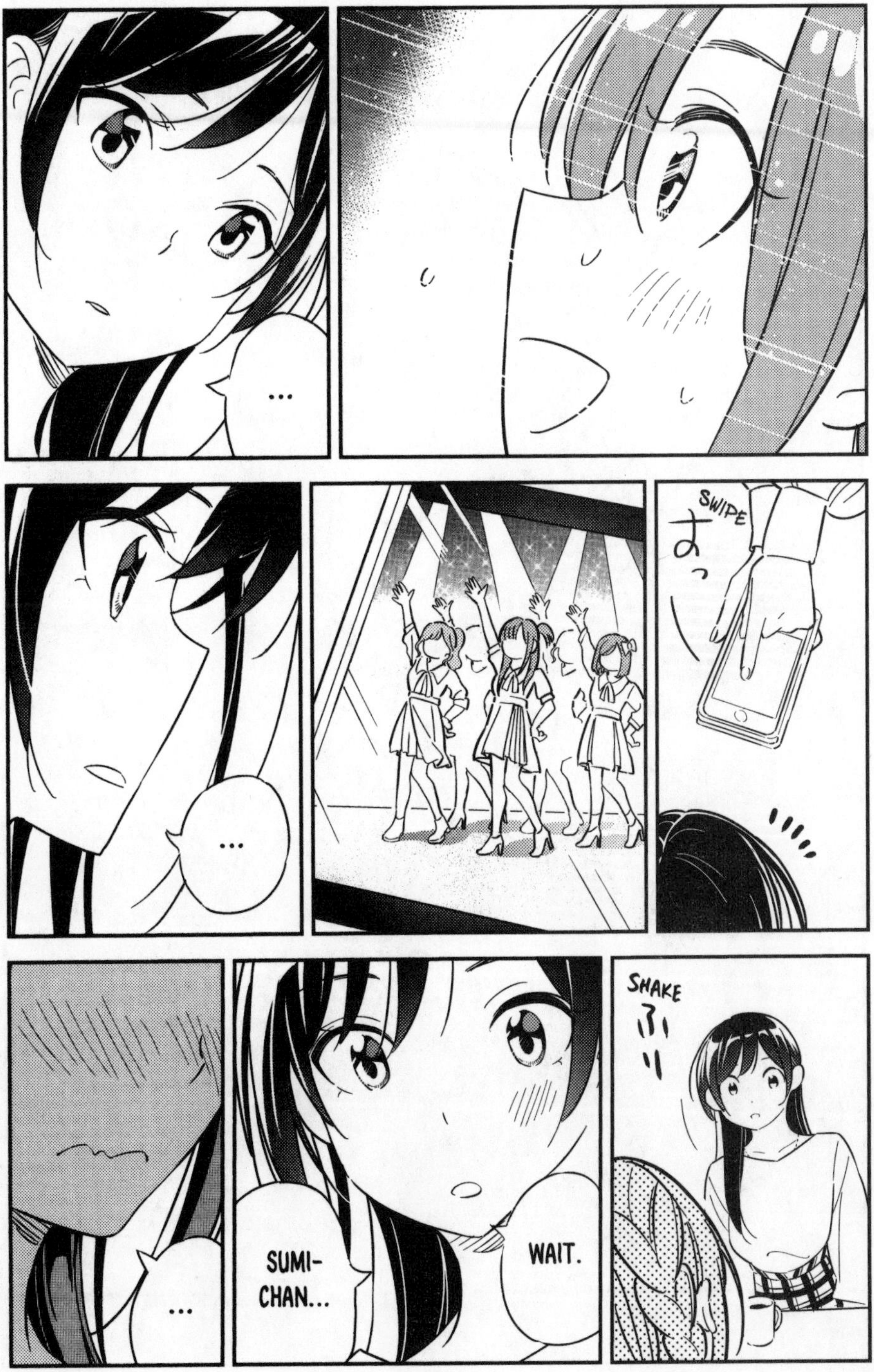
...
SWIPE
...
SHAKE
WAIT.
SUMI-CHAN...
...

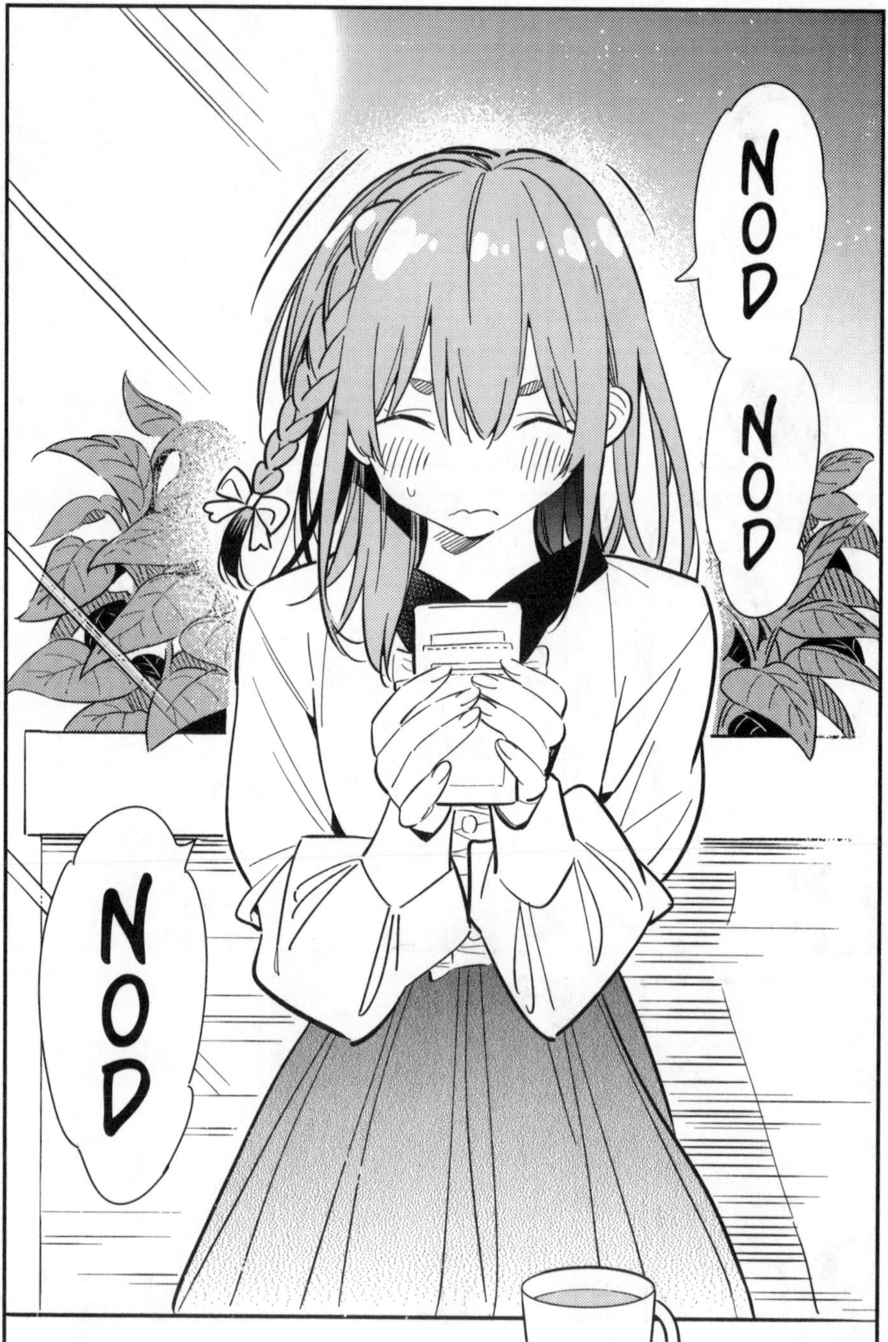
NOD NOD NOD
NOD

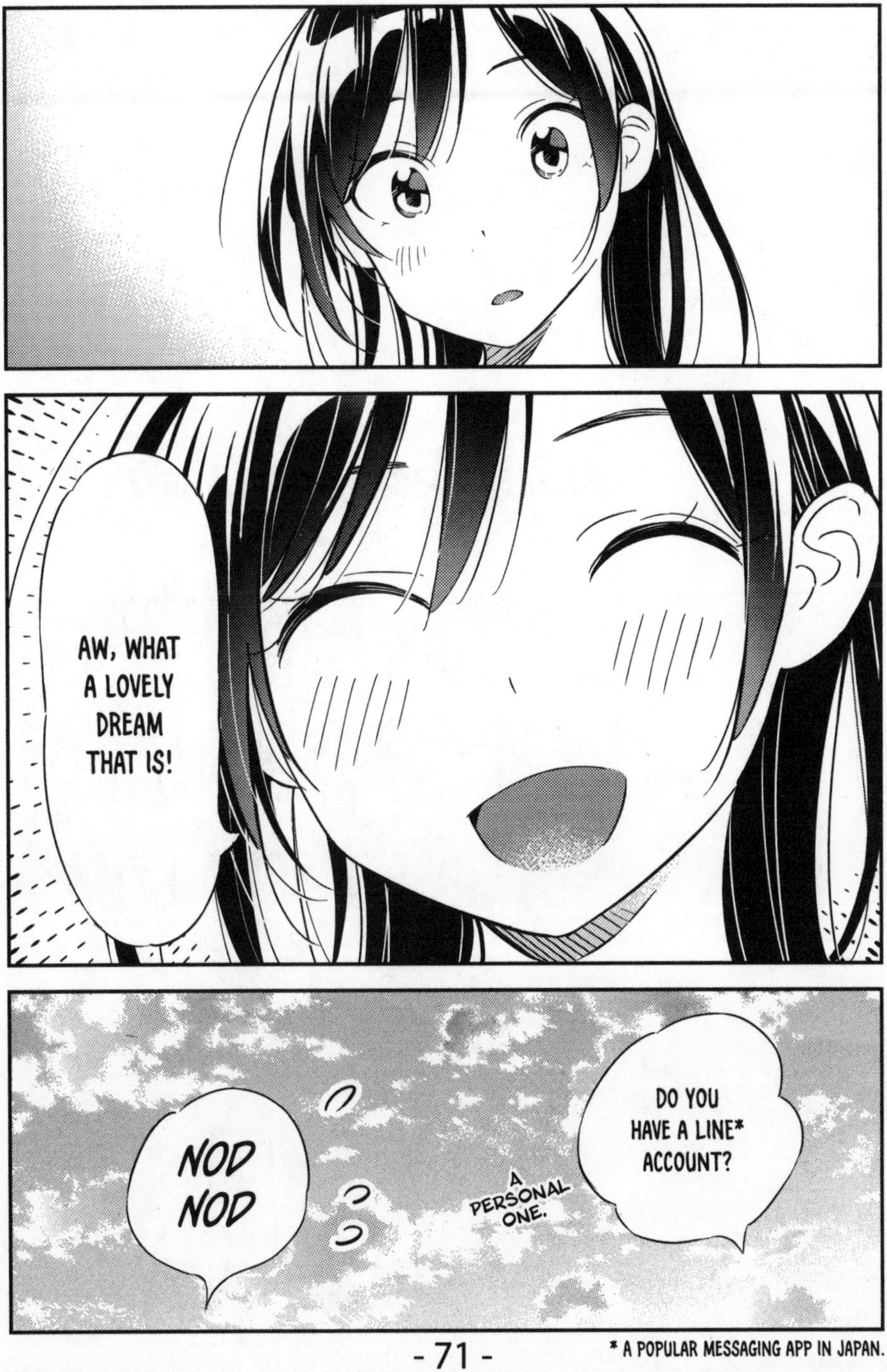
AW, WHAT A LOVELY DREAM THAT IS!
DO YOU HAVE A LINE* ACCOUNT?
A PERSONAL ONE.
NOD NOD

* A POPULAR MESSAGING APP IN JAPAN.

SUMI'S ROOM DESIGN

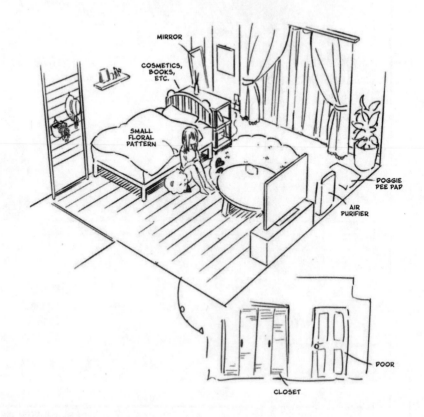

MIRROR

COSMETICS,
BOOKS,
ETC.

SMALL
FLORAL
PATTERN

DOGGIE
PEE PAD

AIR
PURIFIER

DOOR

CLOSET

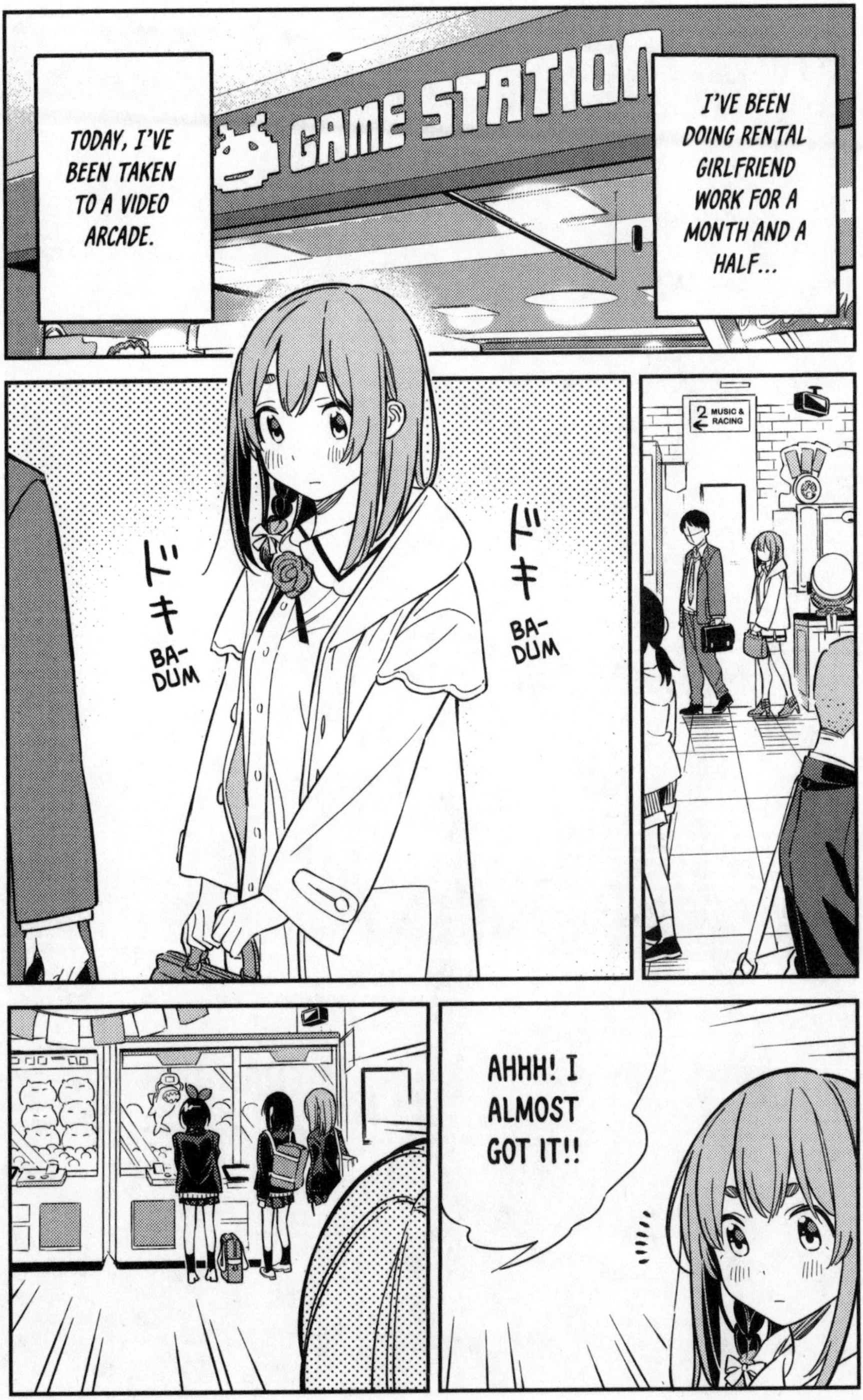
I'VE BEEN DOING RENTAL GIRLFRIEND WORK FOR A MONTH AND A HALF...
GAME STATION
TODAY, I'VE BEEN TAKEN TO A VIDEO ARCADE.
2 MUSIC & RACING
ドキ
BA-DUM
ドキ
BA-DUM
AHHH! I ALMOST GOT IT!!

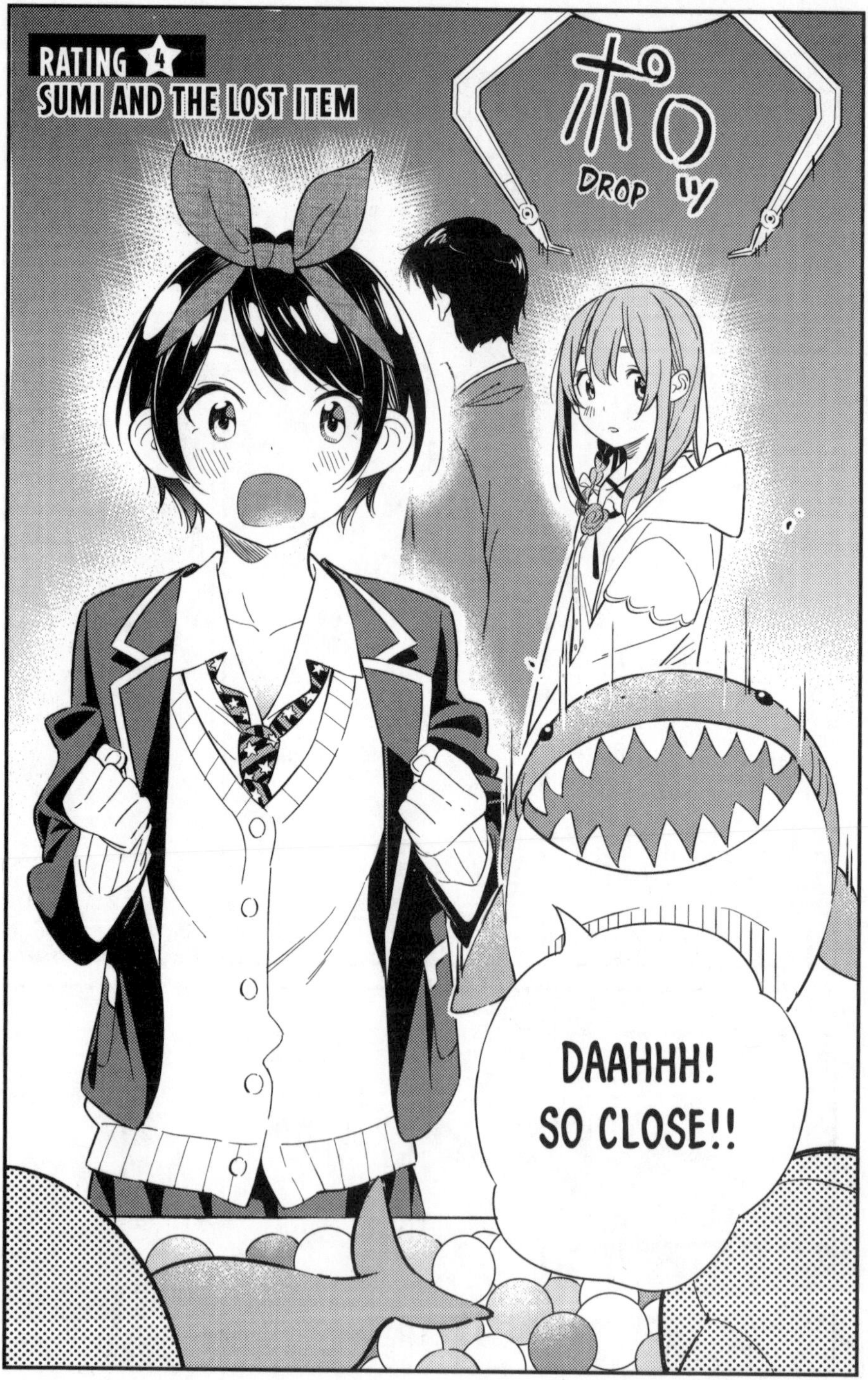
RATING 4
SUMI AND THE LOST ITEM
ポロッ
DROP
DAAHHH! SO CLOSE!!

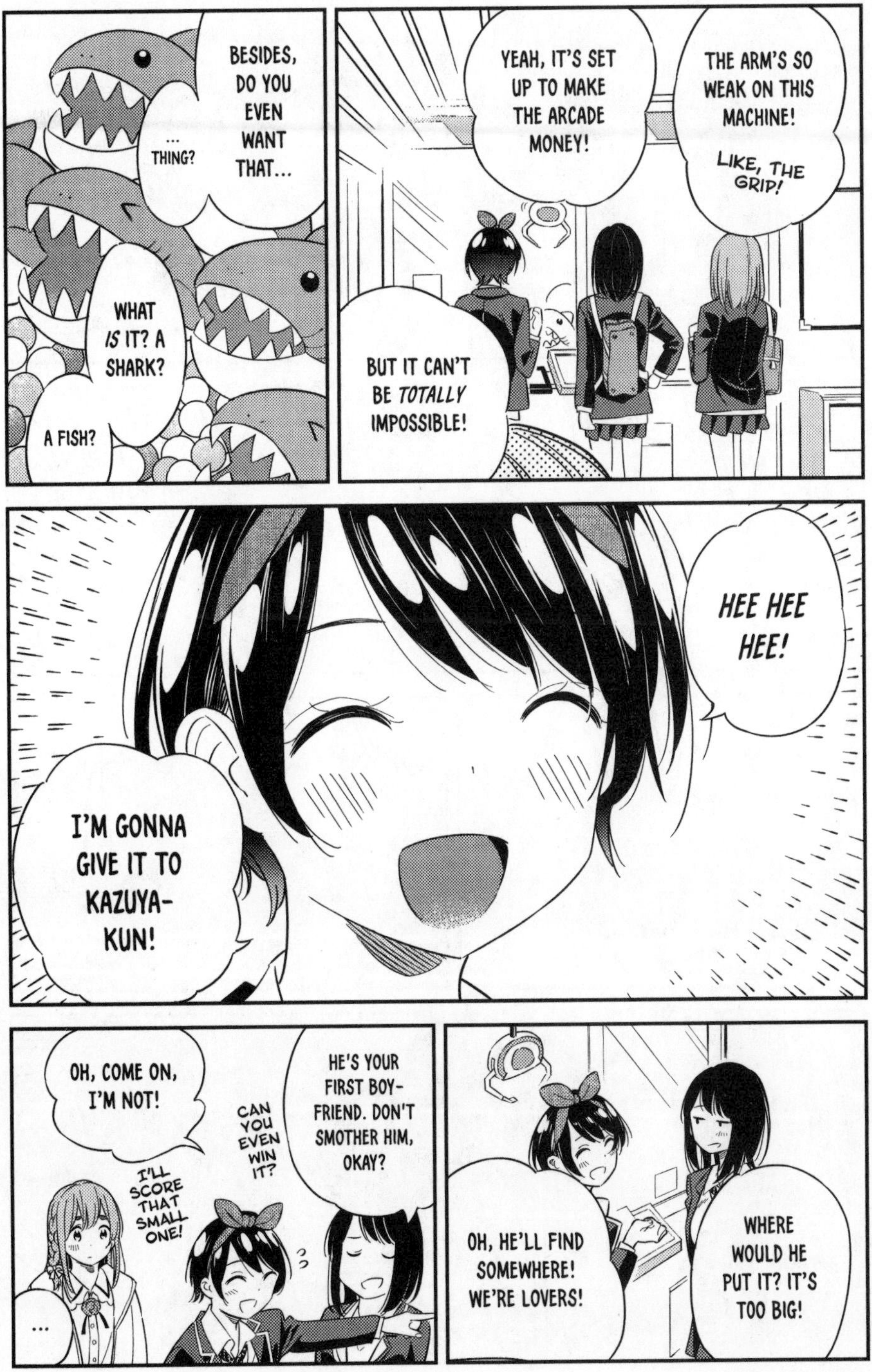
THE ARM'S SO WEAK ON THIS MACHINE!
LIKE, THE GRIP!
YEAH, IT'S SET UP TO MAKE THE ARCADE MONEY!
BUT IT CAN'T BE *TOTALLY* IMPOSSIBLE!
BESIDES, DO YOU EVEN WANT THAT...
...THING?
WHAT *IS* IT? A SHARK?
A FISH?
HEE HEE HEE!
I'M GONNA GIVE IT TO KAZUYA-KUN!
WHERE WOULD HE PUT IT? IT'S TOO BIG!
OH, HE'LL FIND SOMEWHERE! WE'RE LOVERS!
HE'S YOUR FIRST BOY-FRIEND. DON'T SMOTHER HIM, OKAY?
OH, COME ON, I'M NOT!
CAN YOU EVEN WIN IT?
I'LL SCORE THAT SMALL ONE!
...

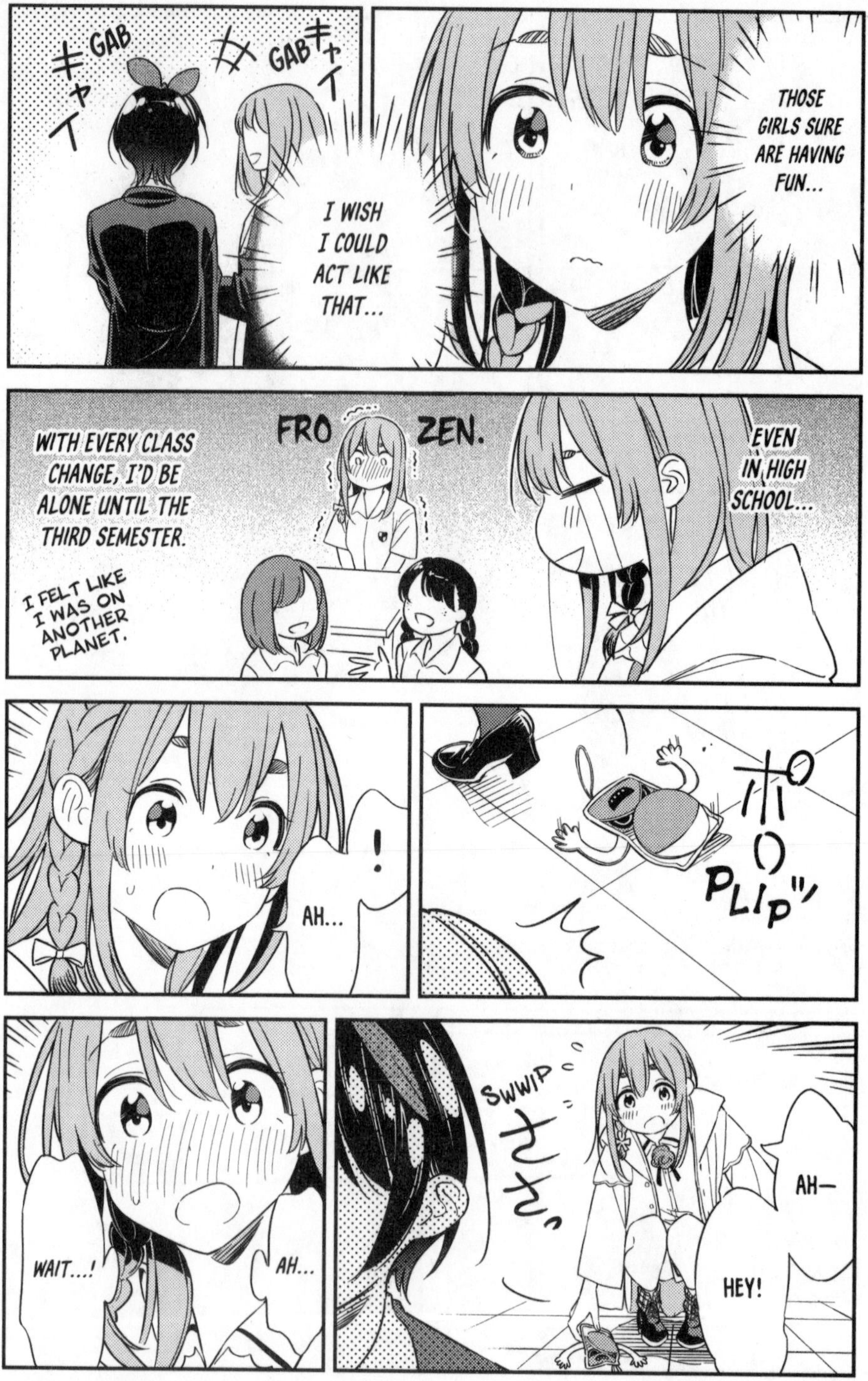
THOSE GIRLS SURE ARE HAVING FUN...
I WISH I COULD ACT LIKE THAT...
GAB キャイ
GAB キャイ
EVEN IN HIGH SCHOOL...
FRO ZEN.
WITH EVERY CLASS CHANGE, I'D BE ALONE UNTIL THE THIRD SEMESTER.
I FELT LIKE I WAS ON ANOTHER PLANET.
ポロッ PLIP
!
AH...
AH—
HEY!
SWWIP さささっ
AH...
WAIT...!

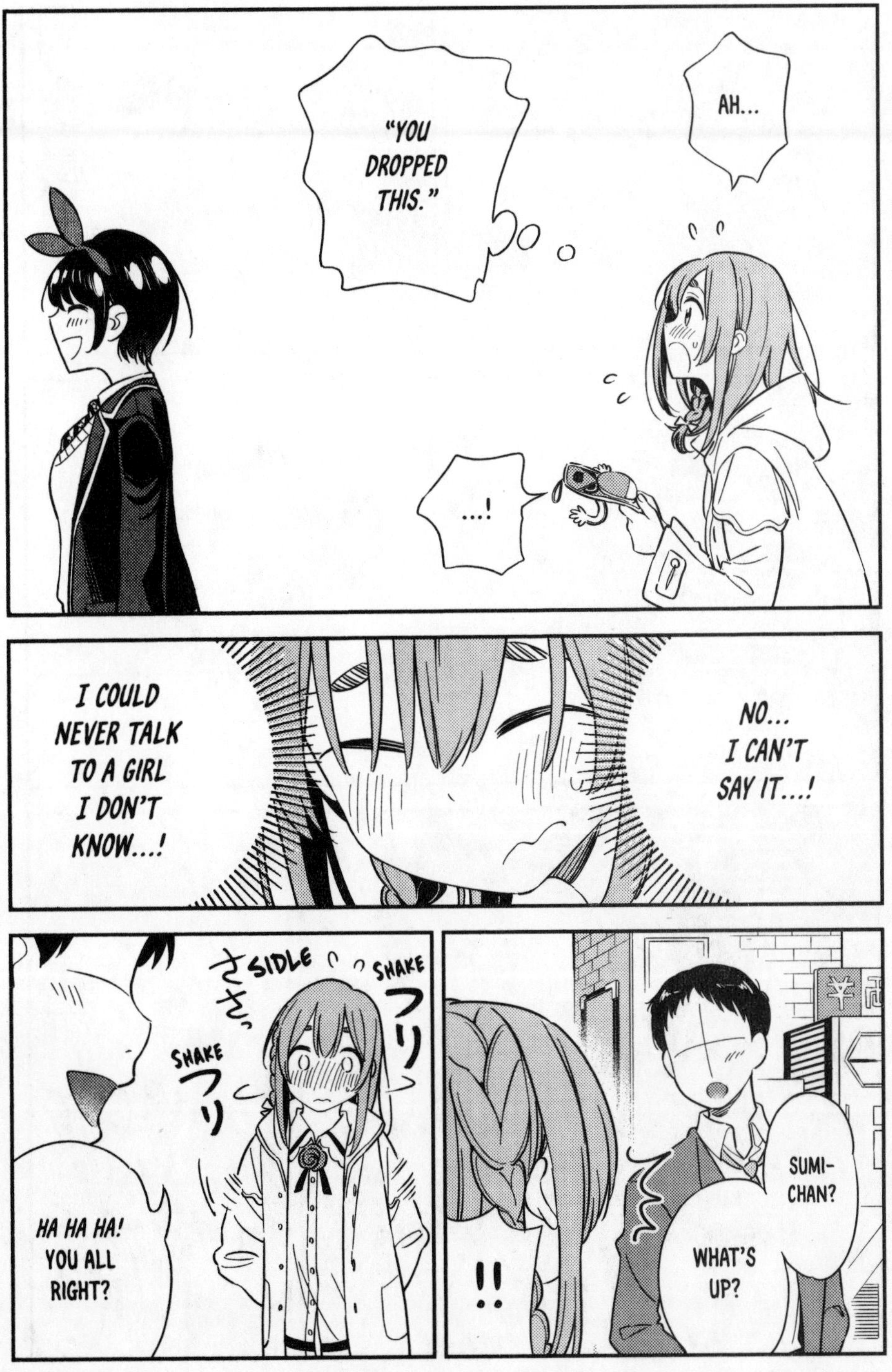
AH...
“YOU DROPPED THIS.”
...!
NO... I CAN’T SAY IT...!
I COULD NEVER TALK TO A GIRL I DON’T KNOW...!
SUMI-CHAN?
WHAT’S UP?
!!
SHAKE フリ
SIDLE ささ
SHAKE フリ
HA HA HA! YOU ALL RIGHT?

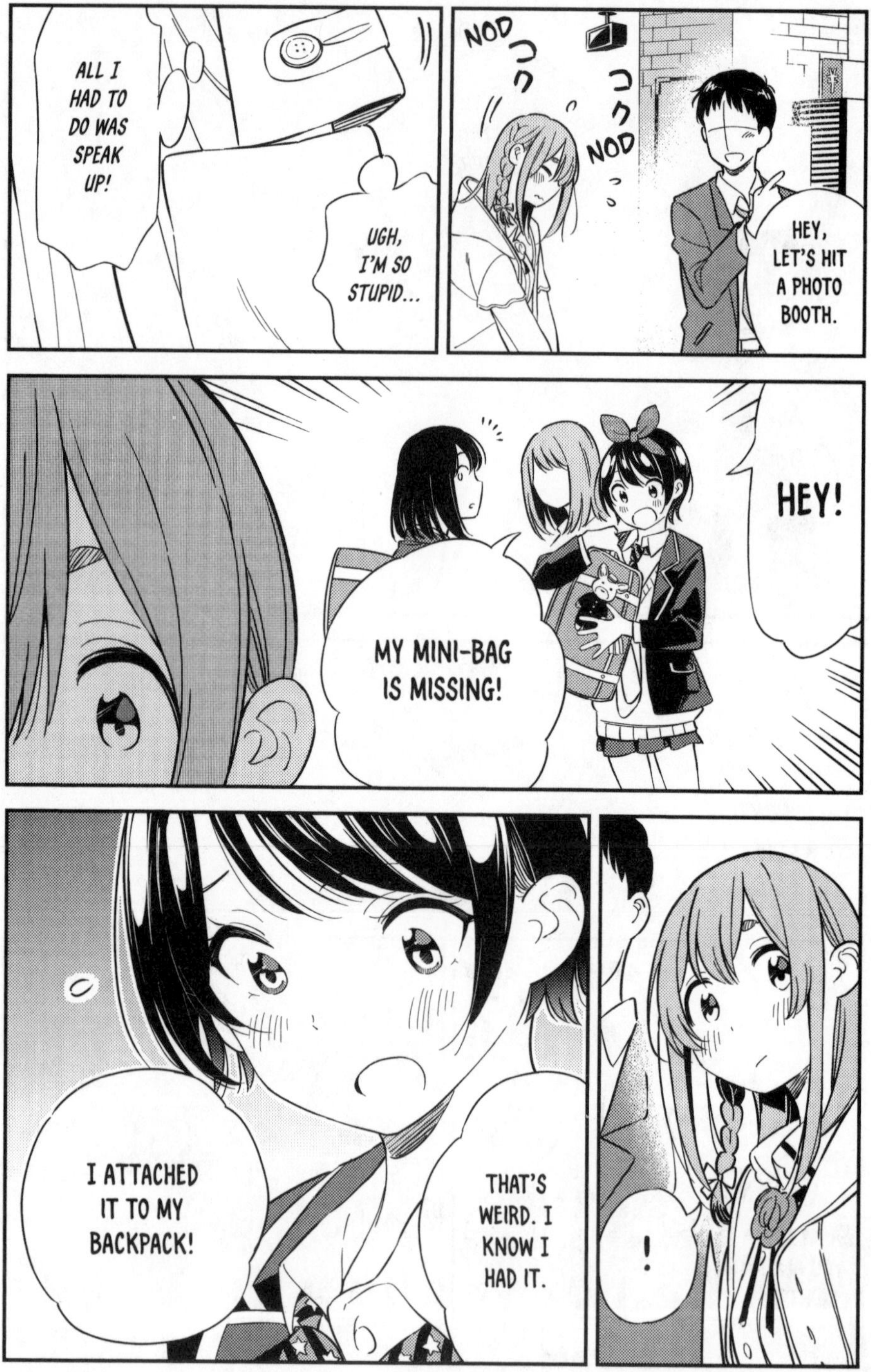
HEY, LET'S HIT A PHOTO BOOTH.
コク NOD
NOD コク
ALL I HAD TO DO WAS SPEAK UP!
UGH, I'M SO STUPID...
HEY!
MY MINI-BAG IS MISSING!
!
THAT'S WEIRD. I KNOW I HAD IT.
I ATTACHED IT TO MY BACKPACK!

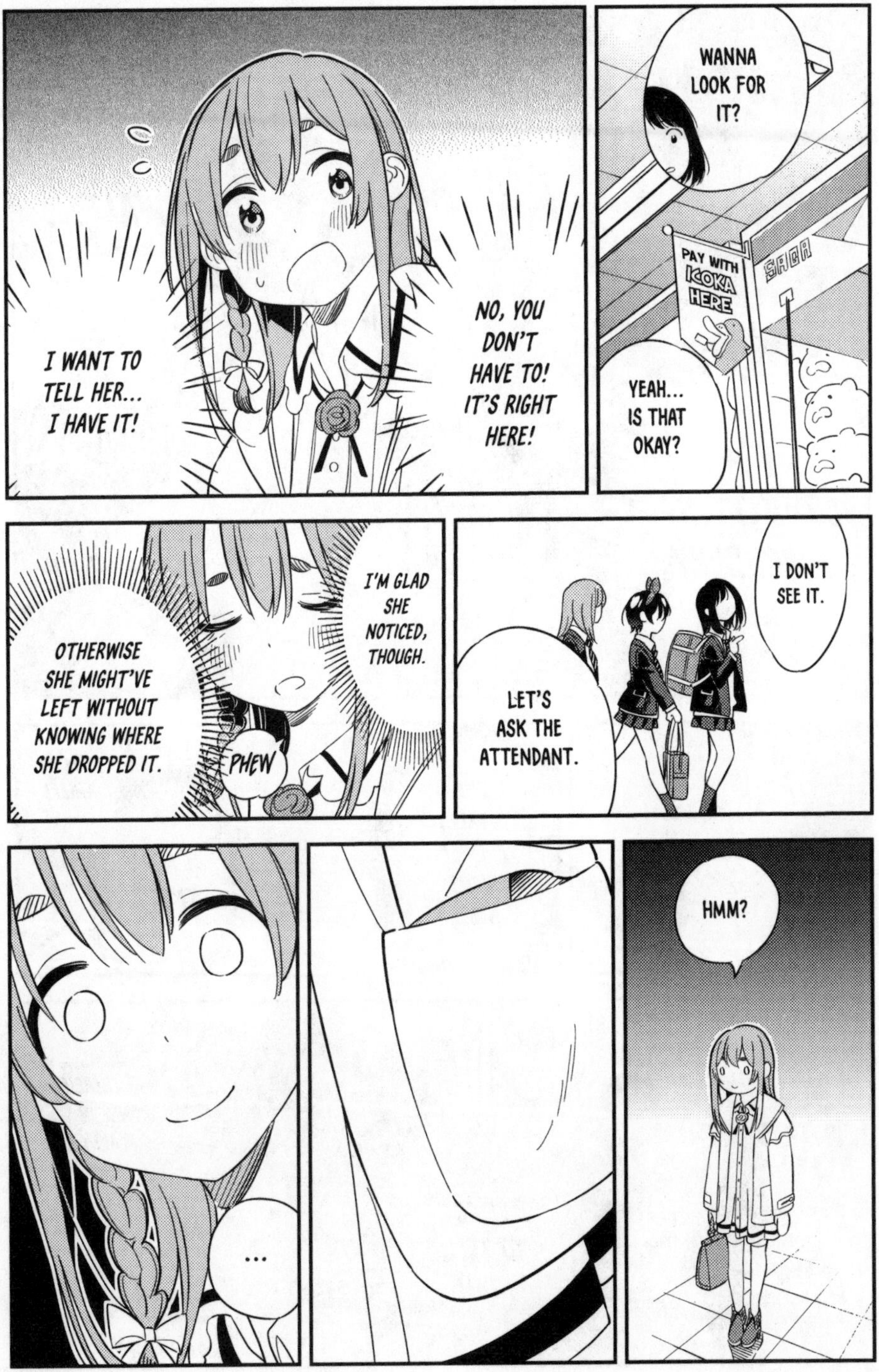
WANNA LOOK FOR IT?
PAY WITH ICOKA HERE
SAGA
YEAH... IS THAT OKAY?
NO, YOU DON'T HAVE TO! IT'S RIGHT HERE!
I WANT TO TELL HER... I HAVE IT!
I DON'T SEE IT.
LET'S ASK THE ATTENDANT.
I'M GLAD SHE NOTICED, THOUGH.
OTHERWISE SHE MIGHT'VE LEFT WITHOUT KNOWING WHERE SHE DROPPED IT.
PHEW
HMM?
...

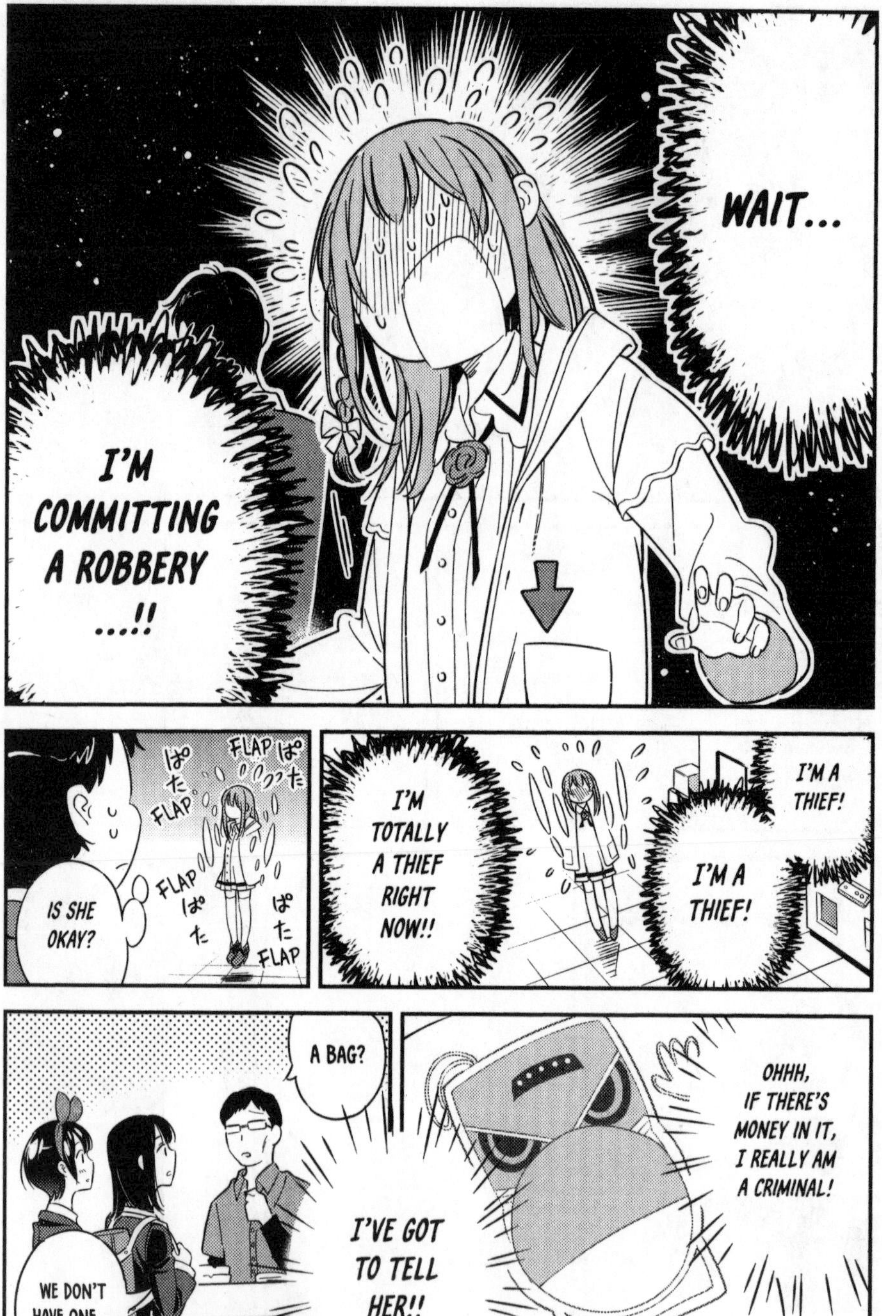
WAIT...
I'M COMMITTING A ROBBERY ...!!
I'M A THIEF!
I'M A THIEF!
I'M TOTALLY A THIEF RIGHT NOW!!
ぱた FLAP
ぱた FLAP
ぱた FLAP
ぱた FLAP
IS SHE OKAY?
OHHH, IF THERE'S MONEY IN IT, I REALLY AM A CRIMINAL!
I'VE GOT TO TELL HER!!
A BAG?
WE DON'T HAVE ONE...

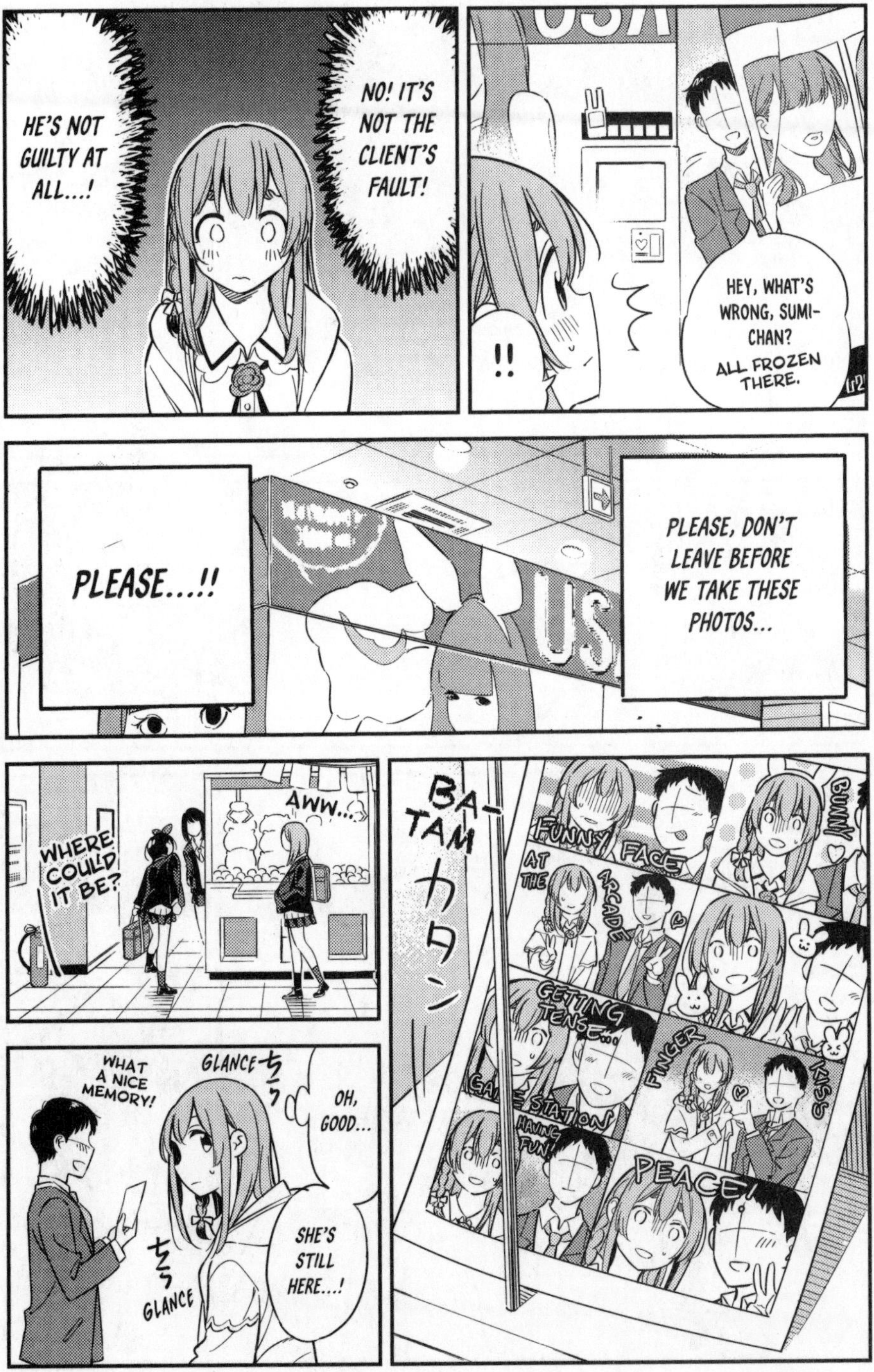
HEY, WHAT'S WRONG, SUMI-CHAN? ALL FROZEN THERE.
!!
NO! IT'S NOT THE CLIENT'S FAULT!
HE'S NOT GUILTY AT ALL...!
PLEASE, DON'T LEAVE BEFORE WE TAKE THESE PHOTOS...
PLEASE...!!
BA-TAM
カタン
BUNNY
FUNNY FACE
AT THE ARCADE
GETTING TENSE...
FINGER KISS
GAME STATION
HAVING FUN
PEACE!
AWW...
WHERE COULD IT BE?
OH, GOOD...
GLANCE ちら
WHAT A NICE MEMORY!
SHE'S STILL HERE...!
ちら GLANCE

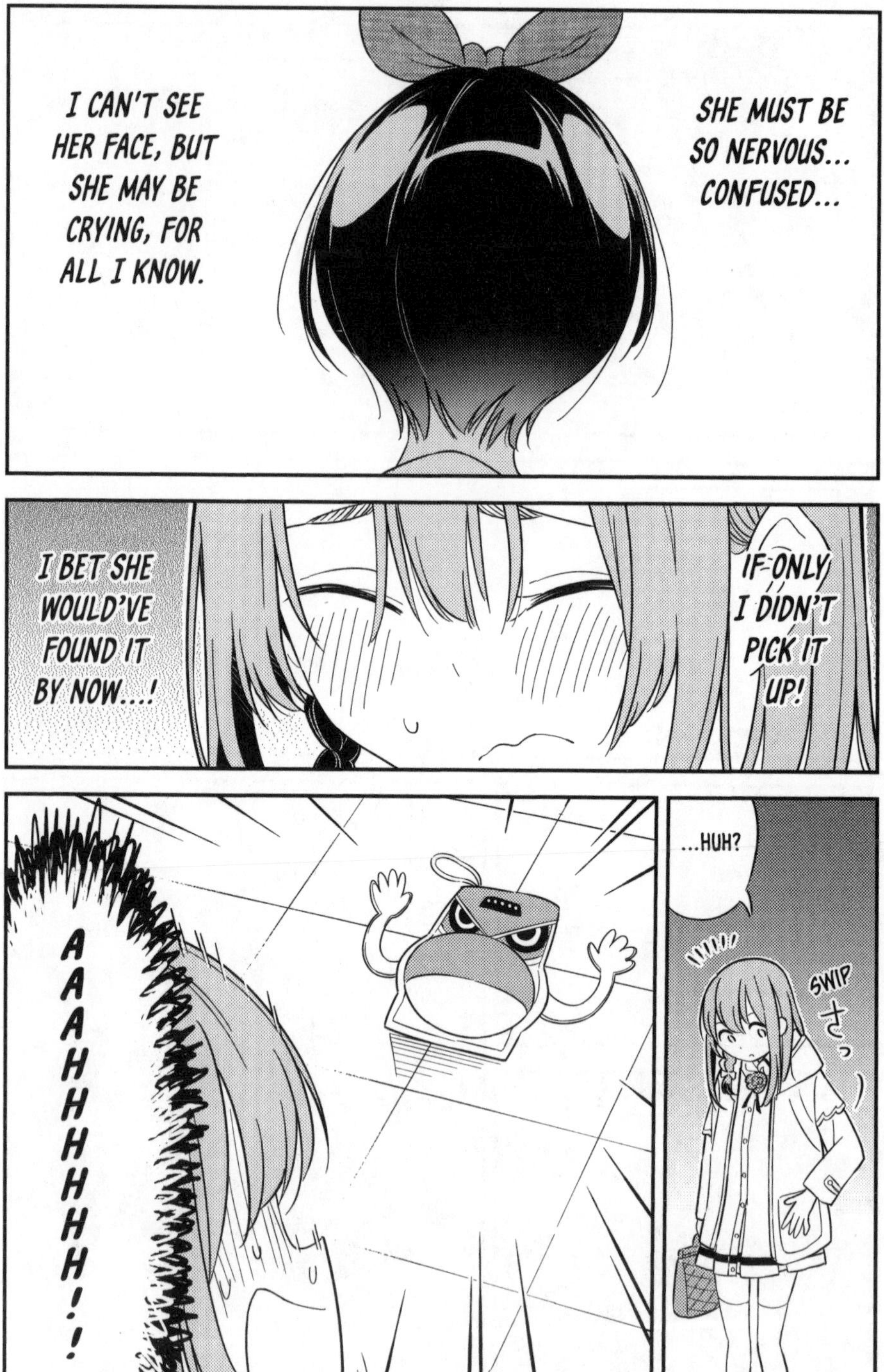
SHE MUST BE SO NERVOUS... CONFUSED...
I CAN'T SEE HER FACE, BUT SHE MAY BE CRYING, FOR ALL I KNOW.
IF ONLY I DIDN'T PICK IT UP!
I BET SHE WOULD'VE FOUND IT BY NOW...!
...HUH?
SWIP
さっ
AAAHHHHHH!!

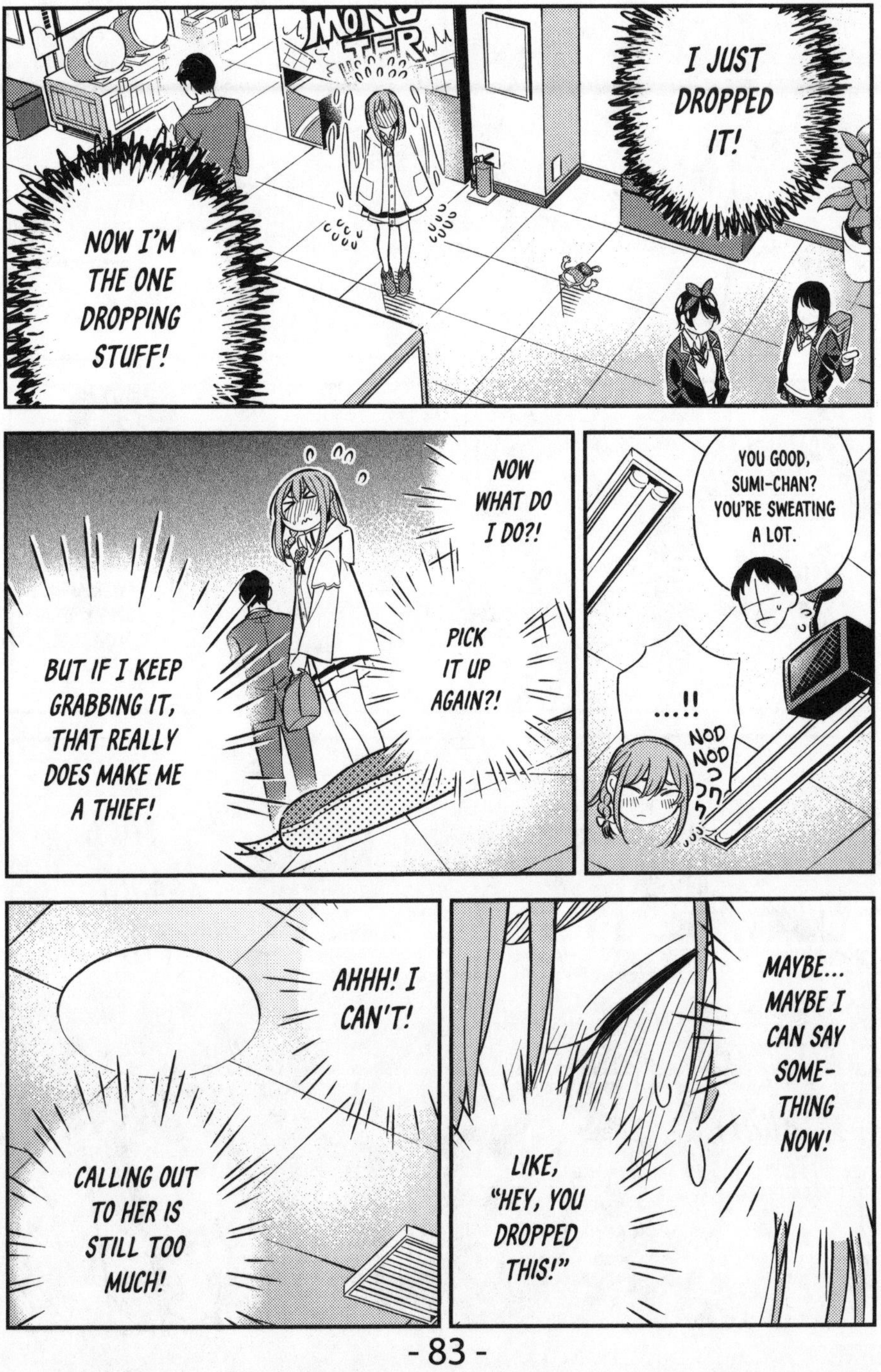
I JUST DROPPED IT!
NOW I'M THE ONE DROPPING STUFF!
YOU GOOD, SUMI-CHAN? YOU'RE SWEATING A LOT.
...!!
NOD NOD
NOW WHAT DO I DO?!
PICK IT UP AGAIN?!
BUT IF I KEEP GRABBING IT, THAT REALLY DOES MAKE ME A THIEF!
MAYBE... MAYBE I CAN SAY SOME-THING NOW!
LIKE, "HEY, YOU DROPPED THIS!"
AHHH! I CAN'T!
CALLING OUT TO HER IS STILL TOO MUCH!

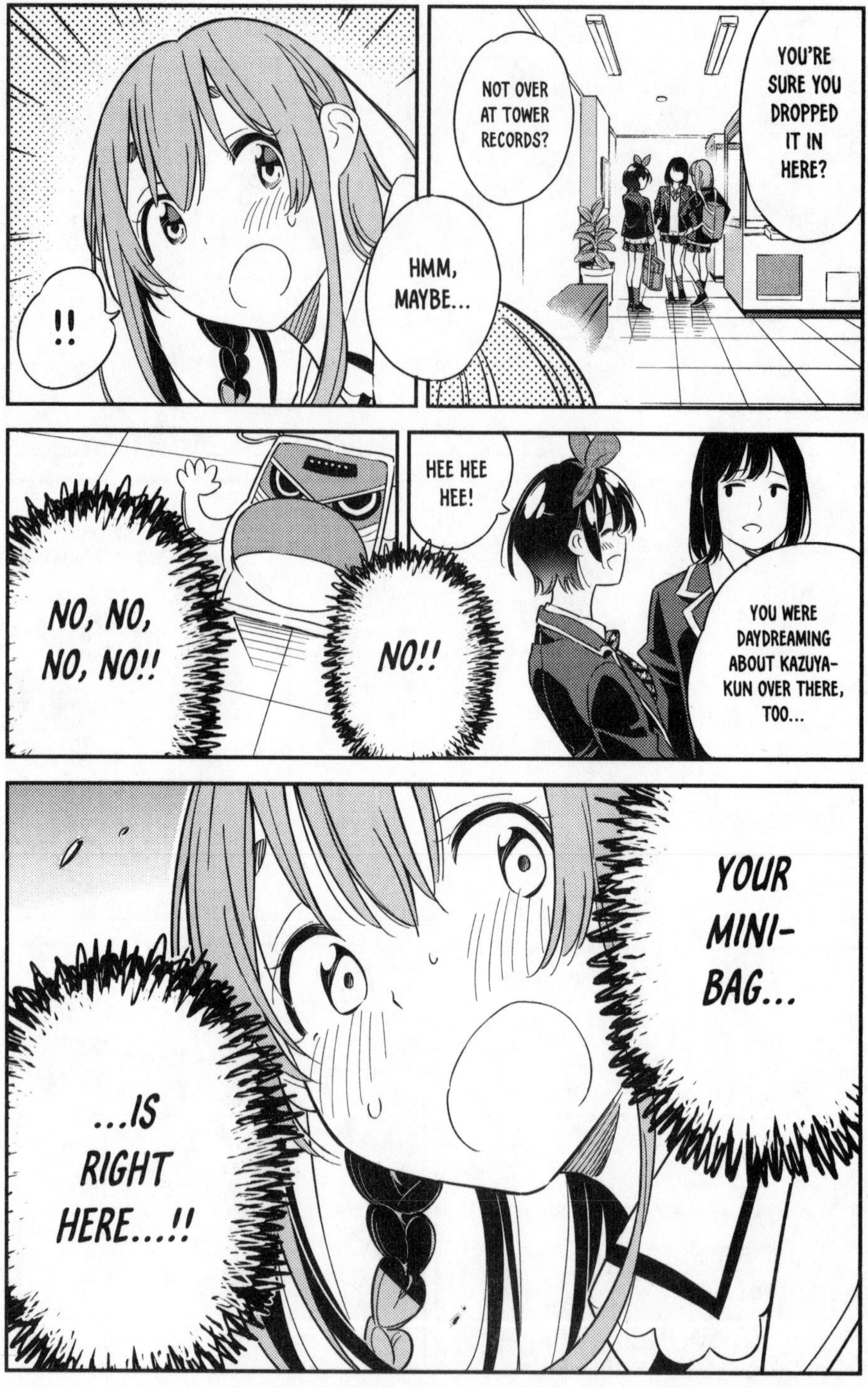
YOU'RE SURE YOU DROPPED IT IN HERE?
NOT OVER AT TOWER RECORDS?
HMM, MAYBE...
!!
YOU WERE DAYDREAMING ABOUT KAZUYA-KUN OVER THERE, TOO...
HEE HEE HEE!
NO!!
NO, NO, NO, NO!!
YOUR MINI-BAG...
...IS RIGHT HERE...!!

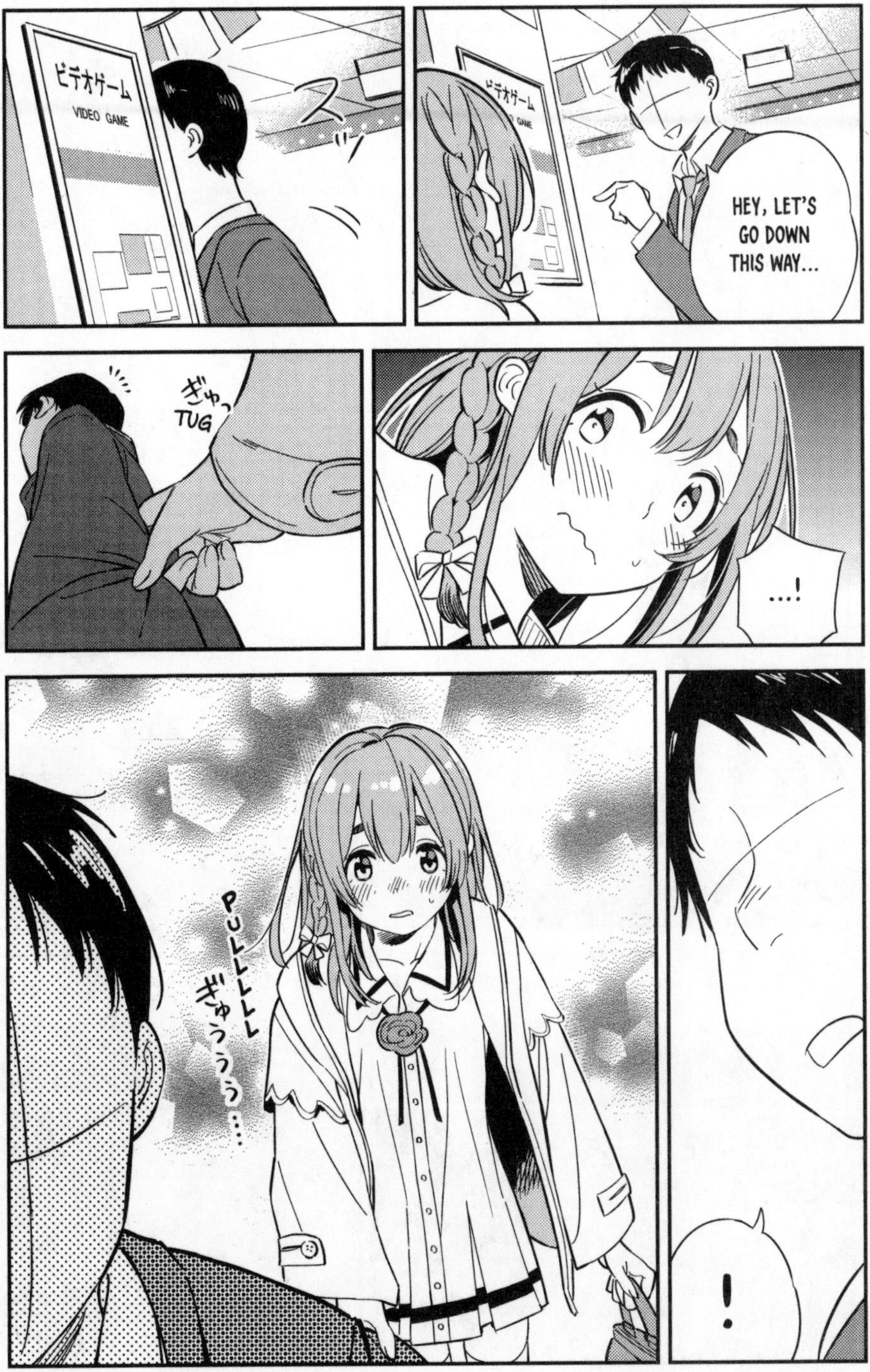

ビデオゲーム
HEY, LET'S GO DOWN THIS WAY...
ビデオゲーム
VIDEO GAME
スッ
...!
ぎゅっ
TUG
!
PULLLLLLL
ぎゅううう…

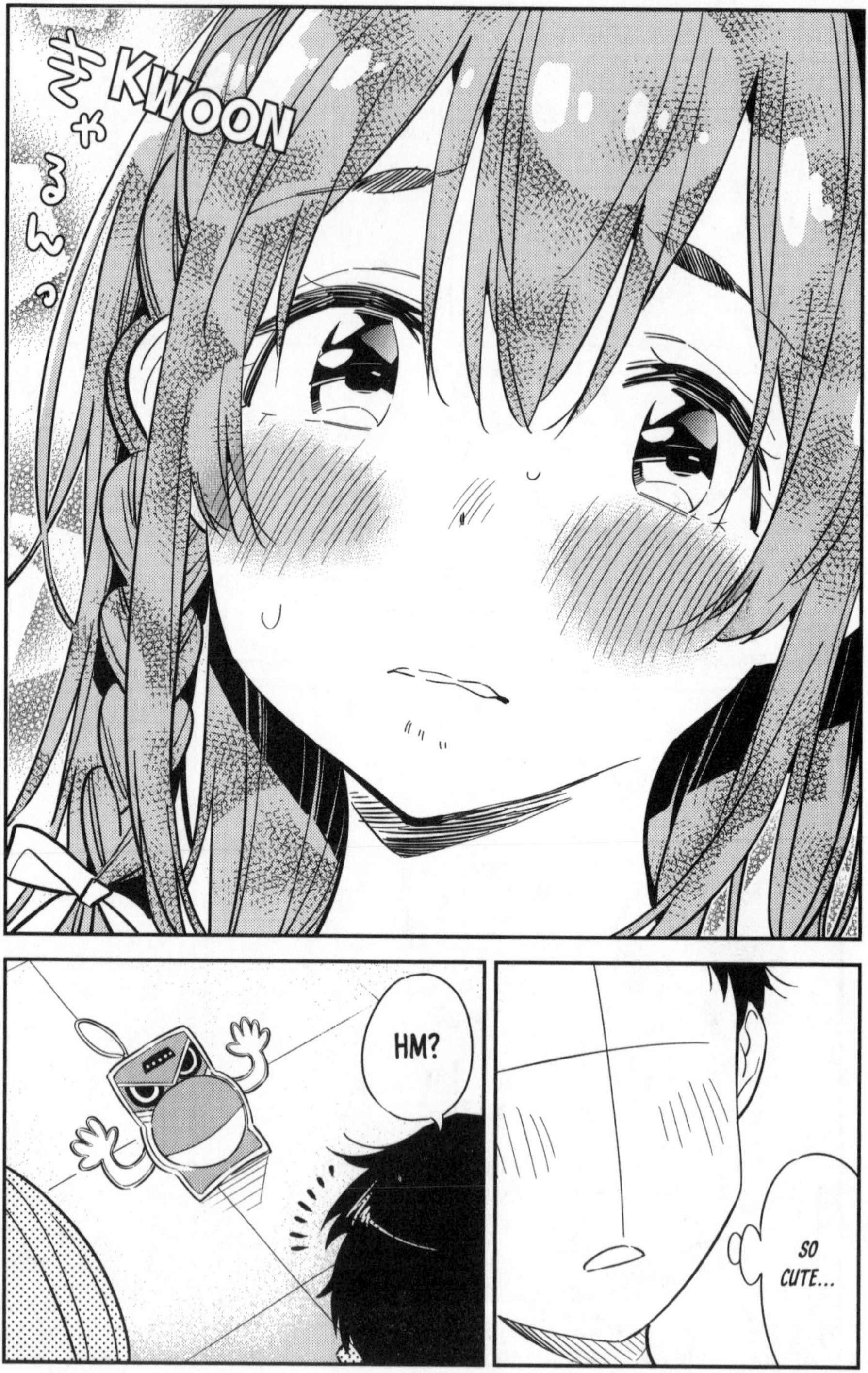
ぎゅるんっ
KWOON
SO CUTE...
HM?

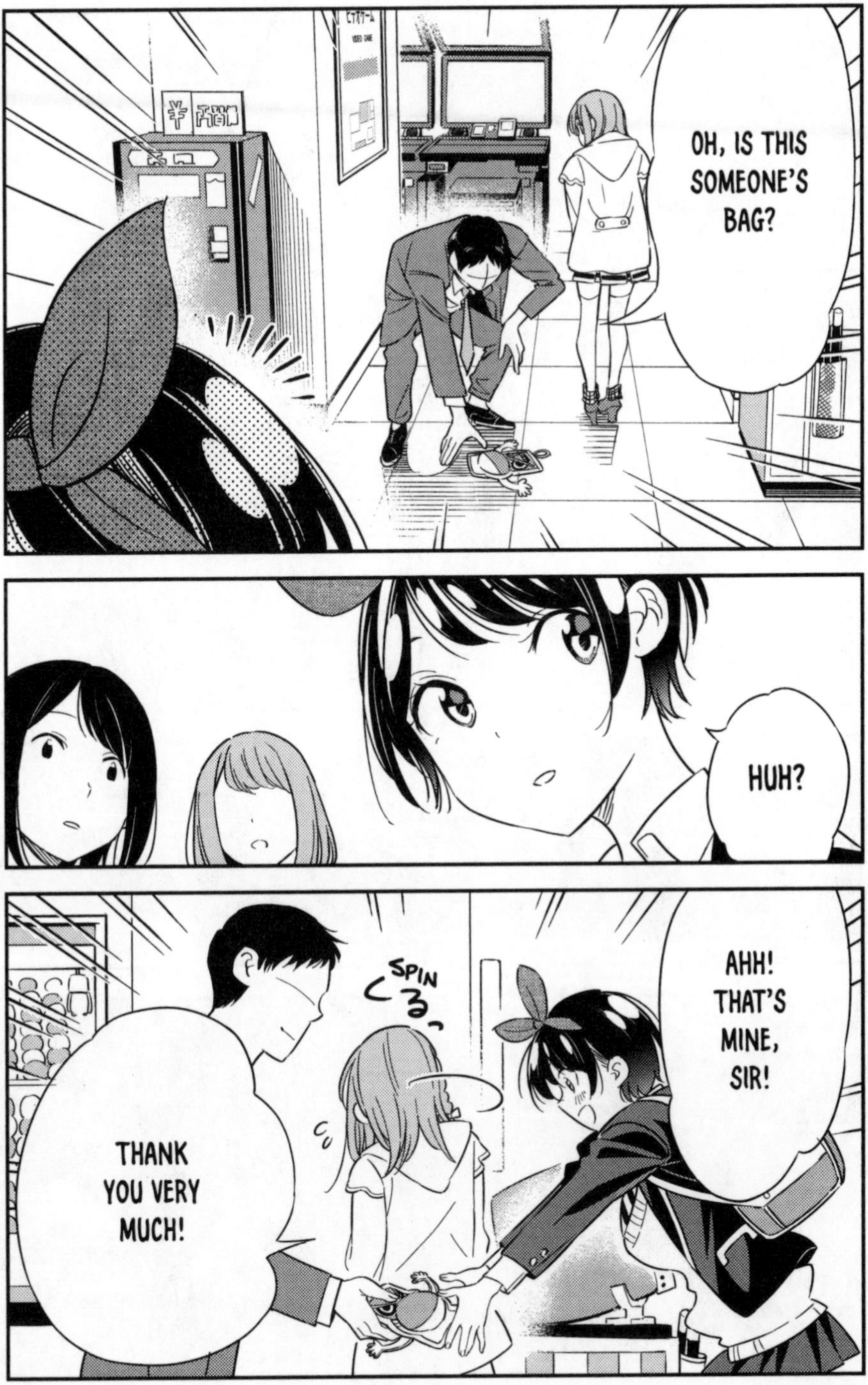
OH, IS THIS SOMEONE'S BAG?
HUH?
AHH! THAT'S MINE, SIR!
SPIN くるっ
THANK YOU VERY MUCH!

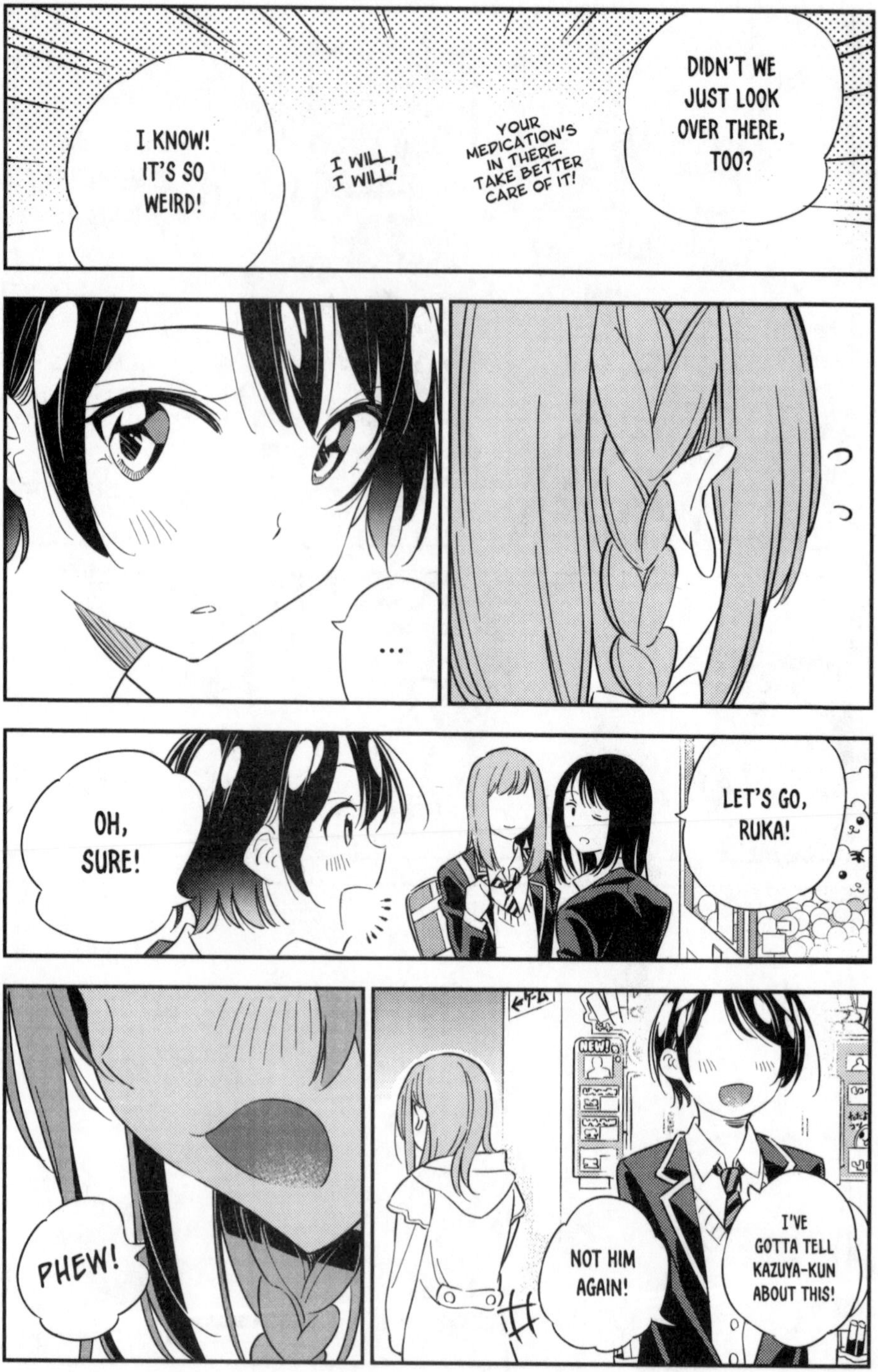
DIDN'T WE JUST LOOK OVER THERE, TOO?
YOUR MEDICATION'S IN THERE. TAKE BETTER CARE OF IT!
I WILL, I WILL!
I KNOW! IT'S SO WEIRD!
...
LET'S GO, RUKA!
OH, SURE!
I'VE GOTTA TELL KAZUYA-KUN ABOUT THIS!
NOT HIM AGAIN!
PHEW!

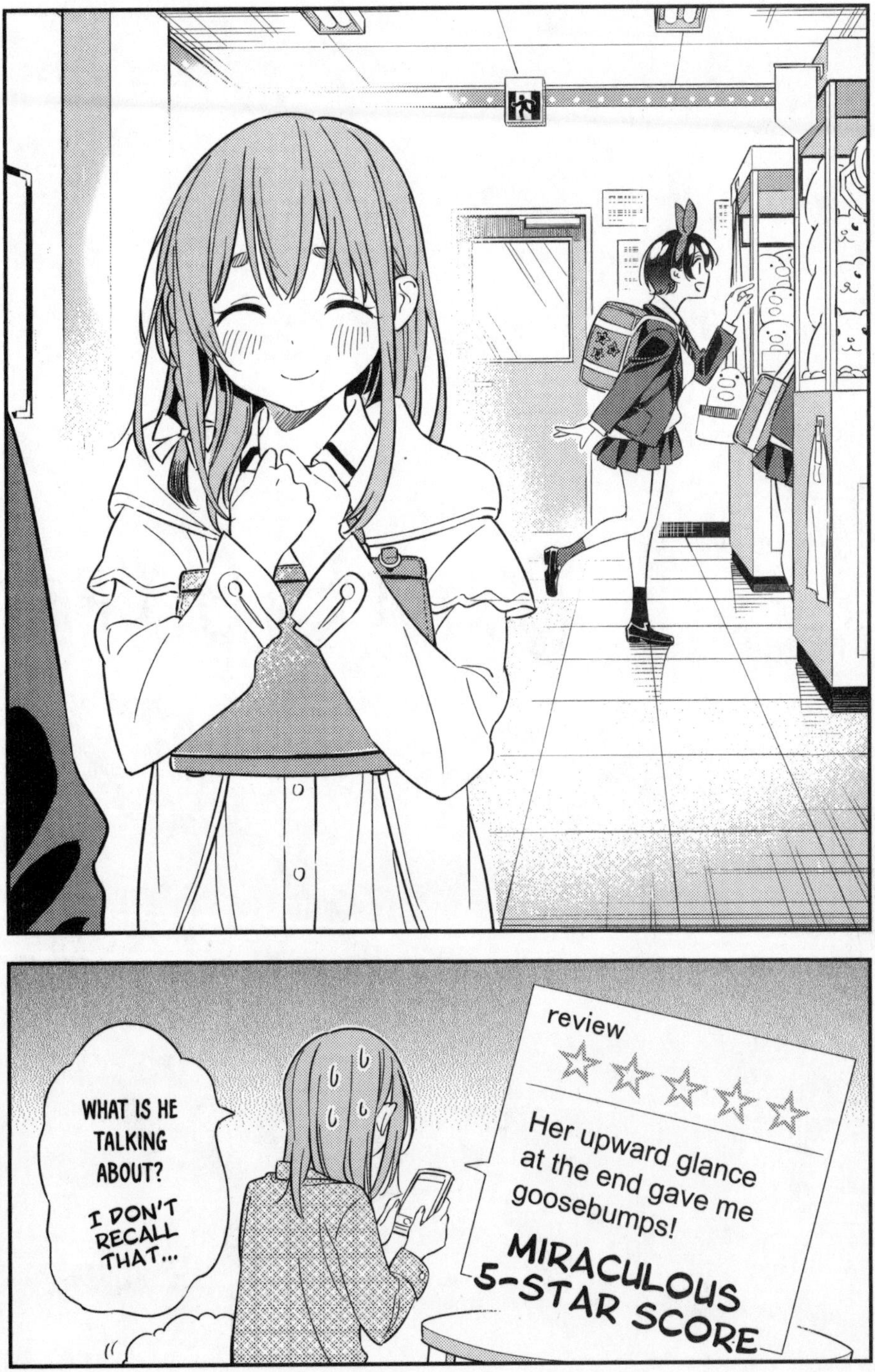
review
Her upward glance at the end gave me goosebumps!
MIRACULOUS 5-STAR SCORE
WHAT IS HE TALKING ABOUT?
I DON'T RECALL THAT...

RENT-A-(REALLY-SHY!)-GIRLFRIEND

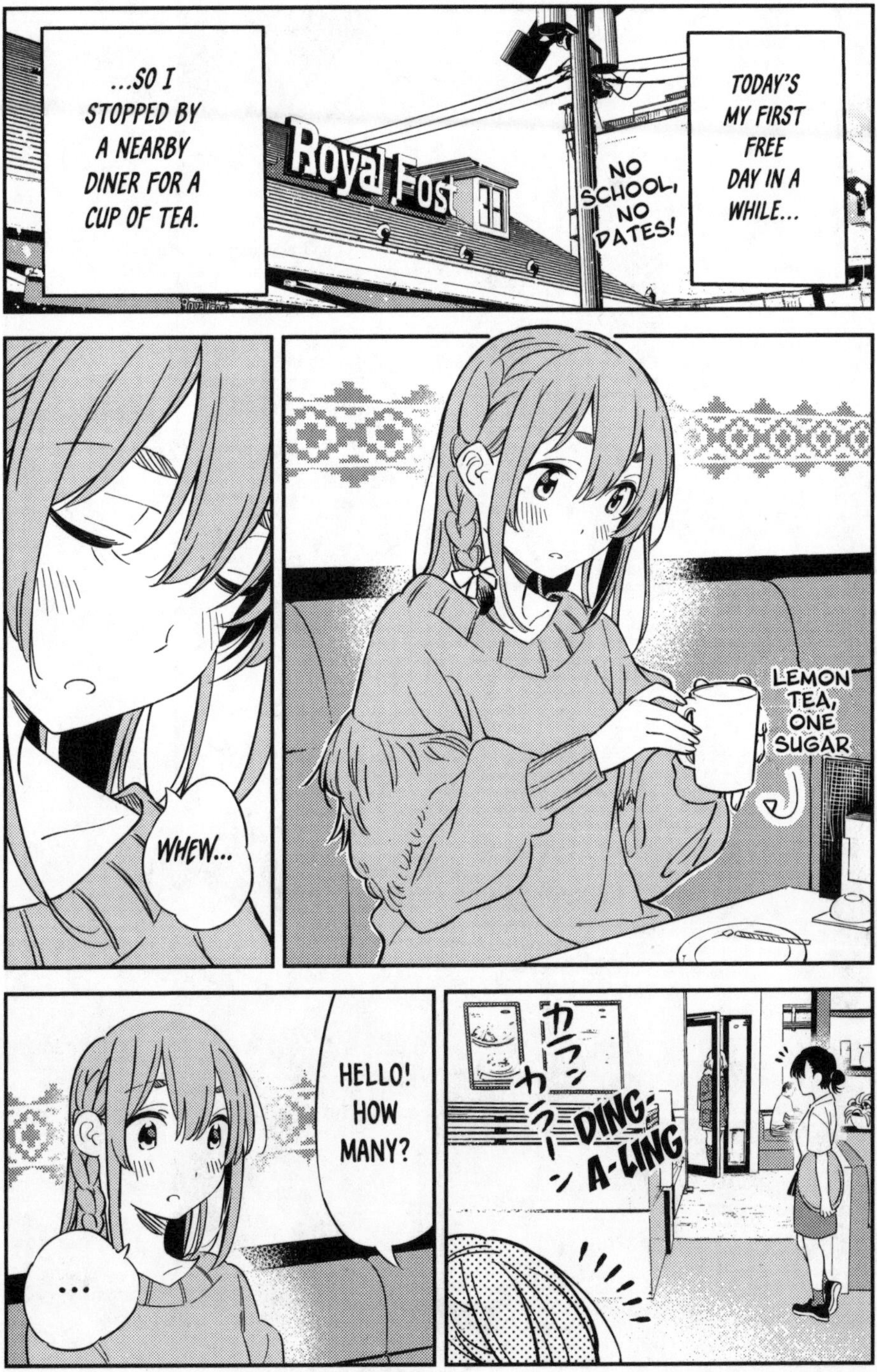
TODAY'S MY FIRST FREE DAY IN A WHILE...
NO SCHOOL, NO DATES!
Royal Fost
...SO I STOPPED BY A NEARBY DINER FOR A CUP OF TEA.
LEMON TEA, ONE SUGAR
WHEW...
カランカラーン
DING-A-LING
HELLO! HOW MANY?
...

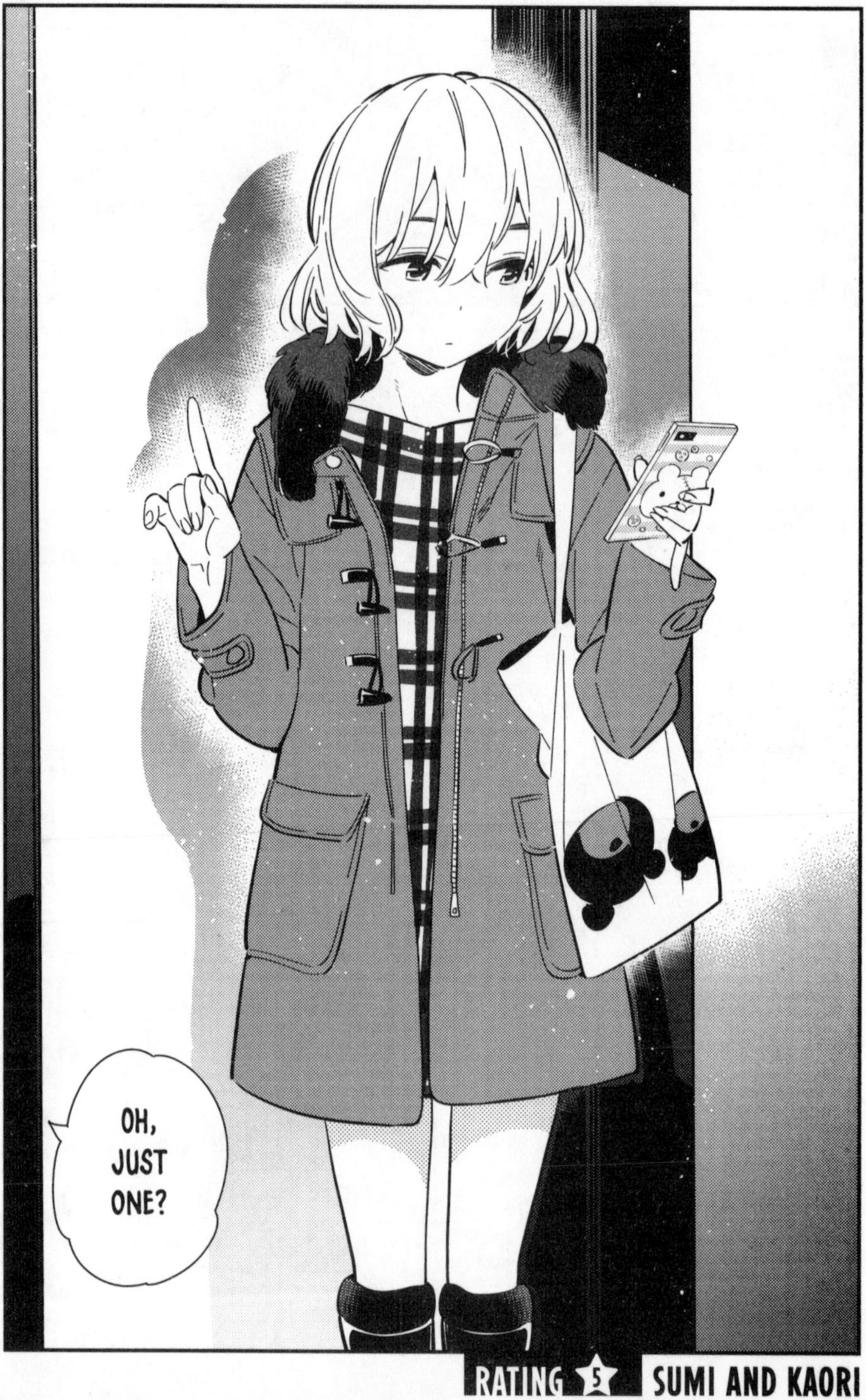
OH, JUST ONE?

RATING 5 SUMI AND KAORI

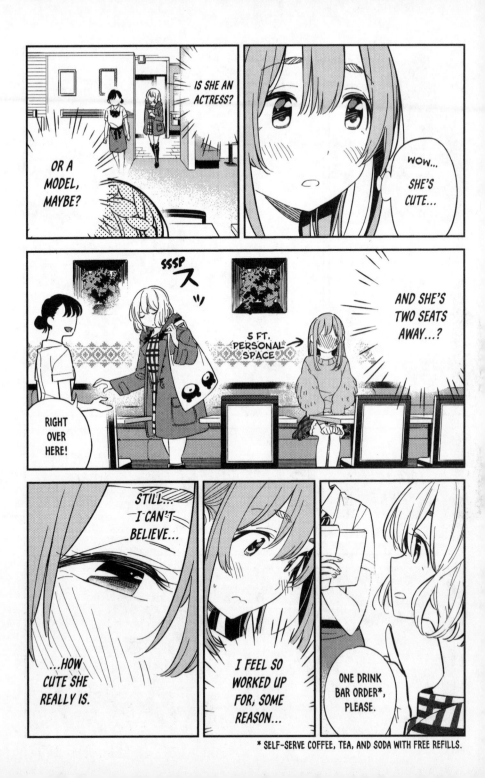

WOW... SHE'S CUTE...
IS SHE AN ACTRESS?
OR A MODEL, MAYBE?
AND SHE'S TWO SEATS AWAY...?
5 FT. PERSONAL SPACE
SSSP
RIGHT OVER HERE!
ONE DRINK BAR ORDER*, PLEASE.
I FEEL SO WORKED UP FOR, SOME REASON...
STILL... I CAN'T BELIEVE...
...HOW CUTE SHE REALLY IS.

* SELF-SERVE COFFEE, TEA, AND SODA WITH FREE REFILLS.

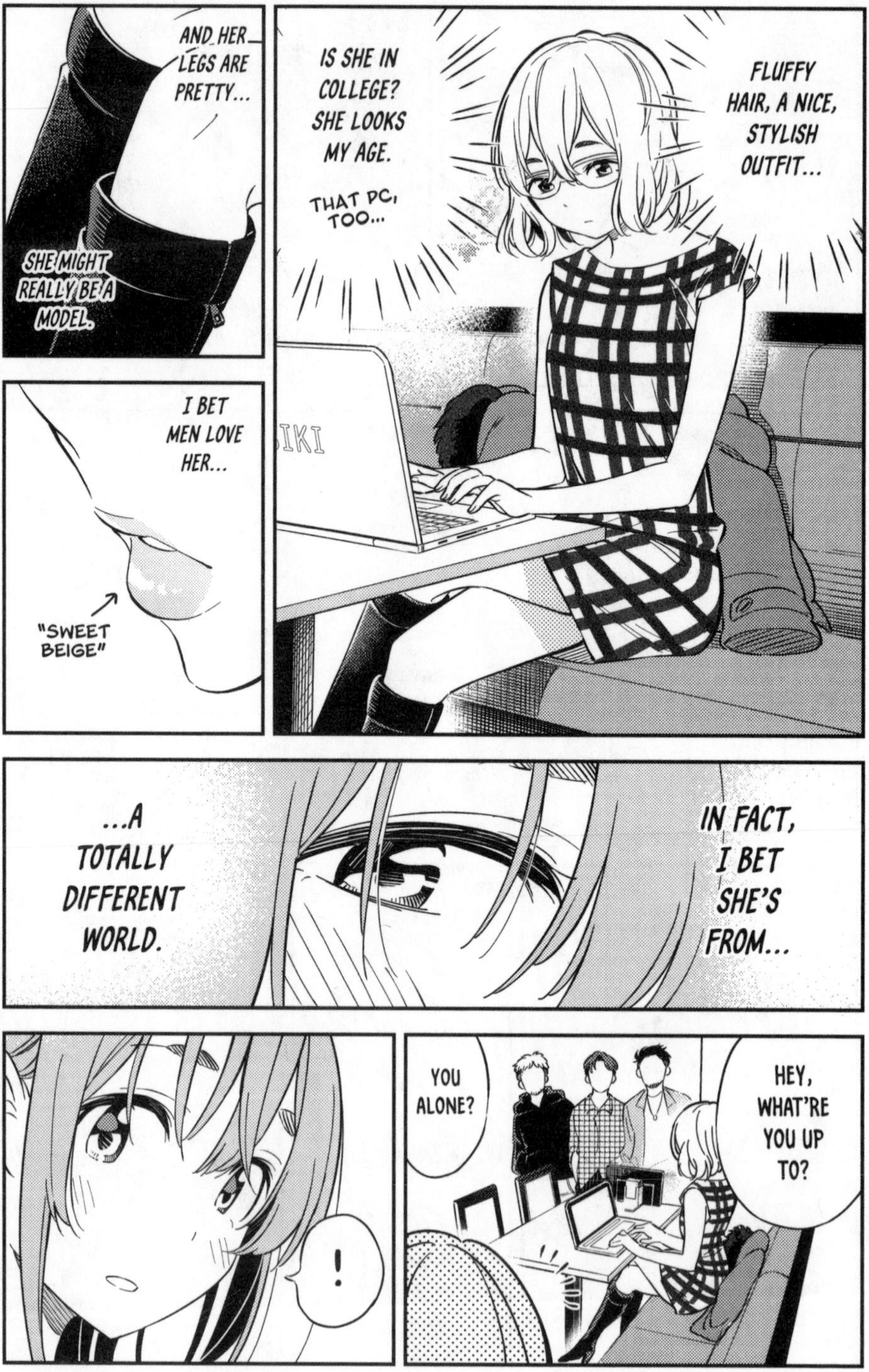
FLUFFY HAIR, A NICE, STYLISH OUTFIT...
IS SHE IN COLLEGE? SHE LOOKS MY AGE.
THAT PC, TOO...
AND HER LEGS ARE PRETTY...
SHE MIGHT REALLY BE A MODEL.
I BET MEN LOVE HER...
"SWEET BEIGE"
IN FACT, I BET SHE'S FROM...
...A TOTALLY DIFFERENT WORLD.
HEY, WHAT'RE YOU UP TO?
YOU ALONE?
!

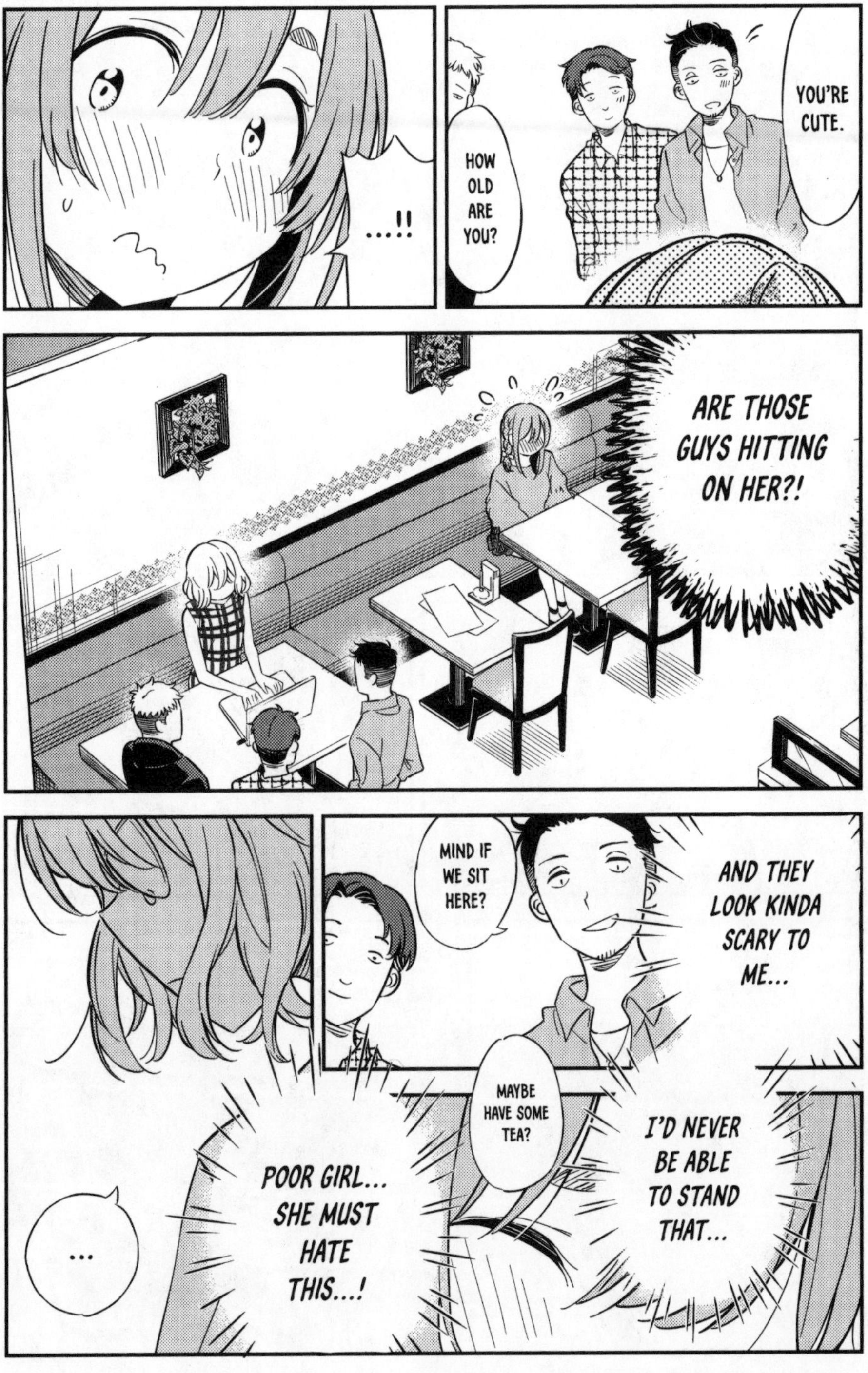
YOU'RE CUTE.
HOW OLD ARE YOU?
...!!
ARE THOSE GUYS HITTING ON HER?!
AND THEY LOOK KINDA SCARY TO ME...
MIND IF WE SIT HERE?
MAYBE HAVE SOME TEA?
I'D NEVER BE ABLE TO STAND THAT...
POOR GIRL... SHE MUST HATE THIS...!
...

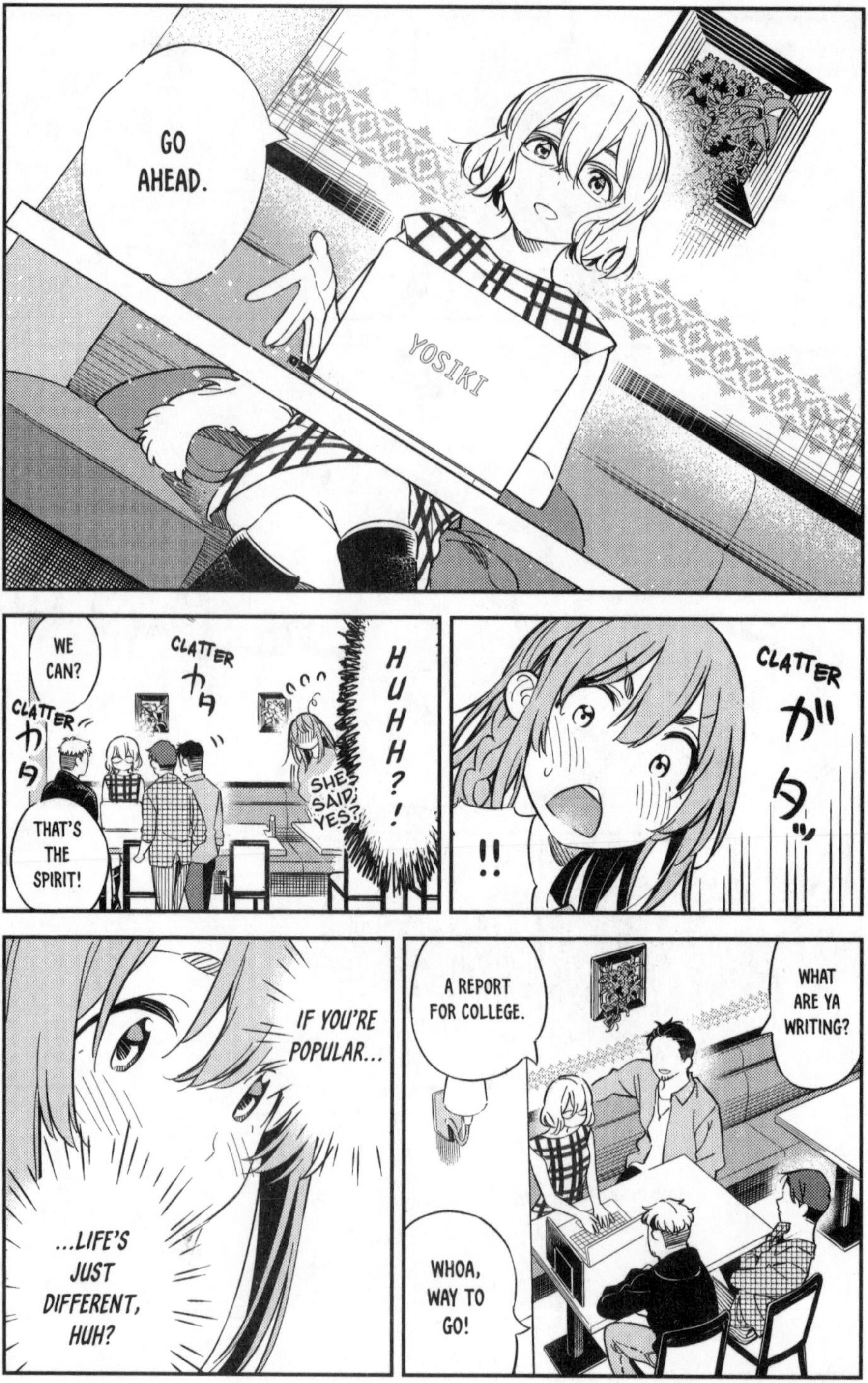
GO AHEAD.
YOSIKI
CLATTER
がタッ
!!
HUHH?!
CLATTER
カタ
WE CAN?
SHE SAID YES?
CLATTER
カタ
THAT'S THE SPIRIT!
WHAT ARE YA WRITING?
A REPORT FOR COLLEGE.
WHOA, WAY TO GO!
IF YOU'RE POPULAR...
...LIFE'S JUST DIFFERENT, HUH?

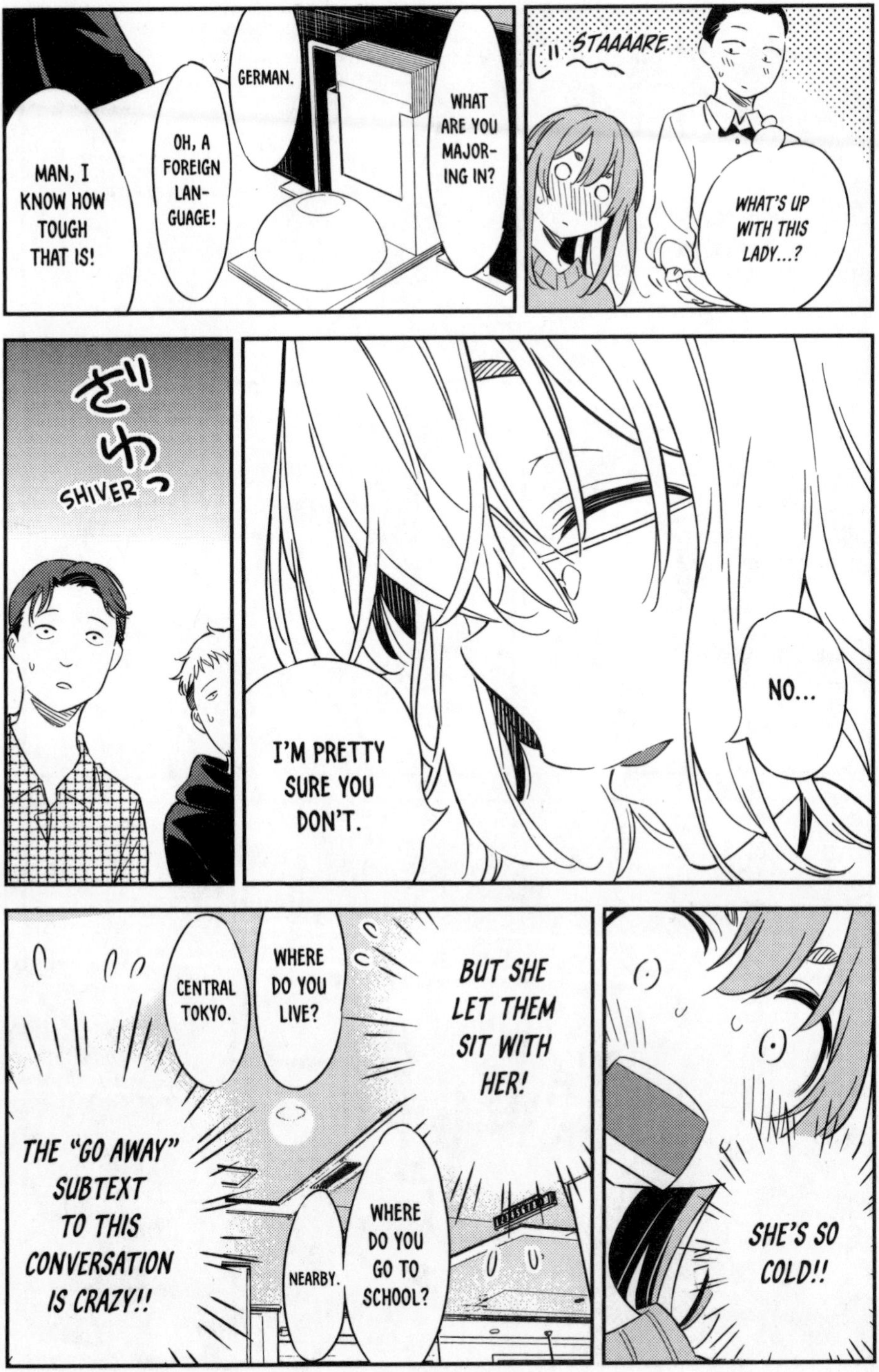
じ STAAAARE
WHAT'S UP WITH THIS LADY...?
WHAT ARE YOU MAJORING IN?
GERMAN.
OH, A FOREIGN LANGUAGE!
MAN, I KNOW HOW TOUGH THAT IS!
NO...
I'M PRETTY SURE YOU DON'T.
ざわっ SHIVER
SHE'S SO COLD!!
BUT SHE LET THEM SIT WITH HER!
WHERE DO YOU LIVE?
CENTRAL TOKYO.
WHERE DO YOU GO TO SCHOOL?
NEARBY.
THE "GO AWAY" SUBTEXT TO THIS CONVERSATION IS CRAZY!!

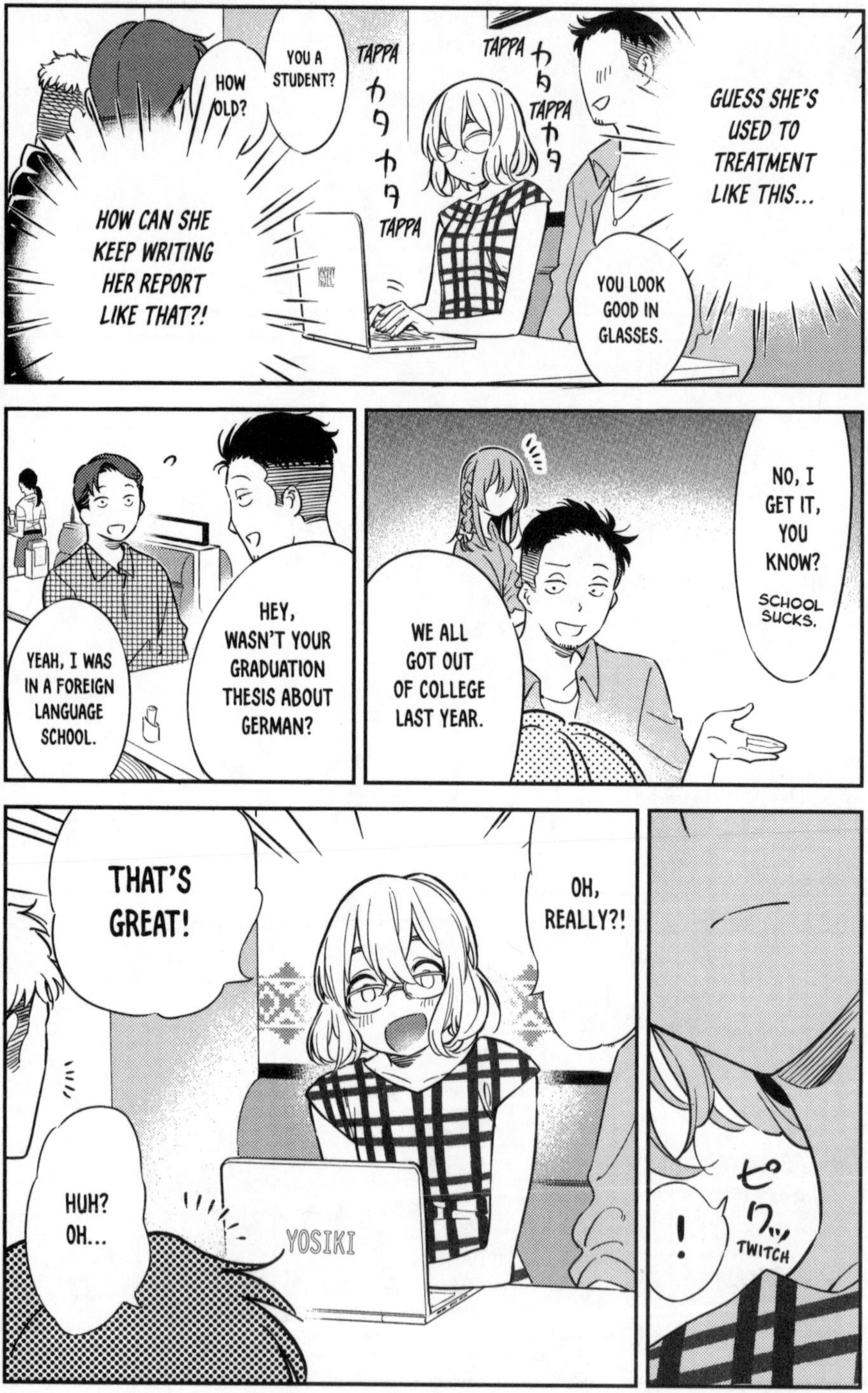

GUESS SHE'S USED TO TREATMENT LIKE THIS...
TAPPA
カタ
TAPPA
カタ
YOU A STUDENT?
TAPPA
カタ
カタ
HOW OLD?
TAPPA
YOU LOOK GOOD IN GLASSES.
HOW CAN SHE KEEP WRITING HER REPORT LIKE THAT?!
NO, I GET IT, YOU KNOW?
SCHOOL SUCKS.
WE ALL GOT OUT OF COLLEGE LAST YEAR.
HEY, WASN'T YOUR GRADUATION THESIS ABOUT GERMAN?
YEAH, I WAS IN A FOREIGN LANGUAGE SCHOOL.
ピクッ
TWITCH
!
OH, REALLY?!
THAT'S GREAT!
YOSIKI
HUH? OH...

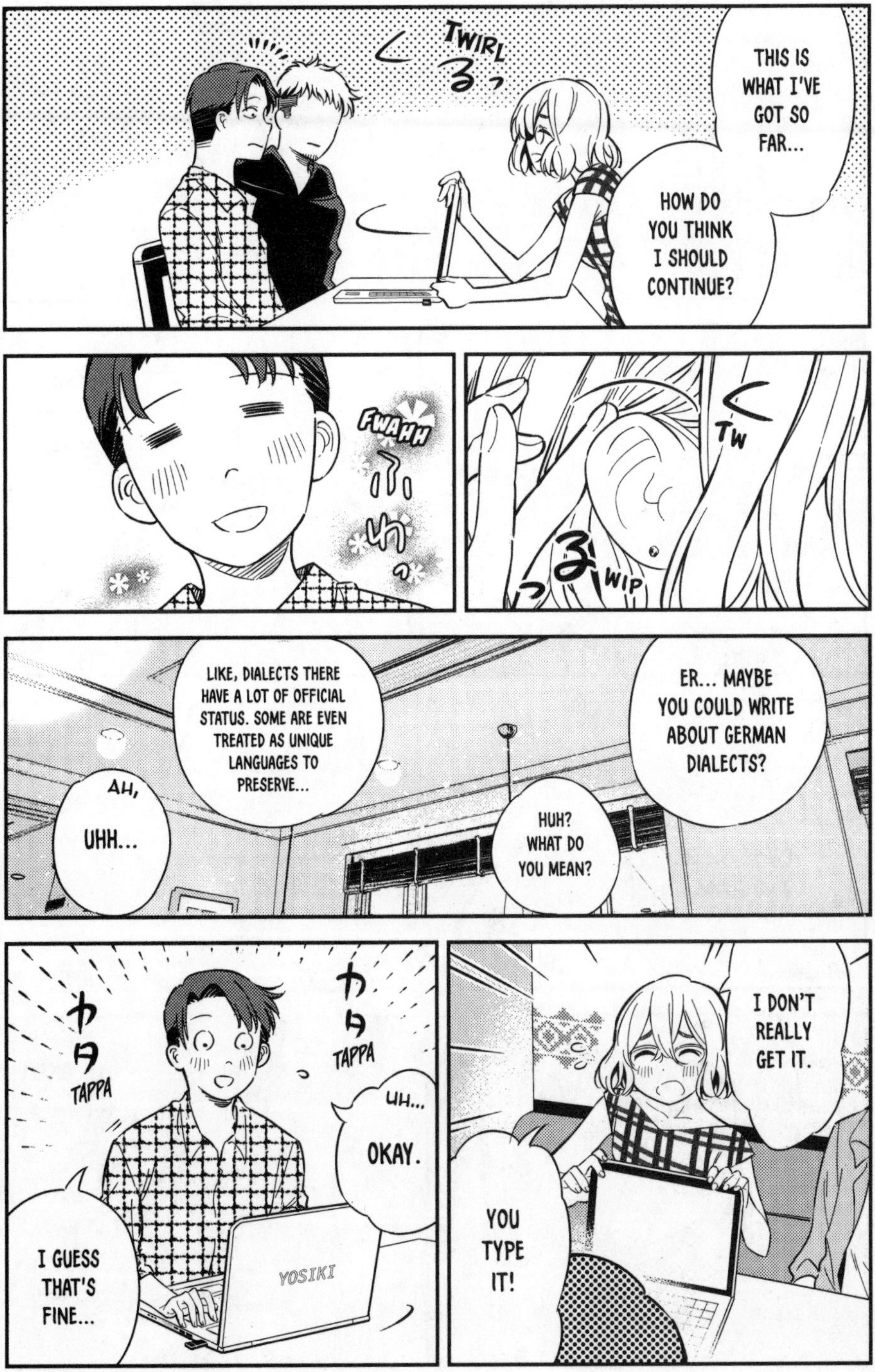
THIS IS WHAT I'VE GOT SO FAR...
HOW DO YOU THINK I SHOULD CONTINUE?
TWIRL
くるっ
TW
WIP
FWAHH
ふわっ
ER... MAYBE YOU COULD WRITE ABOUT GERMAN DIALECTS?
HUH? WHAT DO YOU MEAN?
LIKE, DIALECTS THERE HAVE A LOT OF OFFICIAL STATUS. SOME ARE EVEN TREATED AS UNIQUE LANGUAGES TO PRESERVE...
AH,
UHH...
I DON'T REALLY GET IT.
YOU TYPE IT!
カタ
TAPPA
UH...
OKAY.
カタ
TAPPA
I GUESS THAT'S FINE...
YOSIKI

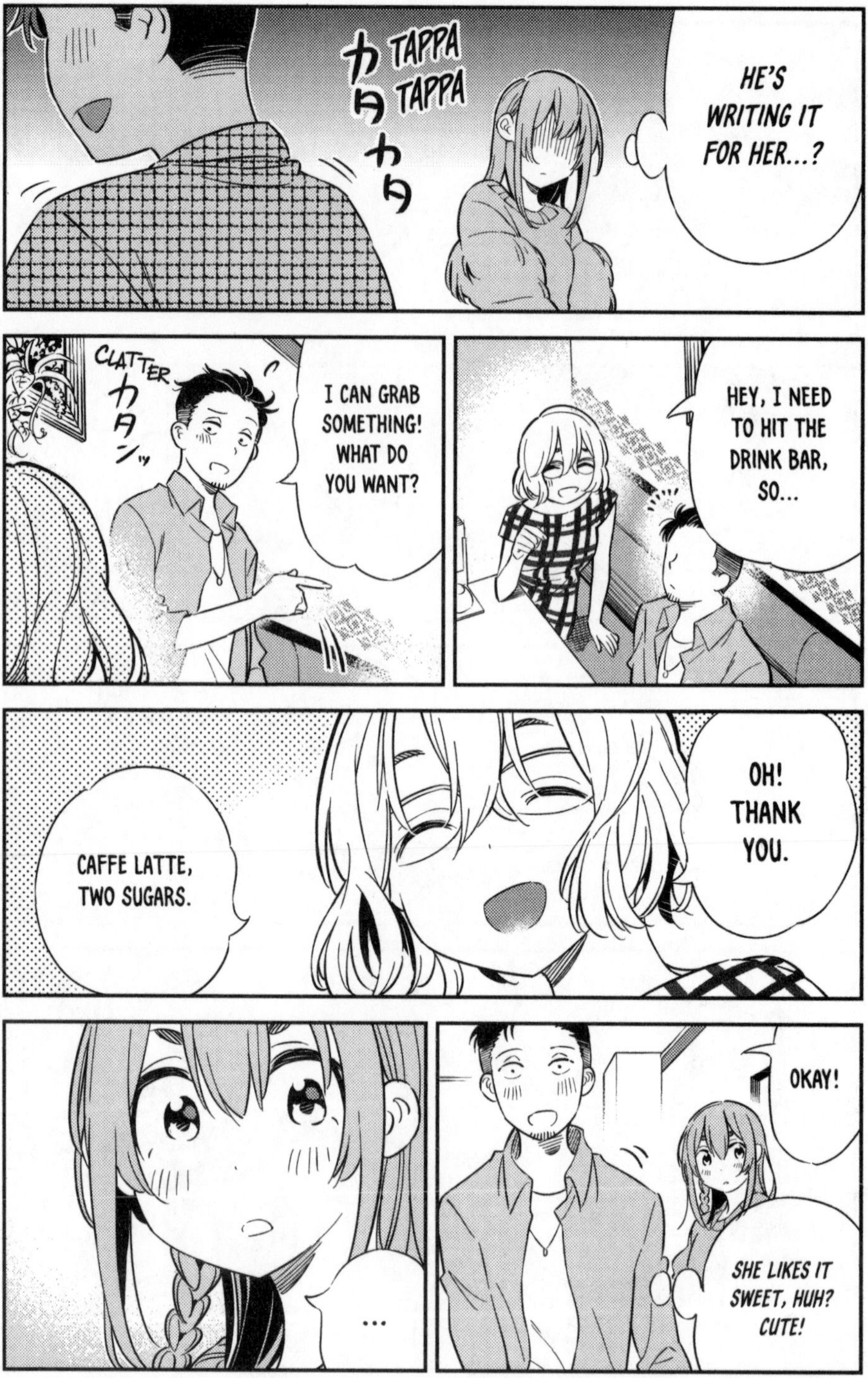
HE'S WRITING IT FOR HER...?
TAPPA TAPPA
カタカタ
HEY, I NEED TO HIT THE DRINK BAR, SO...
CLATTER
カタンッ
I CAN GRAB SOMETHING! WHAT DO YOU WANT?
OH! THANK YOU.
CAFFE LATTE, TWO SUGARS.
OKAY!
SHE LIKES IT SWEET, HUH? CUTE!
...

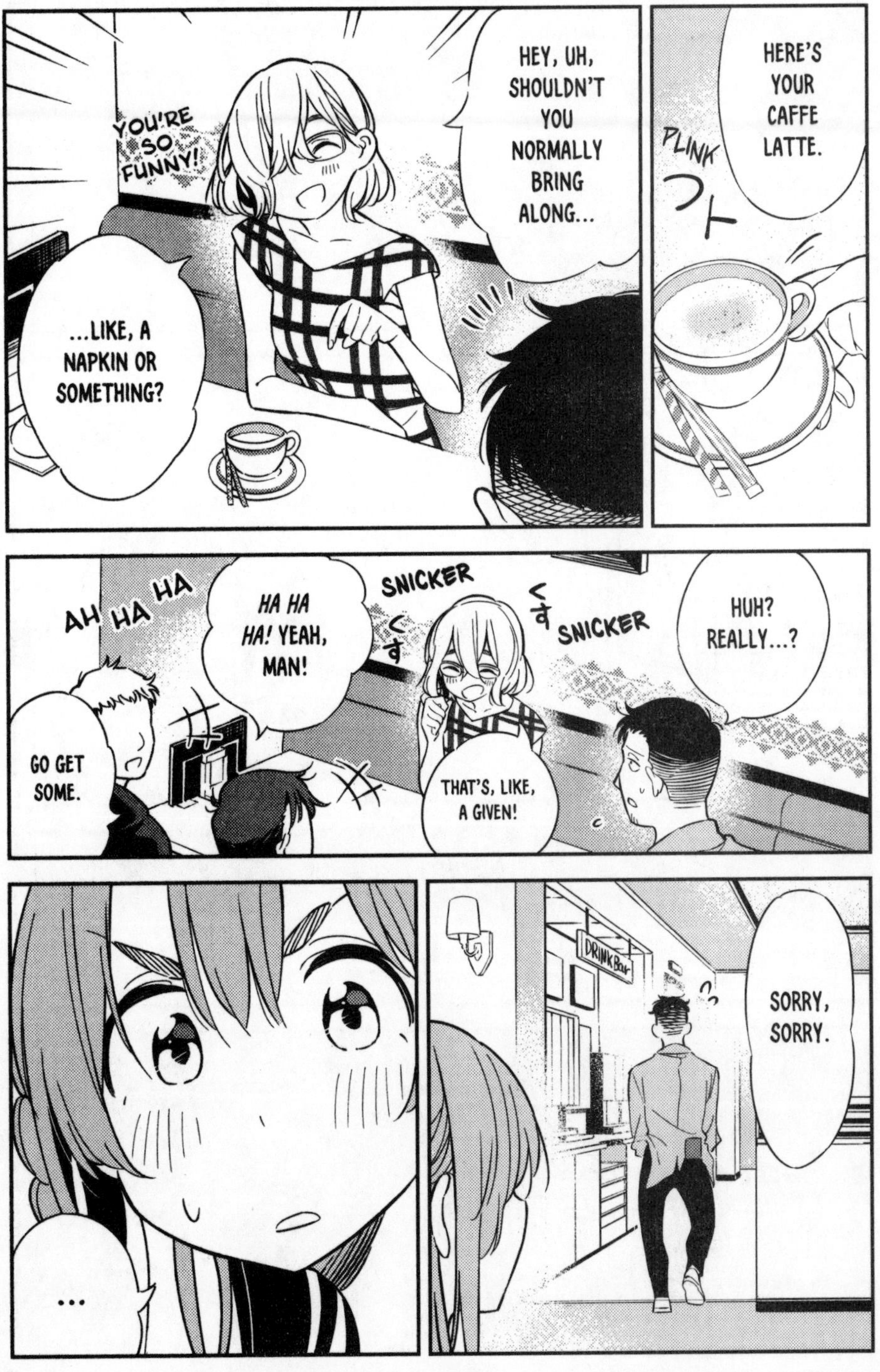
HERE'S YOUR CAFFE LATTE.
PLINK
コト
HEY, UH, SHOULDN'T YOU NORMALLY BRING ALONG...
YOU'RE SO FUNNY!
...LIKE, A NAPKIN OR SOMETHING?
HUH? REALLY...?
SNICKER
くす
SNICKER
くす
THAT'S, LIKE, A GIVEN!
HA HA HA! YEAH, MAN!
AH HA HA
GO GET SOME.
SORRY, SORRY.
DRINK Bar
...

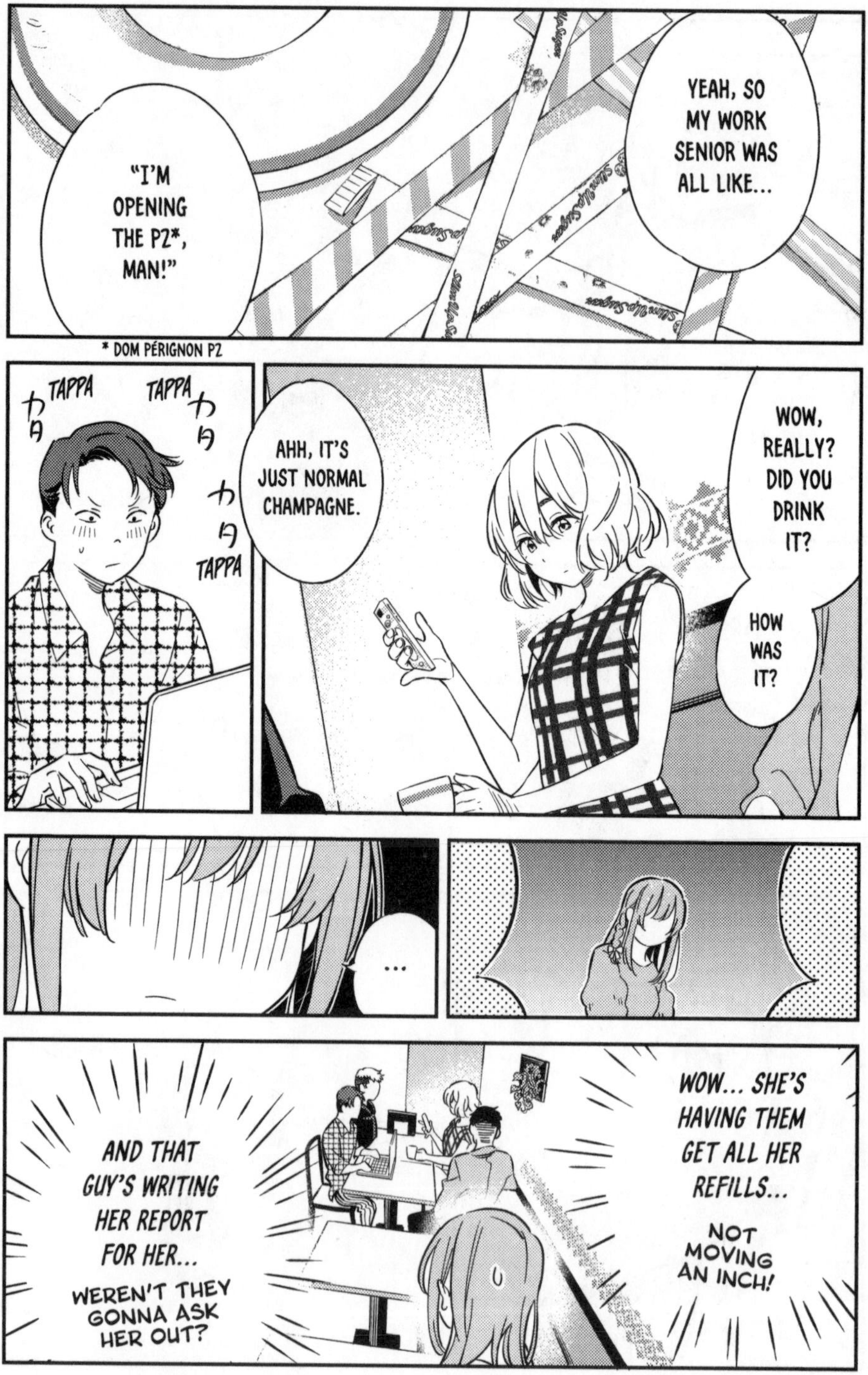
YEAH, SO MY WORK SENIOR WAS ALL LIKE...
"I'M OPENING THE P2*, MAN!"
WOW, REALLY? DID YOU DRINK IT?
HOW WAS IT?
AHH, IT'S JUST NORMAL CHAMPAGNE.
TAPPA
TAPPA
TAPPA
...
WOW... SHE'S HAVING THEM GET ALL HER REFILLS...
NOT MOVING AN INCH!
AND THAT GUY'S WRITING HER REPORT FOR HER...
WEREN'T THEY GONNA ASK HER OUT?

* DOM PÉRIGNON P2

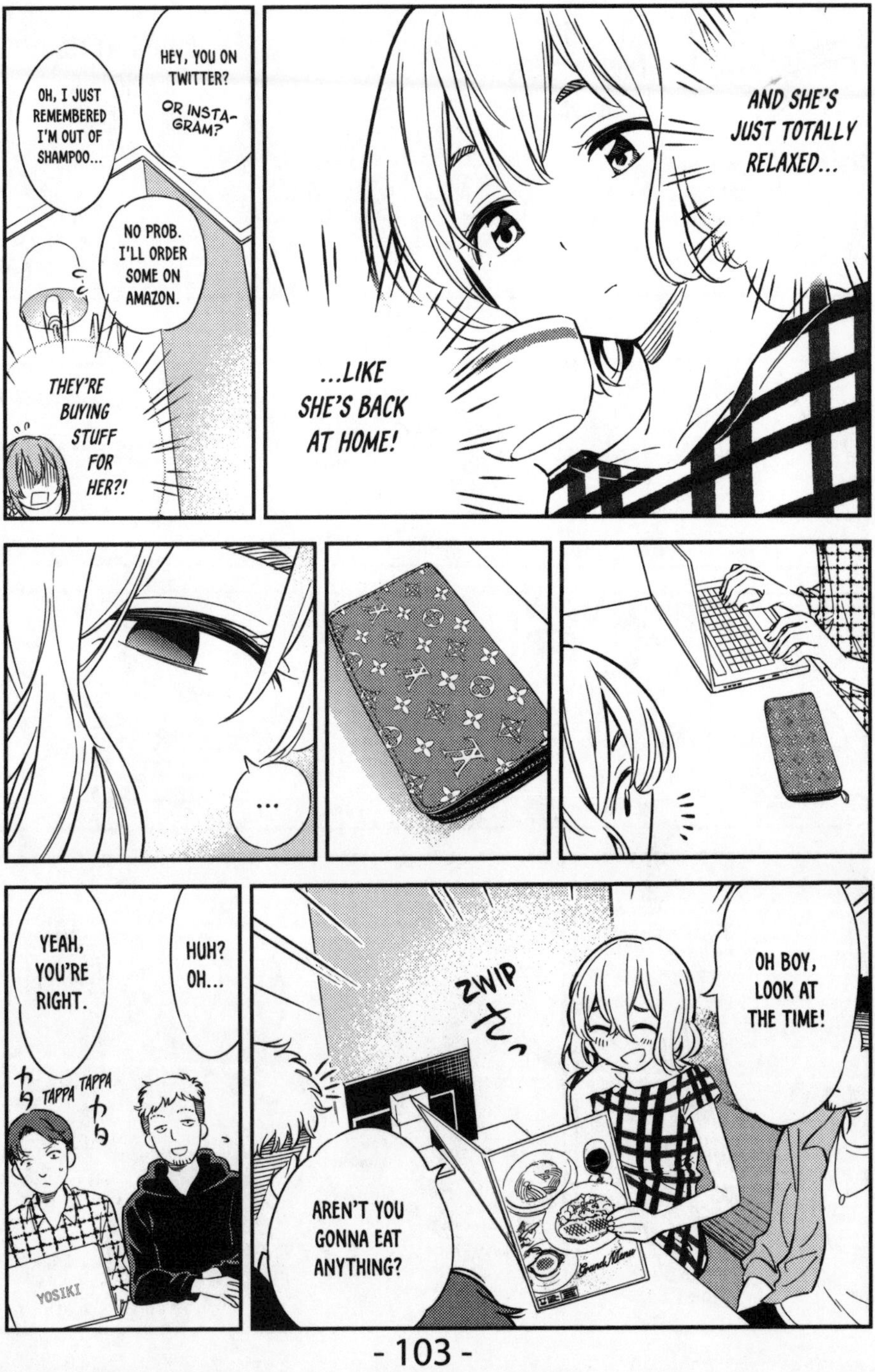

AND SHE'S JUST TOTALLY RELAXED...
...LIKE SHE'S BACK AT HOME!
HEY, YOU ON TWITTER? OR INSTA-GRAM?
OH, I JUST REMEMBERED I'M OUT OF SHAMPOO...
NO PROB. I'LL ORDER SOME ON AMAZON.
THEY'RE BUYING STUFF FOR HER?!
...
OH BOY, LOOK AT THE TIME!
ZWIP
Grand Menu
AREN'T YOU GONNA EAT ANYTHING?
HUH? OH...
YEAH, YOU'RE RIGHT.
TAPPA
TAPPA
YOSIKI

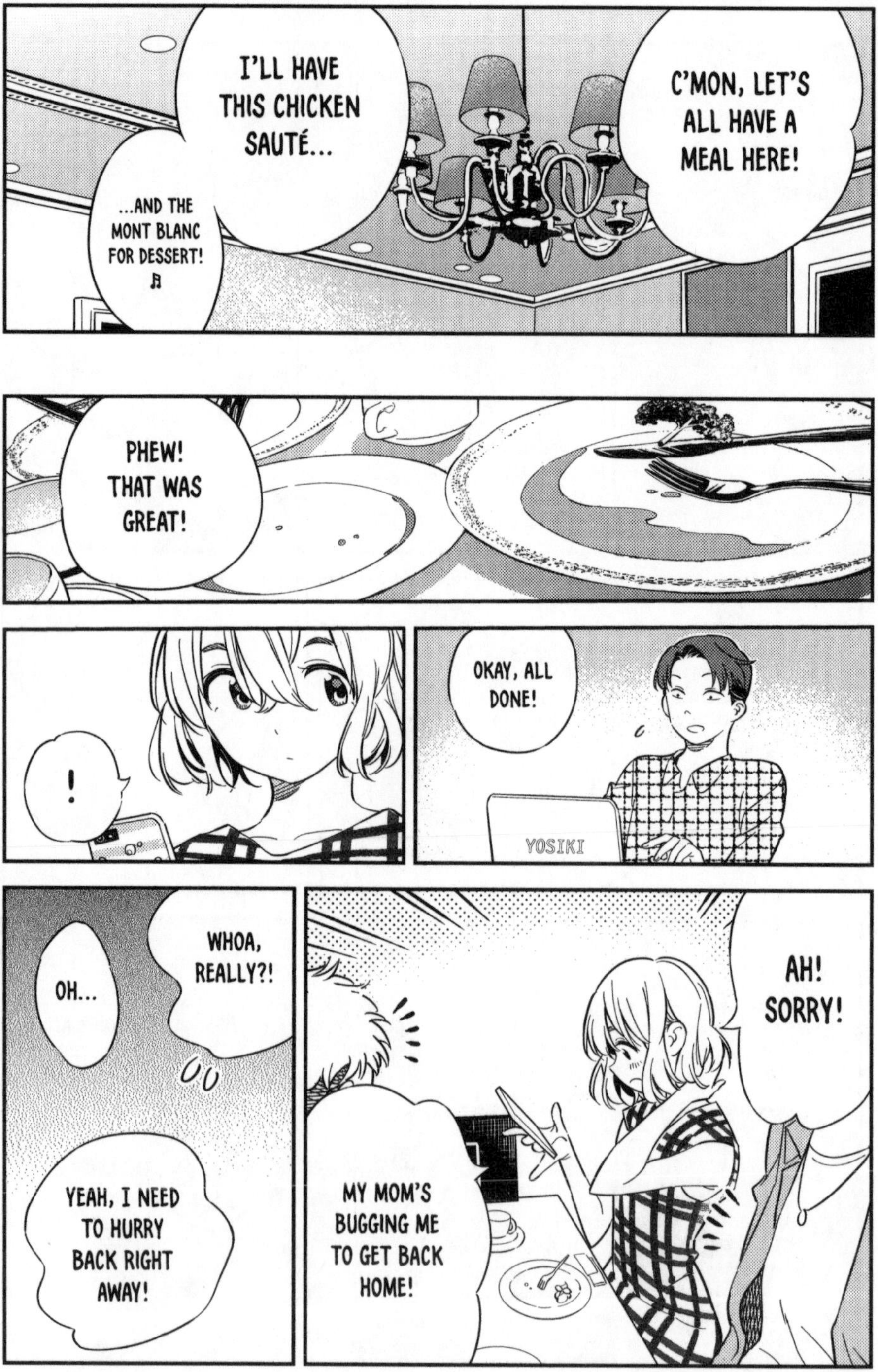
C'MON, LET'S ALL HAVE A MEAL HERE!
I'LL HAVE THIS CHICKEN SAUTÉ...
...AND THE MONT BLANC FOR DESSERT! ♫
PHEW! THAT WAS GREAT!
OKAY, ALL DONE!
YOSIKI
!
AH! SORRY!
MY MOM'S BUGGING ME TO GET BACK HOME!
WHOA, REALLY?!
OH...
YEAH, I NEED TO HURRY BACK RIGHT AWAY!

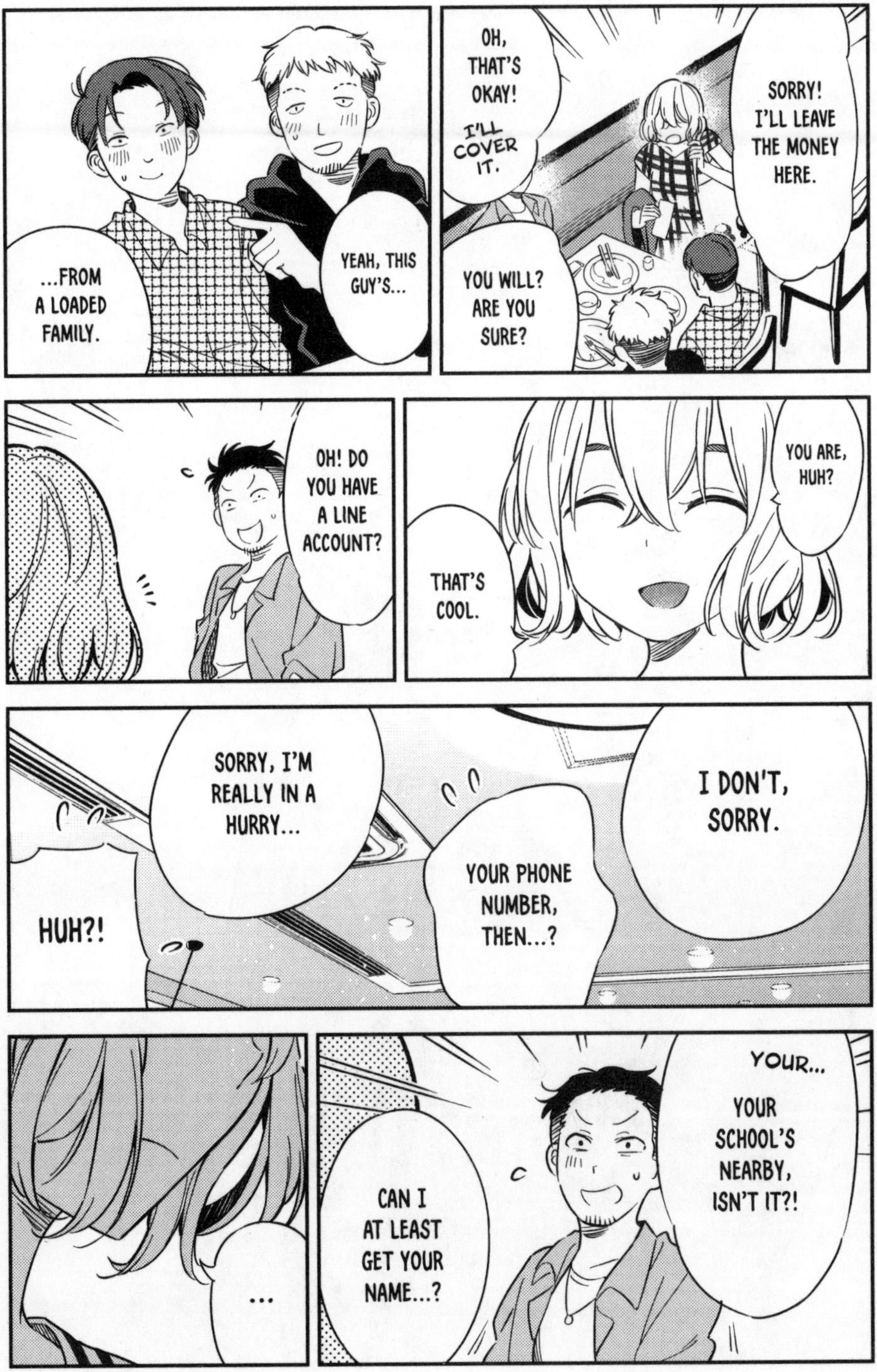
SORRY! I'LL LEAVE THE MONEY HERE.
OH, THAT'S OKAY!
I'LL COVER IT.
YOU WILL? ARE YOU SURE?
YEAH, THIS GUY'S...
...FROM A LOADED FAMILY.
YOU ARE, HUH?
THAT'S COOL.
OH! DO YOU HAVE A LINE ACCOUNT?
I DON'T, SORRY.
YOUR PHONE NUMBER, THEN...?
SORRY, I'M REALLY IN A HURRY...
HUH?!
YOUR...
YOUR SCHOOL'S NEARBY, ISN'T IT?!
CAN I AT LEAST GET YOUR NAME...?
...

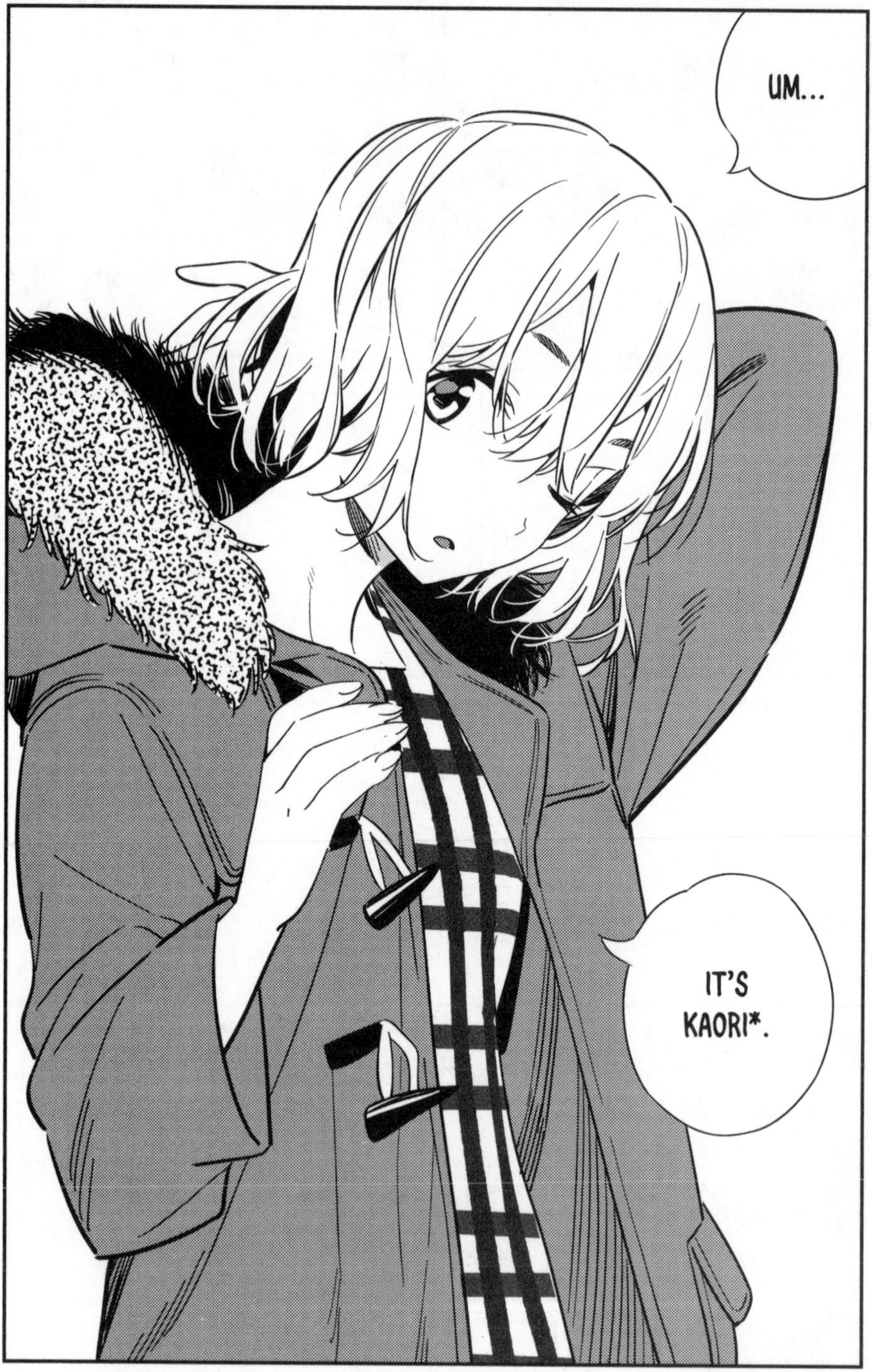
UM...
IT'S KAORI*.

*I.E. A FAKE NAME

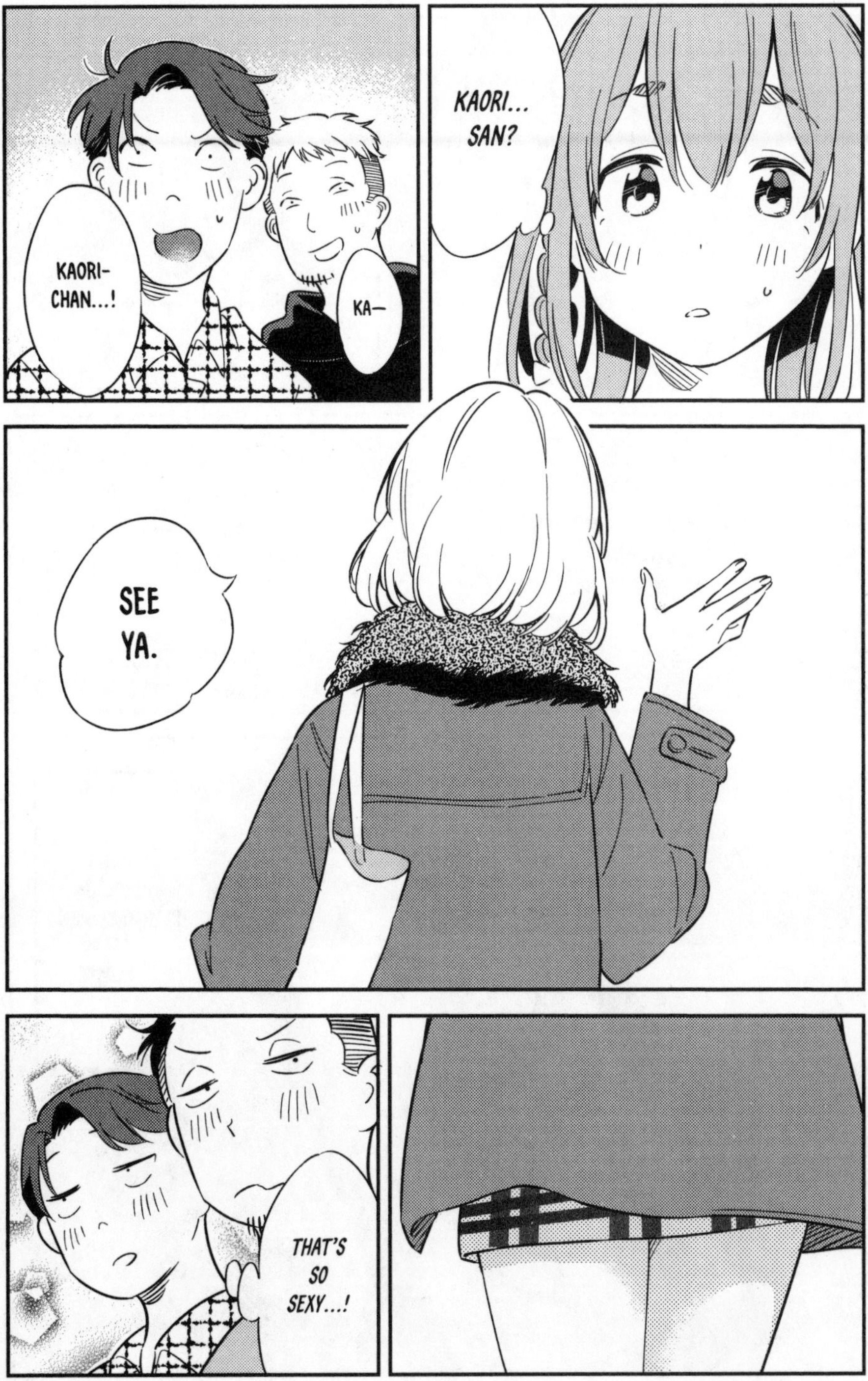
KAORI... SAN?
KAORI-CHAN...!
KA—
SEE YA.
THAT'S SO SEXY...!

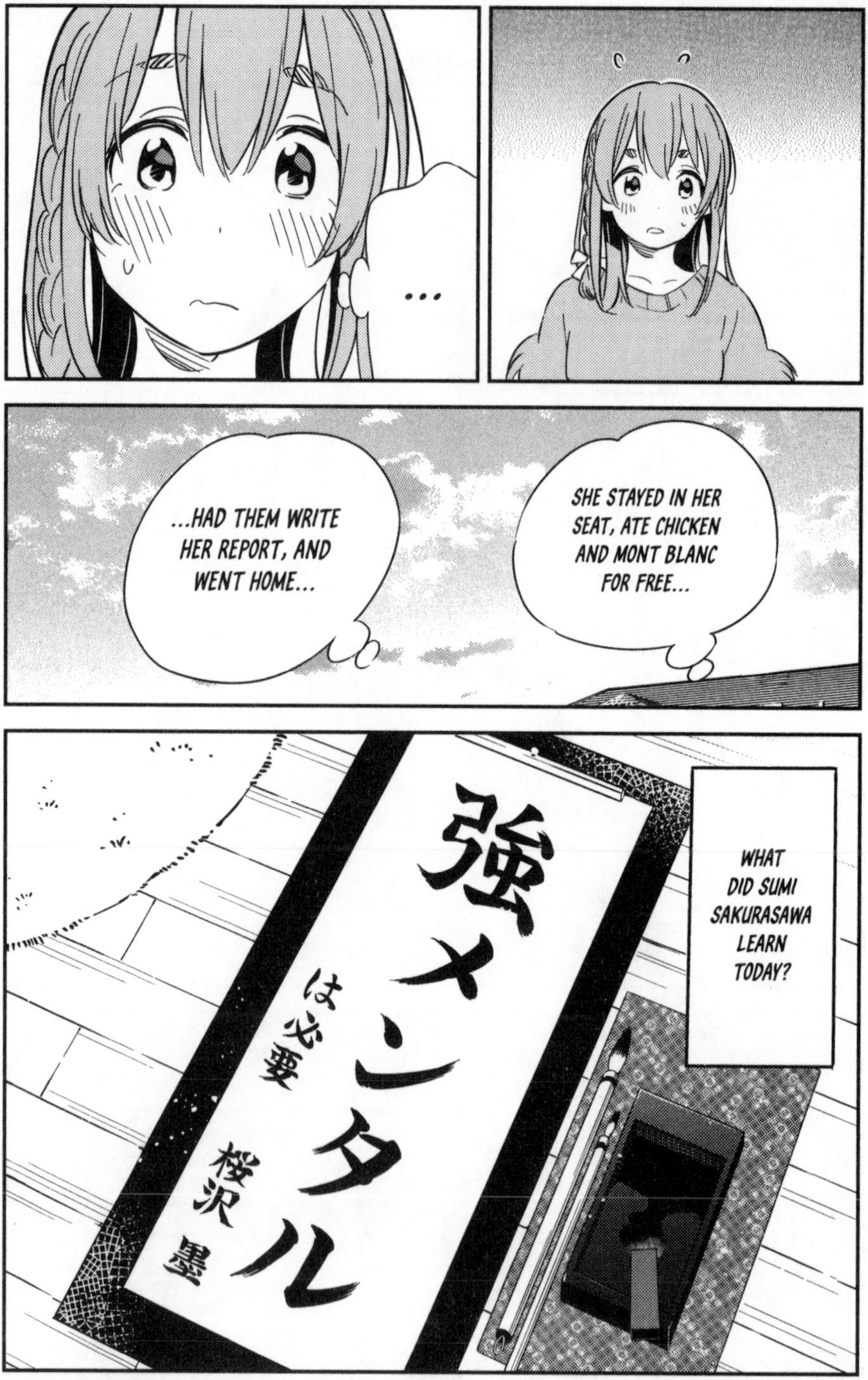
...
SHE STAYED IN HER SEAT, ATE CHICKEN AND MONT BLANC FOR FREE...
...HAD THEM WRITE HER REPORT, AND WENT HOME...
WHAT DID SUMI SAKURASAWA LEARN TODAY?
強メンタルは必要
桜沢墨

BANNER: MENTAL STRENGTH IS EVERYTHING SUMI SAKURASAWA

RENT-A-(REALLY SHY!)-GIRLFRIEND

RENT-A-(REALLY SHY!)-GIRLFRIEND

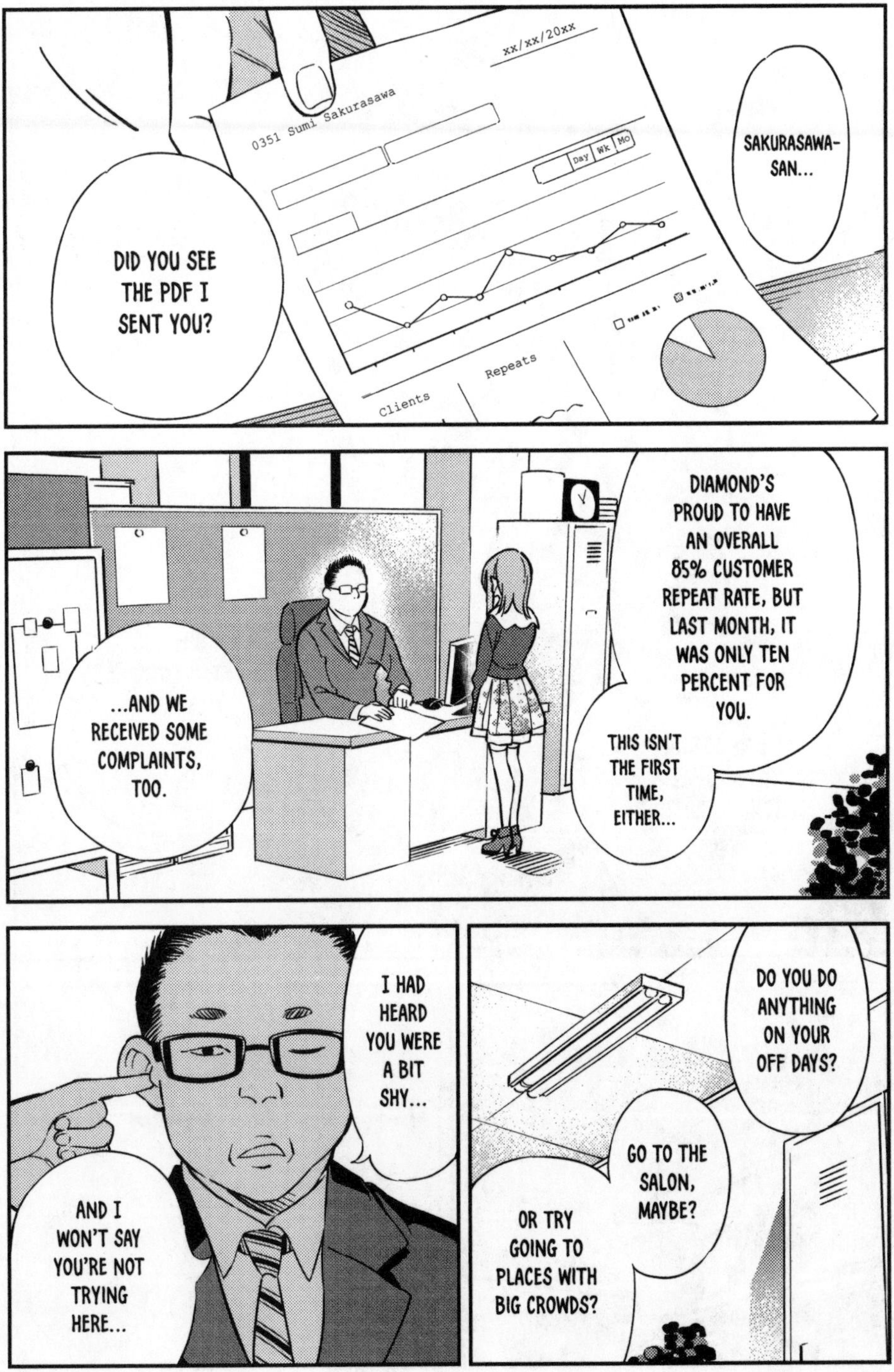
xx/xx/20xx
0351 Sumi Sakurasawa
Day
Wk
Mo
Repeats
Clients
SAKURASAWA-SAN...
DID YOU SEE THE PDF I SENT YOU?
DIAMOND'S PROUD TO HAVE AN OVERALL 85% CUSTOMER REPEAT RATE, BUT LAST MONTH, IT WAS ONLY TEN PERCENT FOR YOU.
THIS ISN'T THE FIRST TIME, EITHER...
...AND WE RECEIVED SOME COMPLAINTS, TOO.
DO YOU DO ANYTHING ON YOUR OFF DAYS?
GO TO THE SALON, MAYBE?
OR TRY GOING TO PLACES WITH BIG CROWDS?
I HAD HEARD YOU WERE A BIT SHY...
AND I WON'T SAY YOU'RE NOT TRYING HERE...

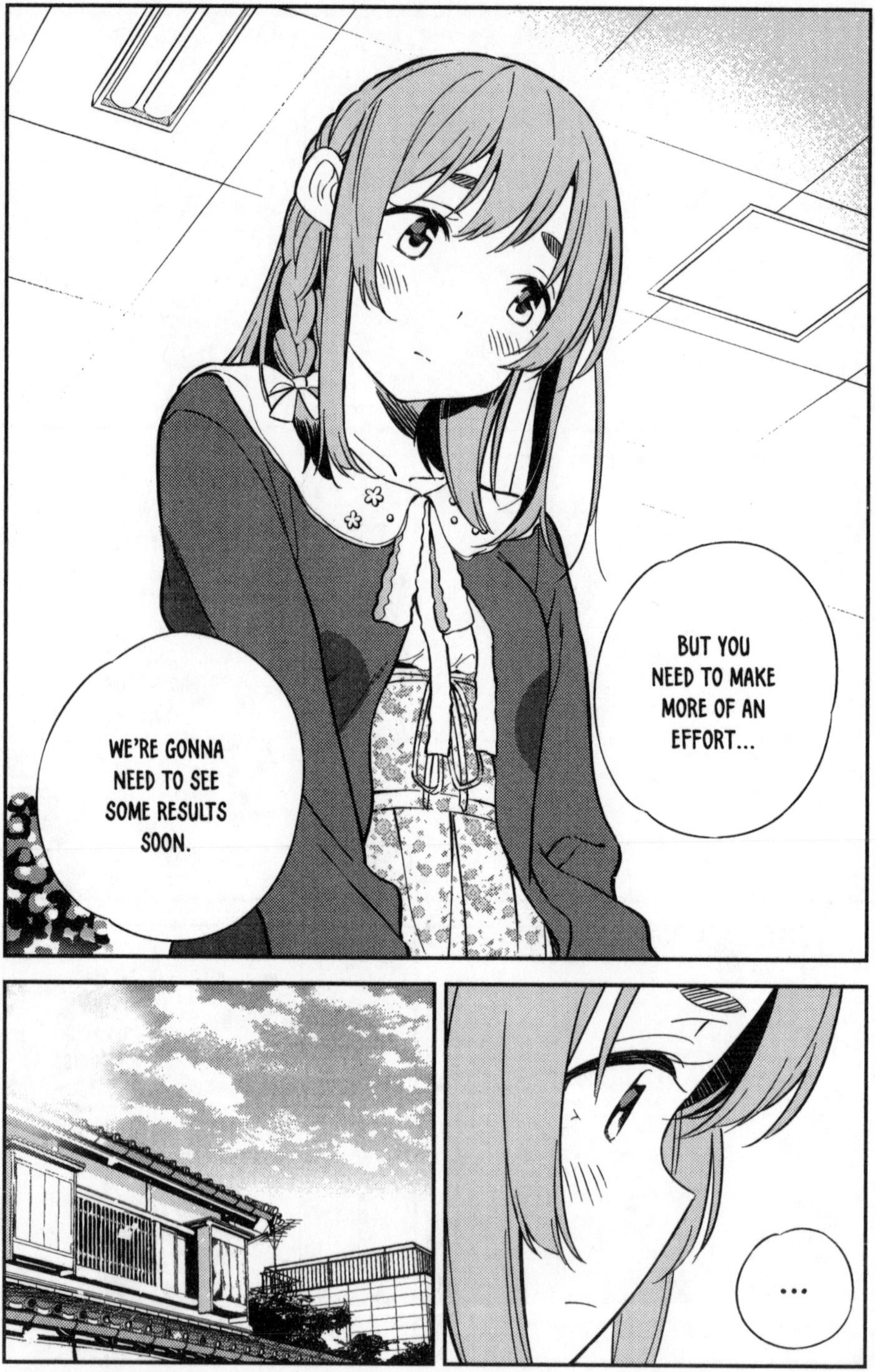
BUT YOU NEED TO MAKE MORE OF AN EFFORT...
WE'RE GONNA NEED TO SEE SOME RESULTS SOON.
...

RATING 6 SUMI AND THE TEARS

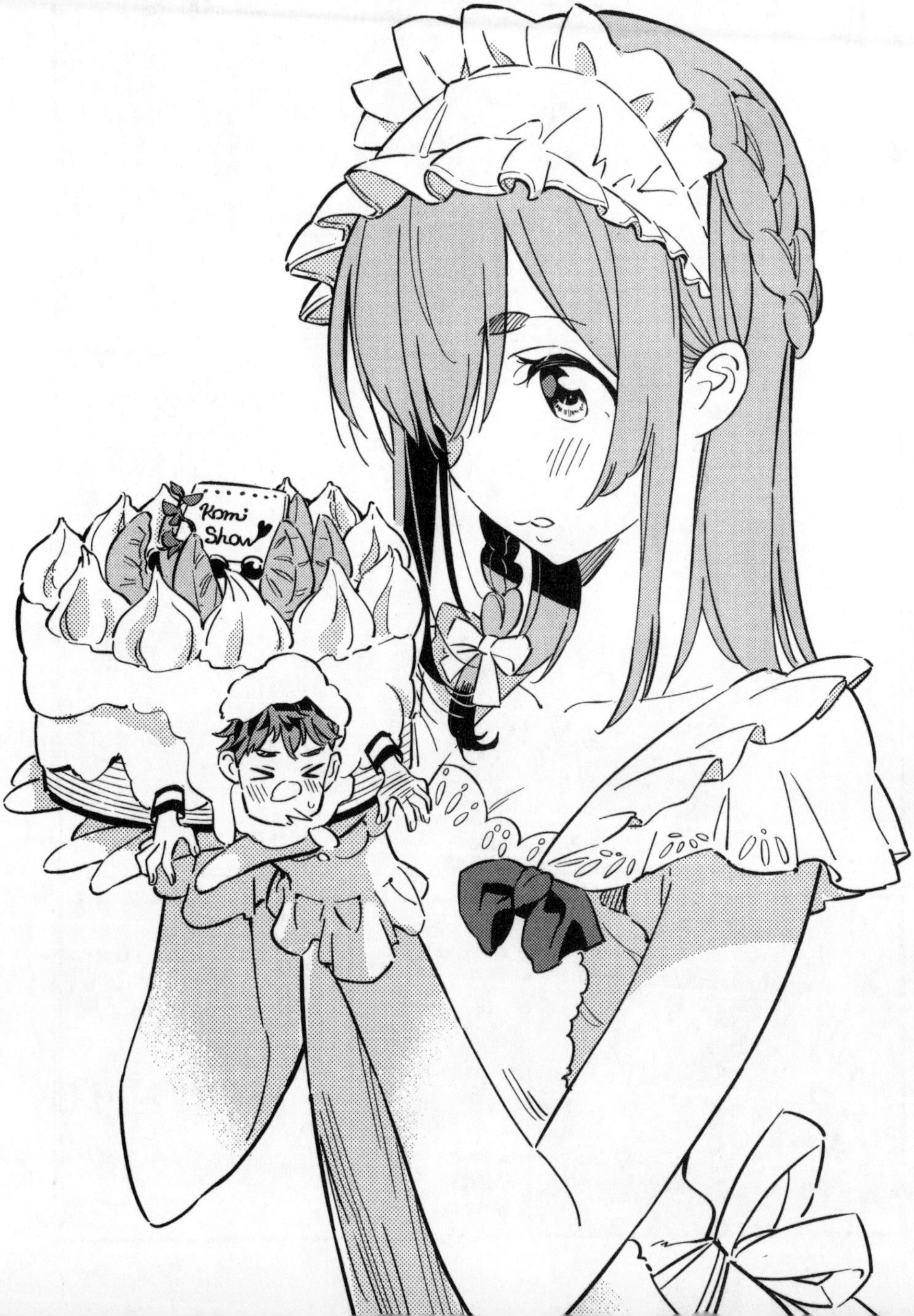
Komi
Show

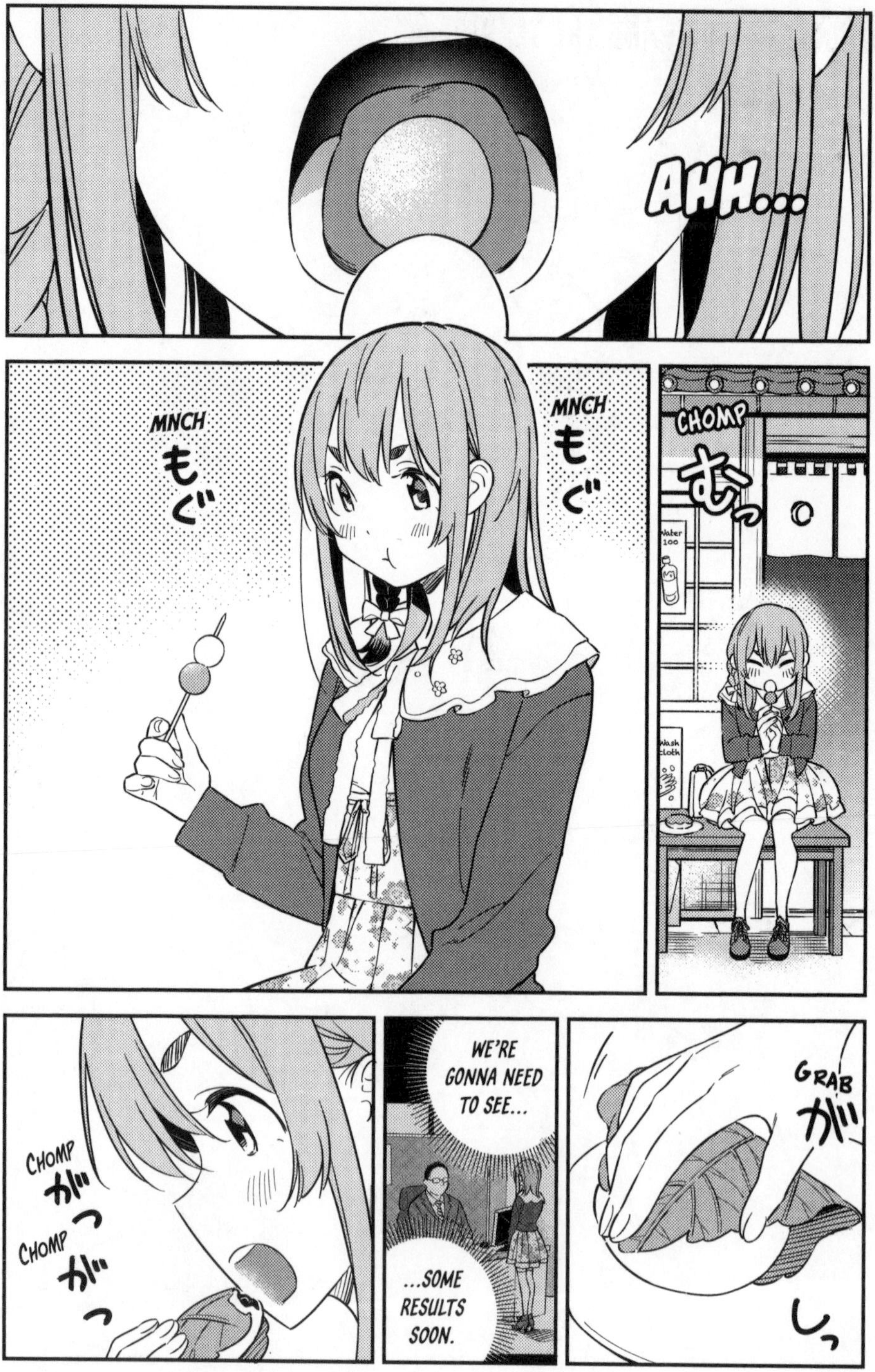
AHH...
CHOMP
むっ
MNCH
もぐ
MNCH
もぐ
GRAB
がい
しっ
WE'RE GONNA NEED TO SEE...
...SOME RESULTS SOON.
CHOMP
がっ
CHOMP
がっ

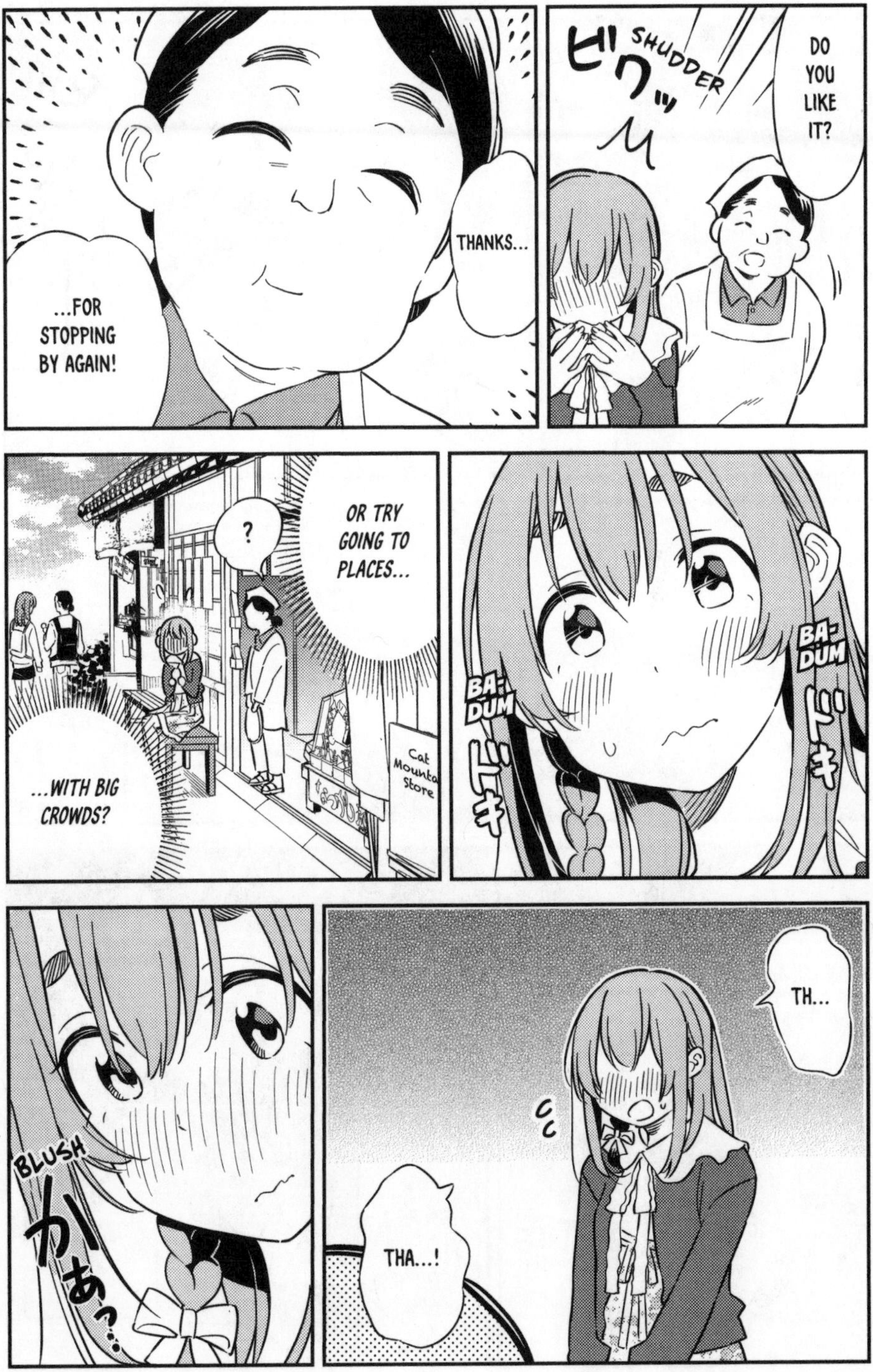
DO YOU LIKE IT?
ビクッ
SHUDDER
THANKS...
...FOR STOPPING BY AGAIN!
ドキ
BA-DUM
ドキ
BA-DUM
OR TRY GOING TO PLACES...
?
...WITH BIG CROWDS?
Cat Mounta Store
TH...
THA...!
かあっ
BLUSH

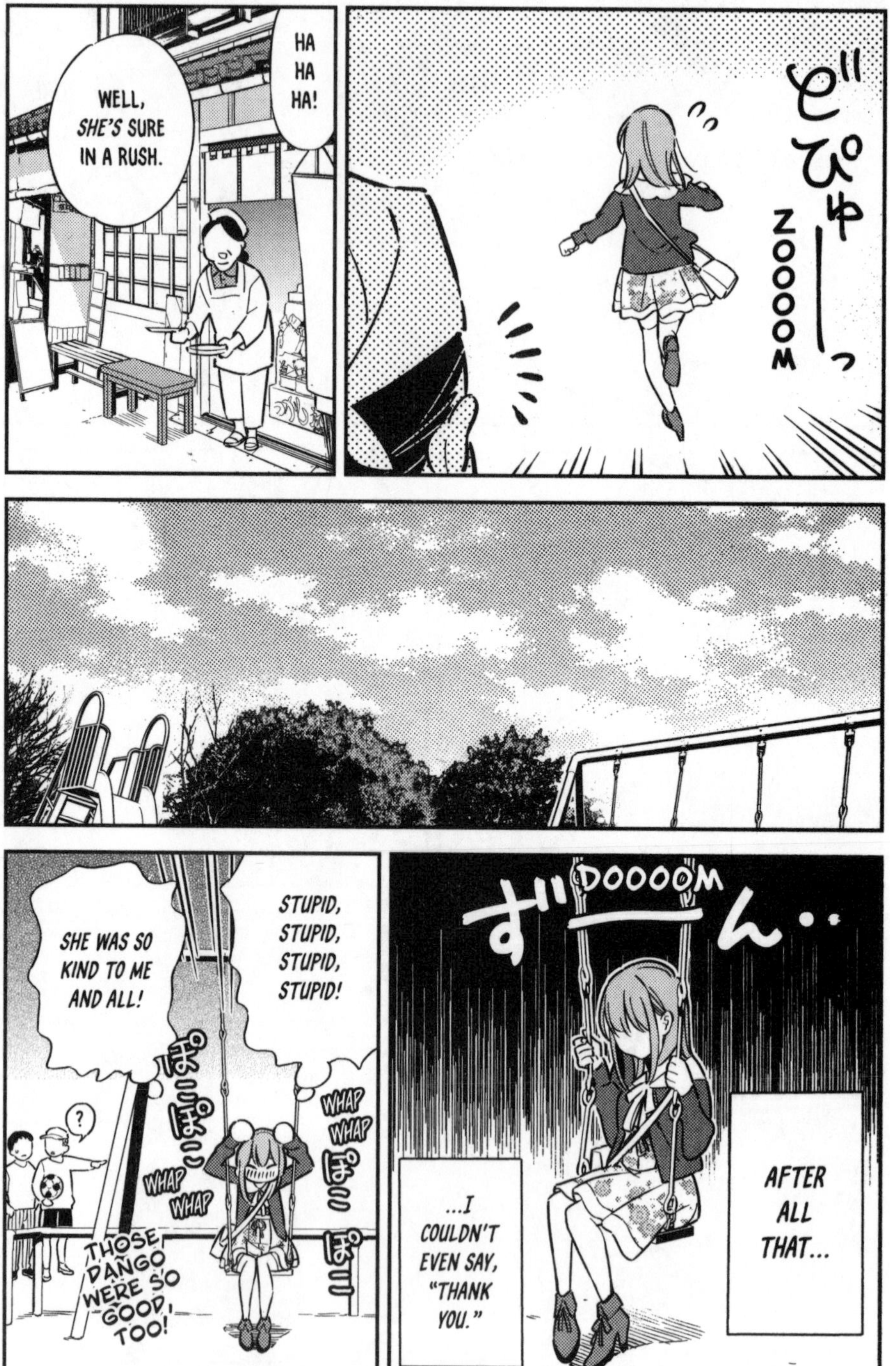
どぴゅーっ
ZOOOOOM
HA HA HA!
WELL, SHE'S SURE IN A RUSH.
ずーん..
DOOOOM
AFTER ALL THAT...
...I COULDN'T EVEN SAY, "THANK YOU."
STUPID, STUPID, STUPID, STUPID!
SHE WAS SO KIND TO ME AND ALL!
ぽこぽこ
WHAP WHAP
ぽこぽこ
WHAP WHAP
?
THOSE DANGO WERE SO GOOD, TOO!

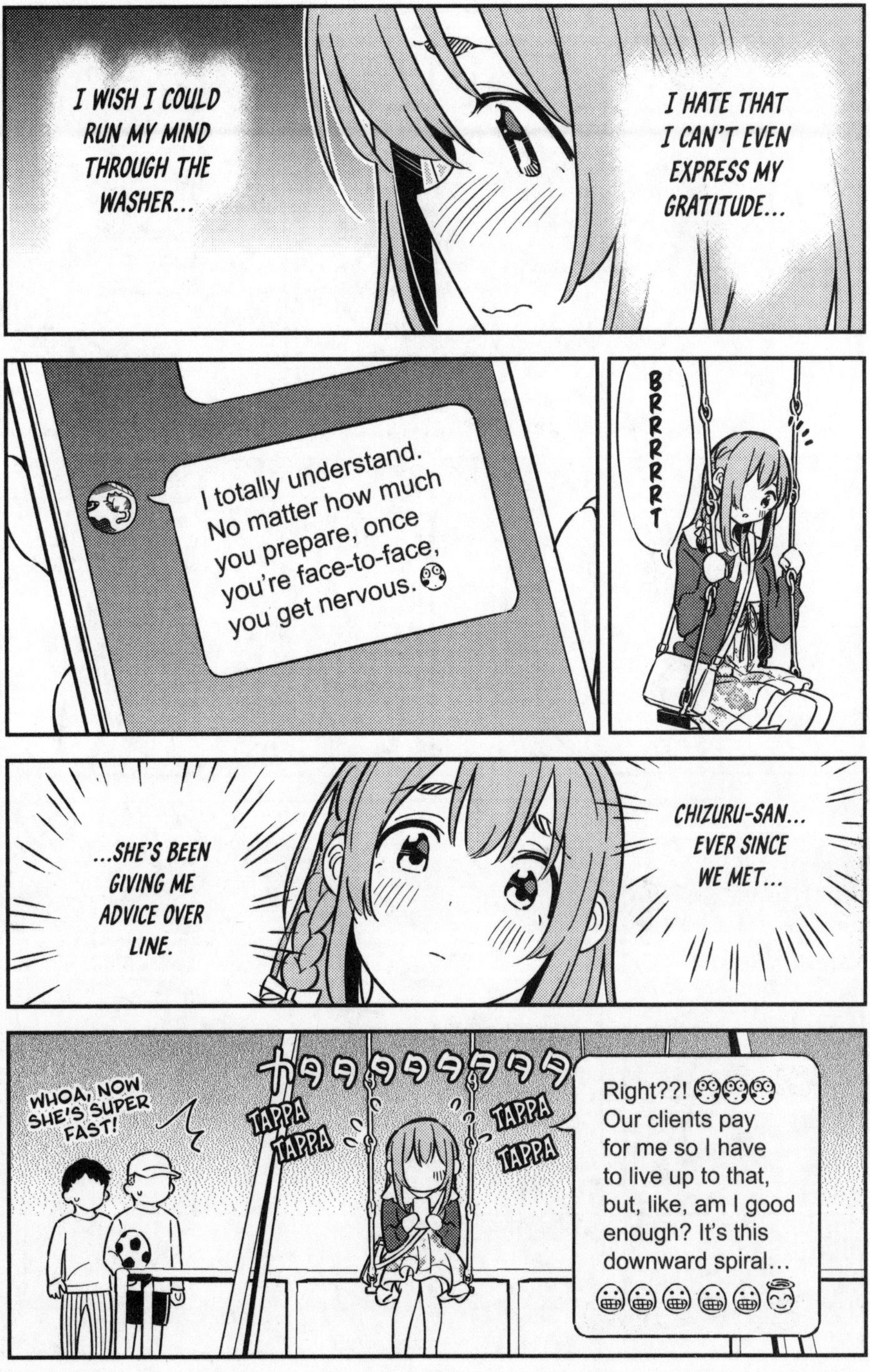

I HATE THAT I CAN'T EVEN EXPRESS MY GRATITUDE...
I WISH I COULD RUN MY MIND THROUGH THE WASHER...
BRRRRRT
I totally understand. No matter how much you prepare, once you're face-to-face, you get nervous.
CHIZURU-SAN... EVER SINCE WE MET...
...SHE'S BEEN GIVING ME ADVICE OVER LINE.
Right??! Our clients pay for me so I have to live up to that, but, like, am I good enough? It's this downward spiral...
TAPPA TAPPA
カタタタタタタタタ
TAPPA TAPPA
WHOA, NOW SHE'S SUPER FAST!

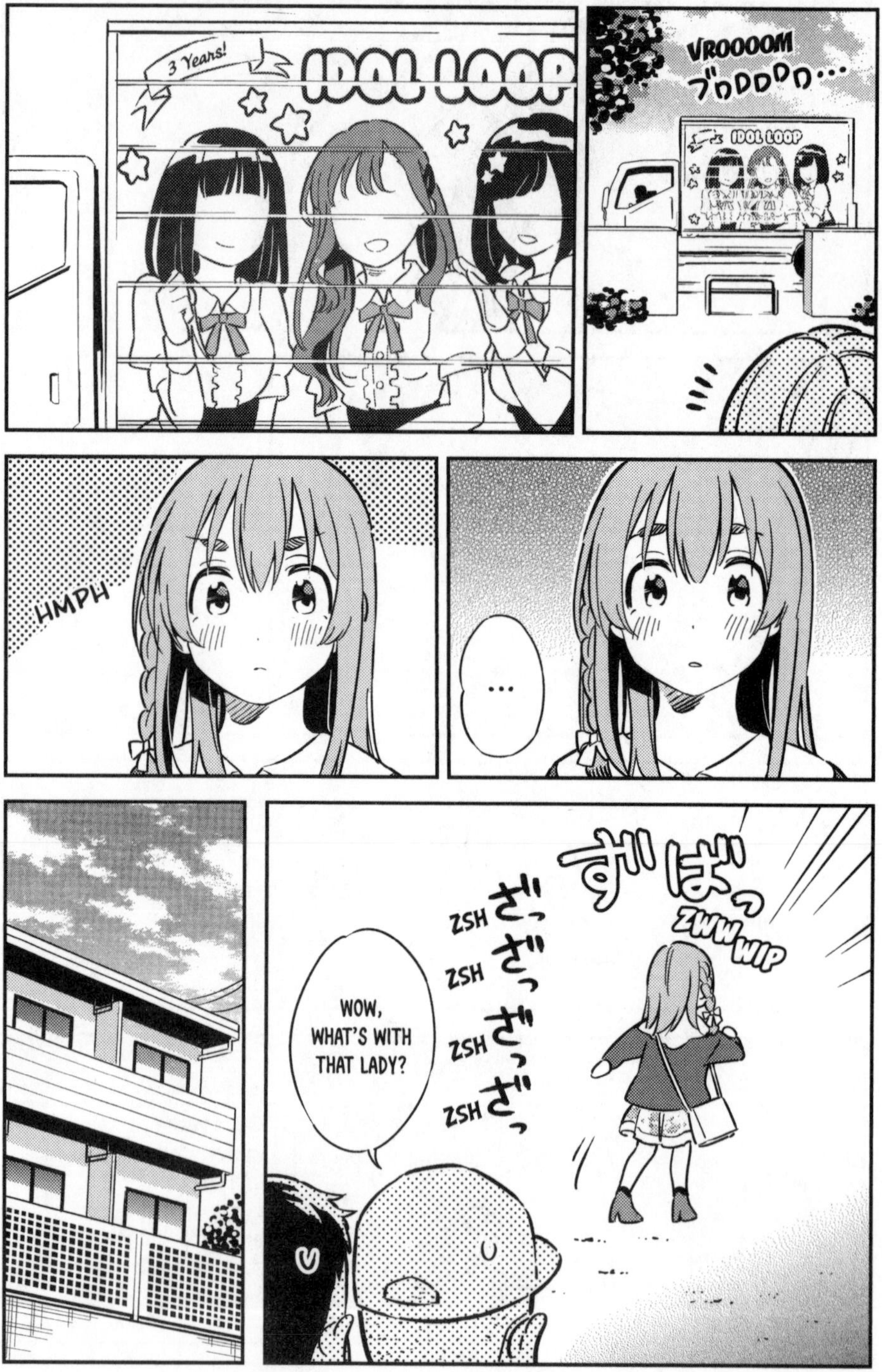

VROOOOM
ブロロロロ…
IDOL LOOP
3 Years!
IDOL LOOP
…
HMPH
すばっ
ZWWWIP
ZSH ざっ
ZSH ざっ
ZSH ざっ
ZSH ざっ
WOW, WHAT'S WITH THAT LADY?

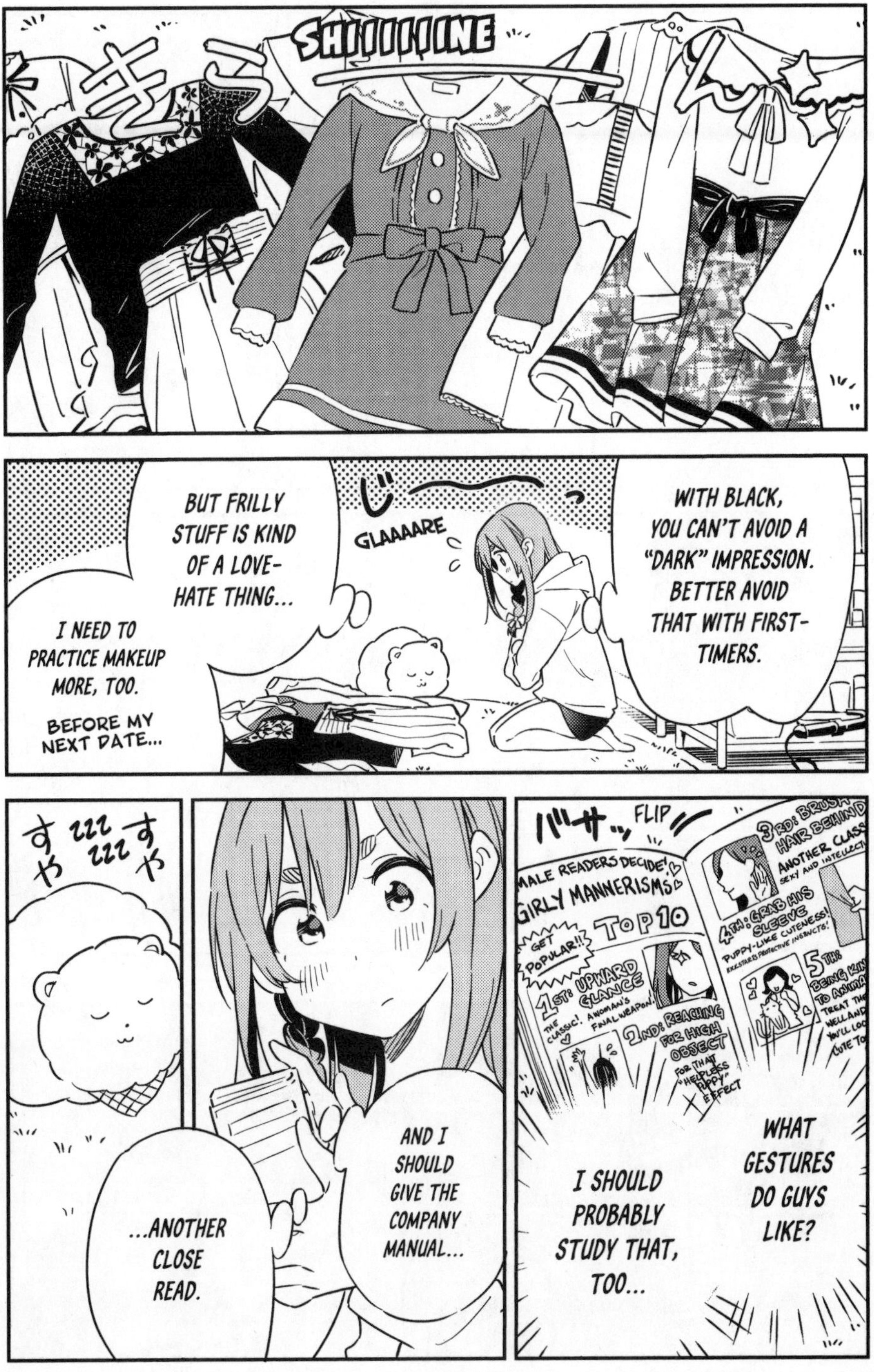
SHIIIIIINE
WITH BLACK, YOU CAN'T AVOID A "DARK" IMPRESSION. BETTER AVOID THAT WITH FIRST-TIMERS.
じーっ
GLAAAARE
BUT FRILLY STUFF IS KIND OF A LOVE-HATE THING...
I NEED TO PRACTICE MAKEUP MORE, TOO.
BEFORE MY NEXT DATE...
バサッ
FLIP
MALE READERS DECIDE!
GIRLY MANNERISMS
TOP 10
GET POPULAR!!
1ST: UPWARD GLANCE
THE CLASSIC! A WOMAN'S FINAL WEAPON.
2ND: REACHING FOR HIGH OBJECT
FOR THAT "HELPLESS PUPPY" EFFECT
3RD: BRUSH HAIR BEHIND
4TH: GRAB HIS SLEEVE
PUPPY-LIKE CUTENESS!
5TH: BEING KIN
WHAT GESTURES DO GUYS LIKE?
I SHOULD PROBABLY STUDY THAT, TOO...
AND I SHOULD GIVE THE COMPANY MANUAL...
...ANOTHER CLOSE READ.
すやすや
ZZZ ZZZ

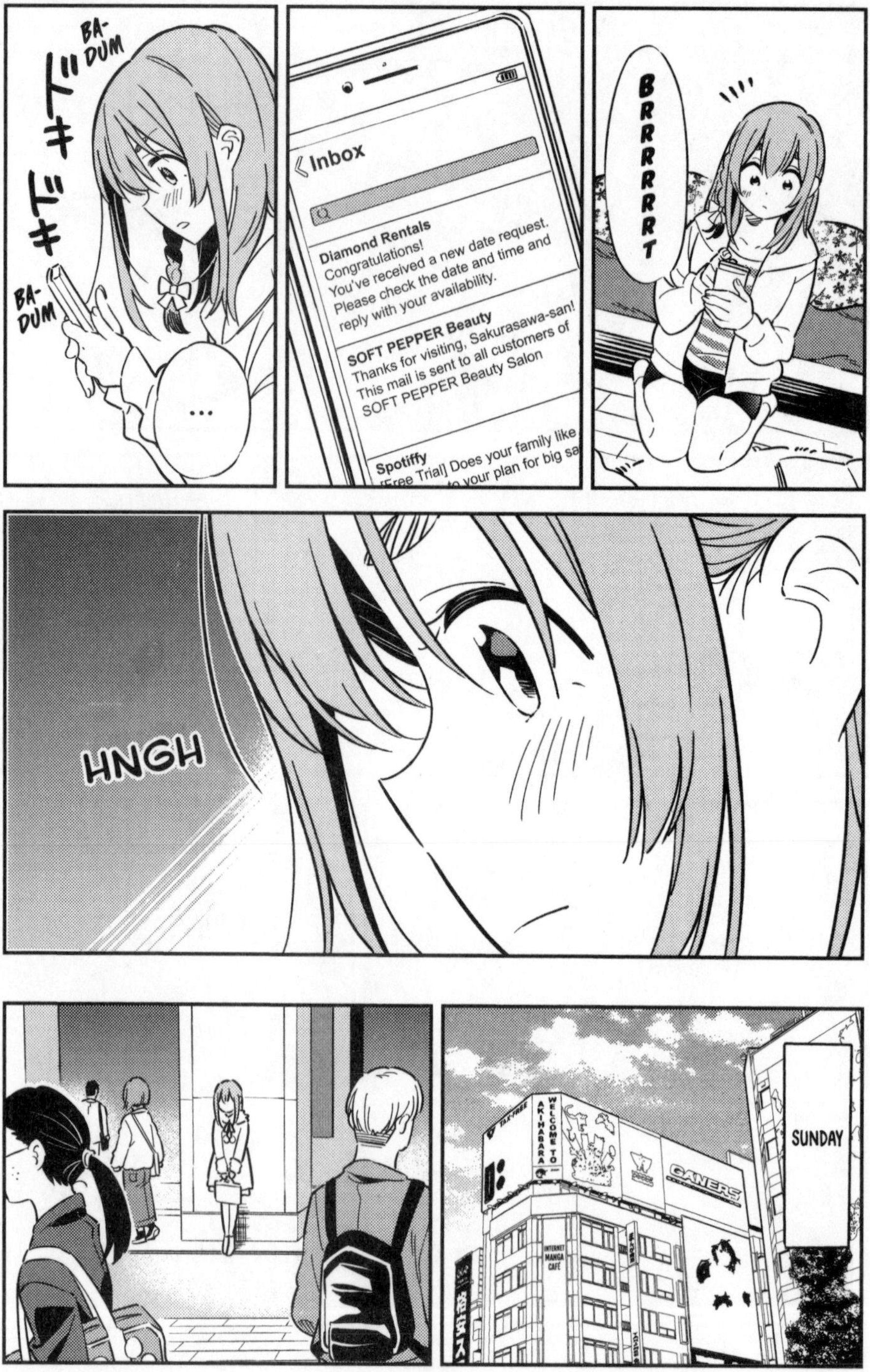
BRRRRRRT
Inbox
Diamond Rentals
Congratulations! You've received a new date request. Please check the date and time and reply with your availability.
SOFT PEPPER Beauty
Thanks for visiting, Sakurasawa-san! This mail is sent to all customers of SOFT PEPPER Beauty Salon
Spotiffy
BA-DUM ドキ
ドキ BA-DUM
...
HNGH
SUNDAY
WELCOME TO AKIHABARA
GAMERS
INTERNET MANGA CAFÉ

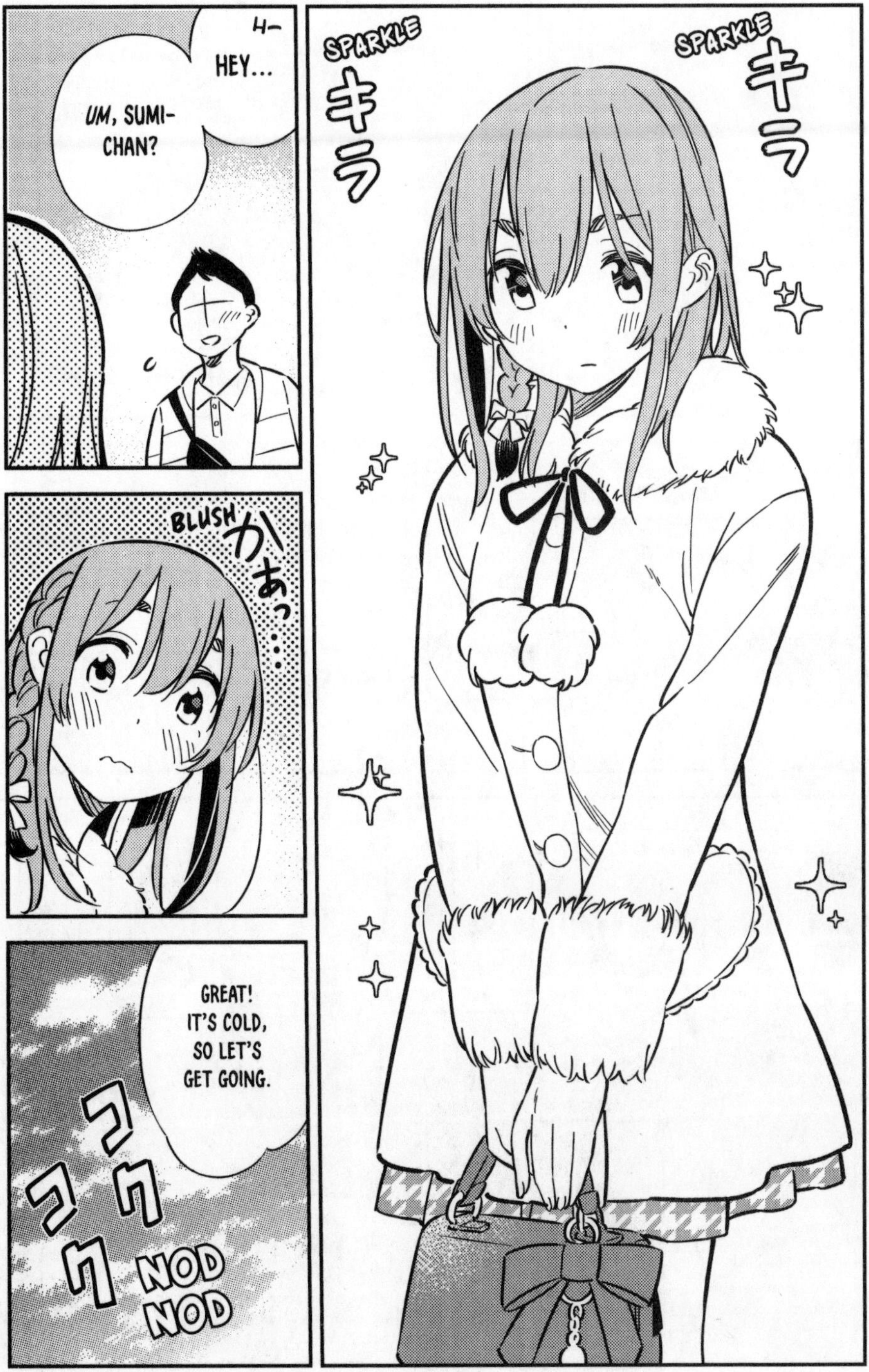
SPARKLE
キラ
SPARKLE
キラ
H- HEY...
UM, SUMI-CHAN?
BLUSH
かあっ...
GREAT! IT'S COLD, SO LET'S GET GOING.
コクコク
NOD NOD

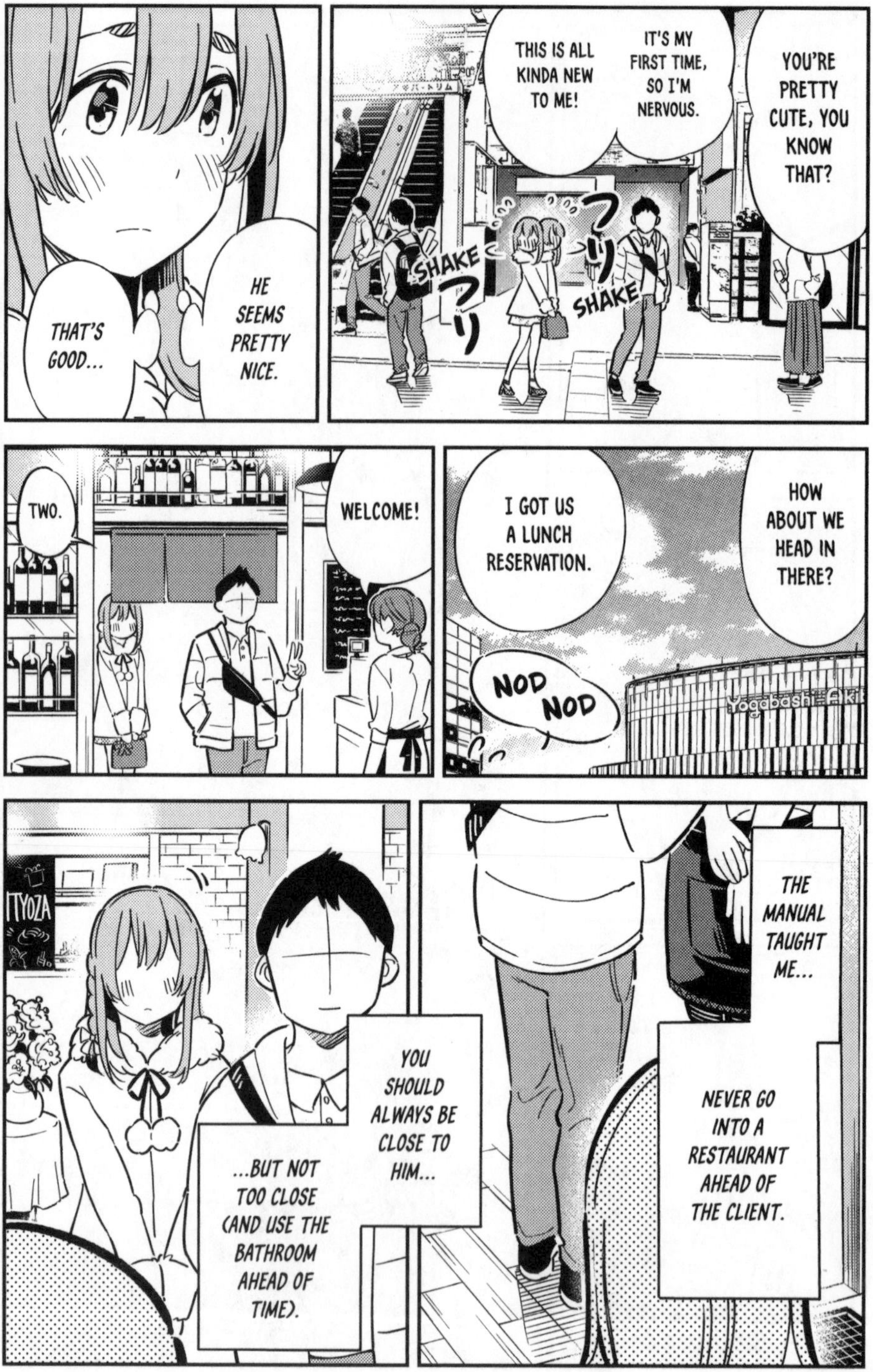
YOU'RE PRETTY CUTE, YOU KNOW THAT?
IT'S MY FIRST TIME, SO I'M NERVOUS.
THIS IS ALL KINDA NEW TO ME!
SHAKE
SHAKE
HE SEEMS PRETTY NICE.
THAT'S GOOD...
HOW ABOUT WE HEAD IN THERE?
I GOT US A LUNCH RESERVATION.
NOD NOD
WELCOME!
TWO.
THE MANUAL TAUGHT ME...
NEVER GO INTO A RESTAURANT AHEAD OF THE CLIENT.
YOU SHOULD ALWAYS BE CLOSE TO HIM...
...BUT NOT TOO CLOSE (AND USE THE BATHROOM AHEAD OF TIME).

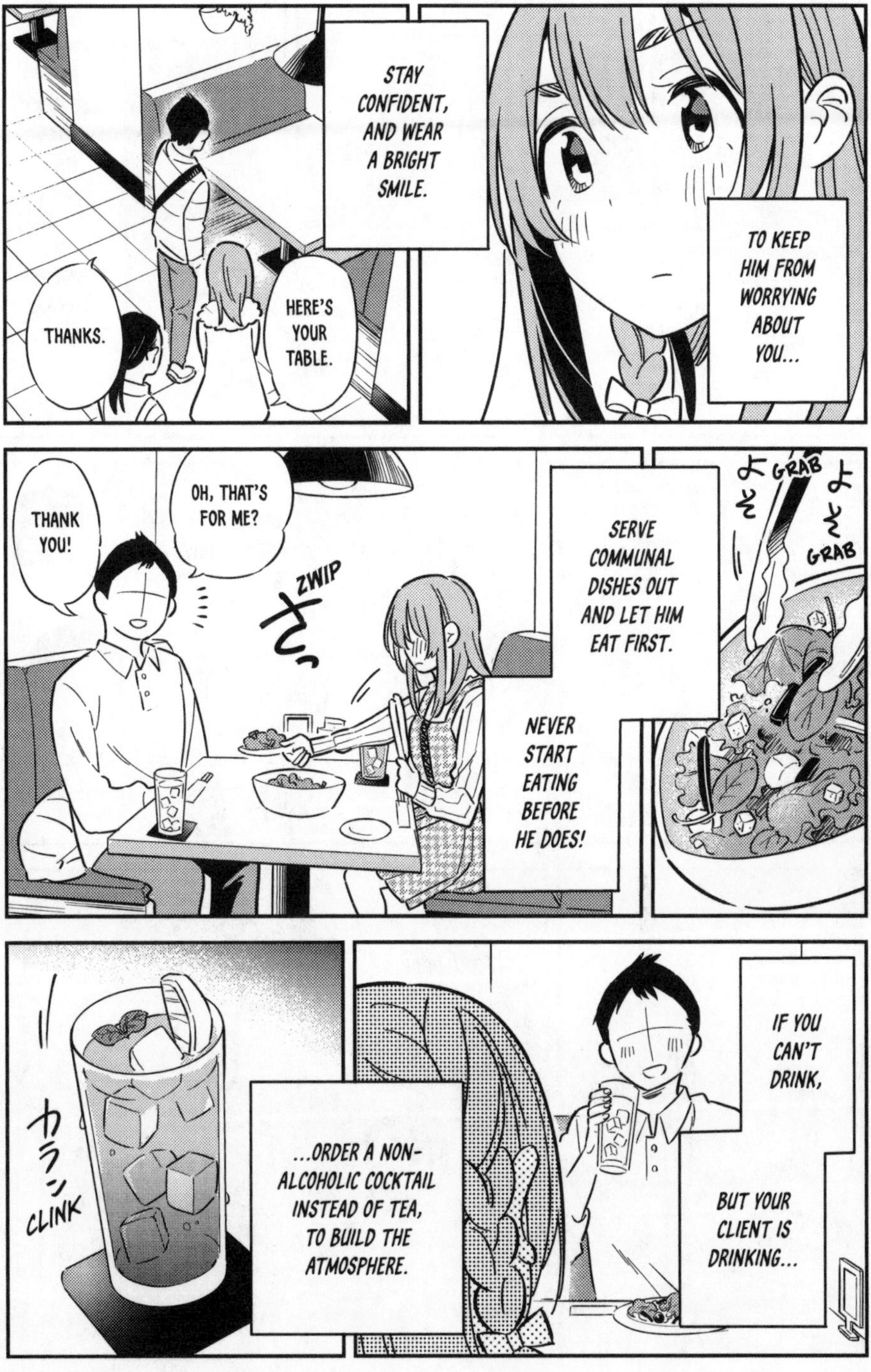
STAY CONFIDENT, AND WEAR A BRIGHT SMILE.
TO KEEP HIM FROM WORRYING ABOUT YOU...
HERE'S YOUR TABLE.
THANKS.
よそ GRAB
よそ GRAB
SERVE COMMUNAL DISHES OUT AND LET HIM EAT FIRST.
NEVER START EATING BEFORE HE DOES!
OH, THAT'S FOR ME?
THANK YOU!
さっ ZWIP
IF YOU CAN'T DRINK,
BUT YOUR CLIENT IS DRINKING...
...ORDER A NON-ALCOHOLIC COCKTAIL INSTEAD OF TEA, TO BUILD THE ATMOSPHERE.
カラン CLINK

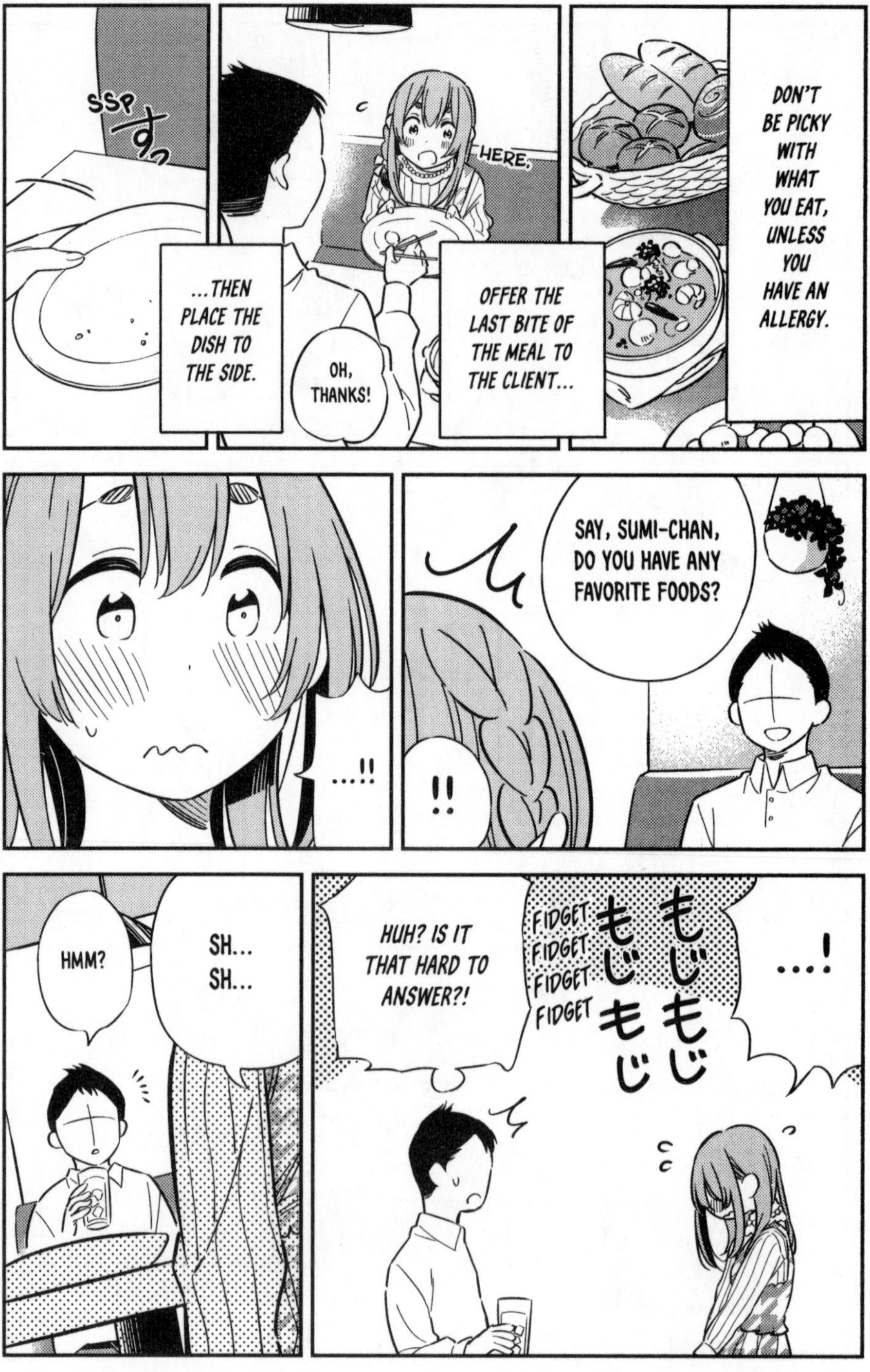
DON'T BE PICKY WITH WHAT YOU EAT, UNLESS YOU HAVE AN ALLERGY.
HERE.
OFFER THE LAST BITE OF THE MEAL TO THE CLIENT...
OH, THANKS!
...THEN PLACE THE DISH TO THE SIDE.
SSP すっ
SAY, SUMI-CHAN, DO YOU HAVE ANY FAVORITE FOODS?
!!
...!!
...!
もじもじ もじもじ
FIDGET FIDGET FIDGET FIDGET
HUH? IS IT THAT HARD TO ANSWER?!
SH... SH...
HMM?

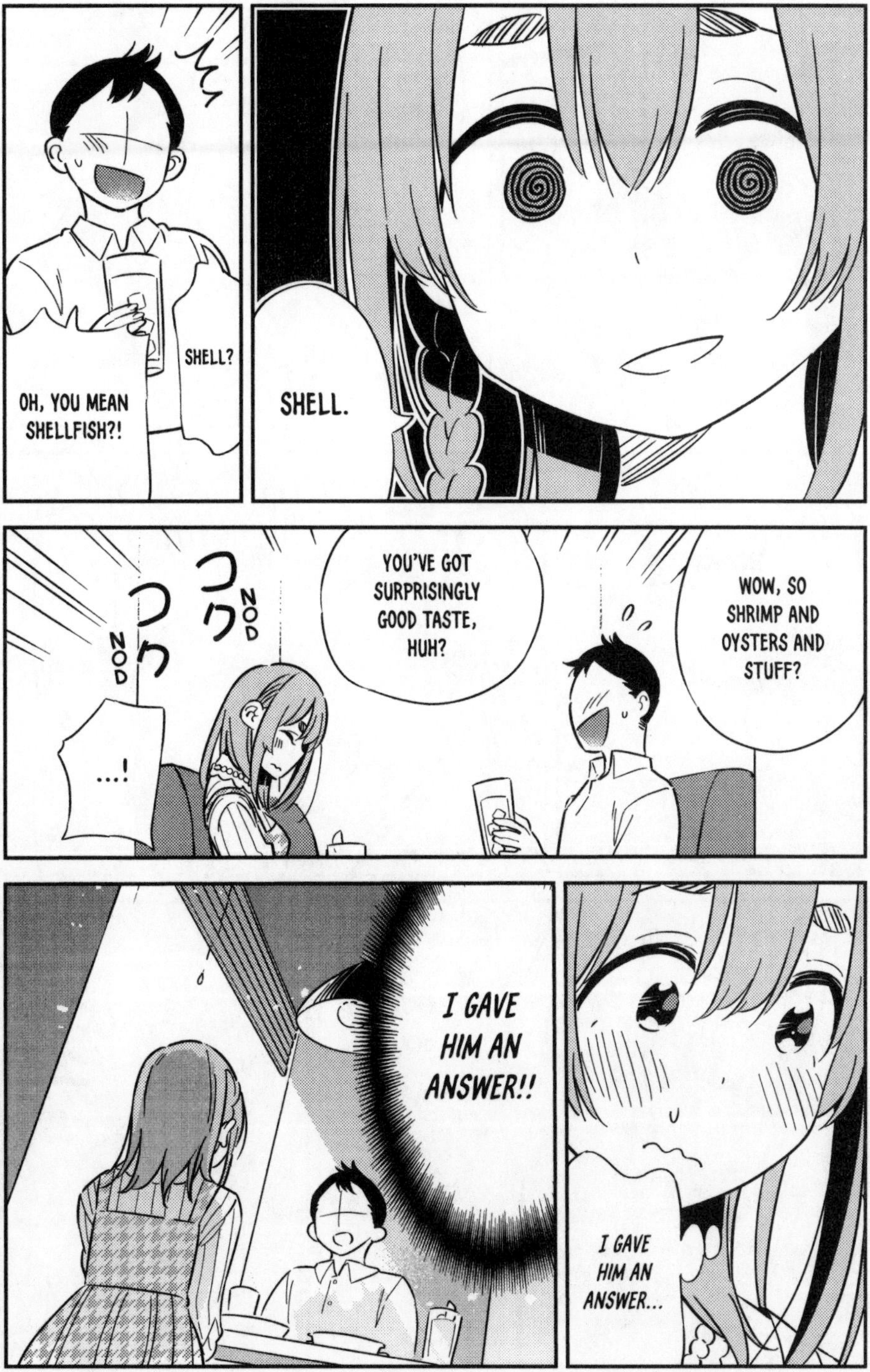
SHELL.
SHELL?
OH, YOU MEAN SHELLFISH?!
WOW, SO SHRIMP AND OYSTERS AND STUFF?
YOU'VE GOT SURPRISINGLY GOOD TASTE, HUH?
コク NOD
コク NOD
...!
I GAVE HIM AN ANSWER...
I GAVE HIM AN ANSWER!!

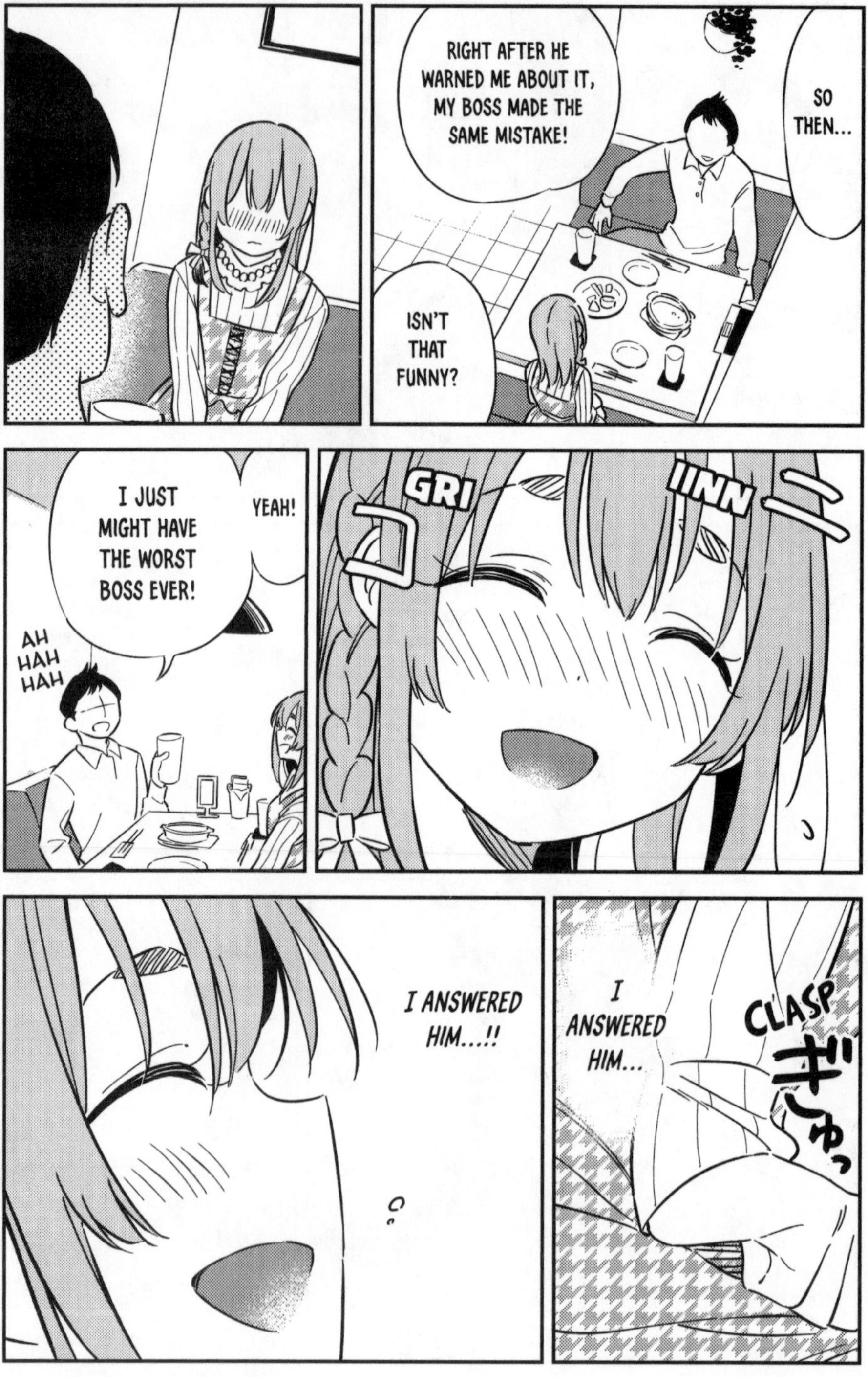
SO THEN...
RIGHT AFTER HE WARNED ME ABOUT IT, MY BOSS MADE THE SAME MISTAKE!
ISN'T THAT FUNNY?
GRI
IINN
YEAH!
I JUST MIGHT HAVE THE WORST BOSS EVER!
AH HAH HAH
CLASP
ぎゅっ
I ANSWERED HIM...
I ANSWERED HIM...!!

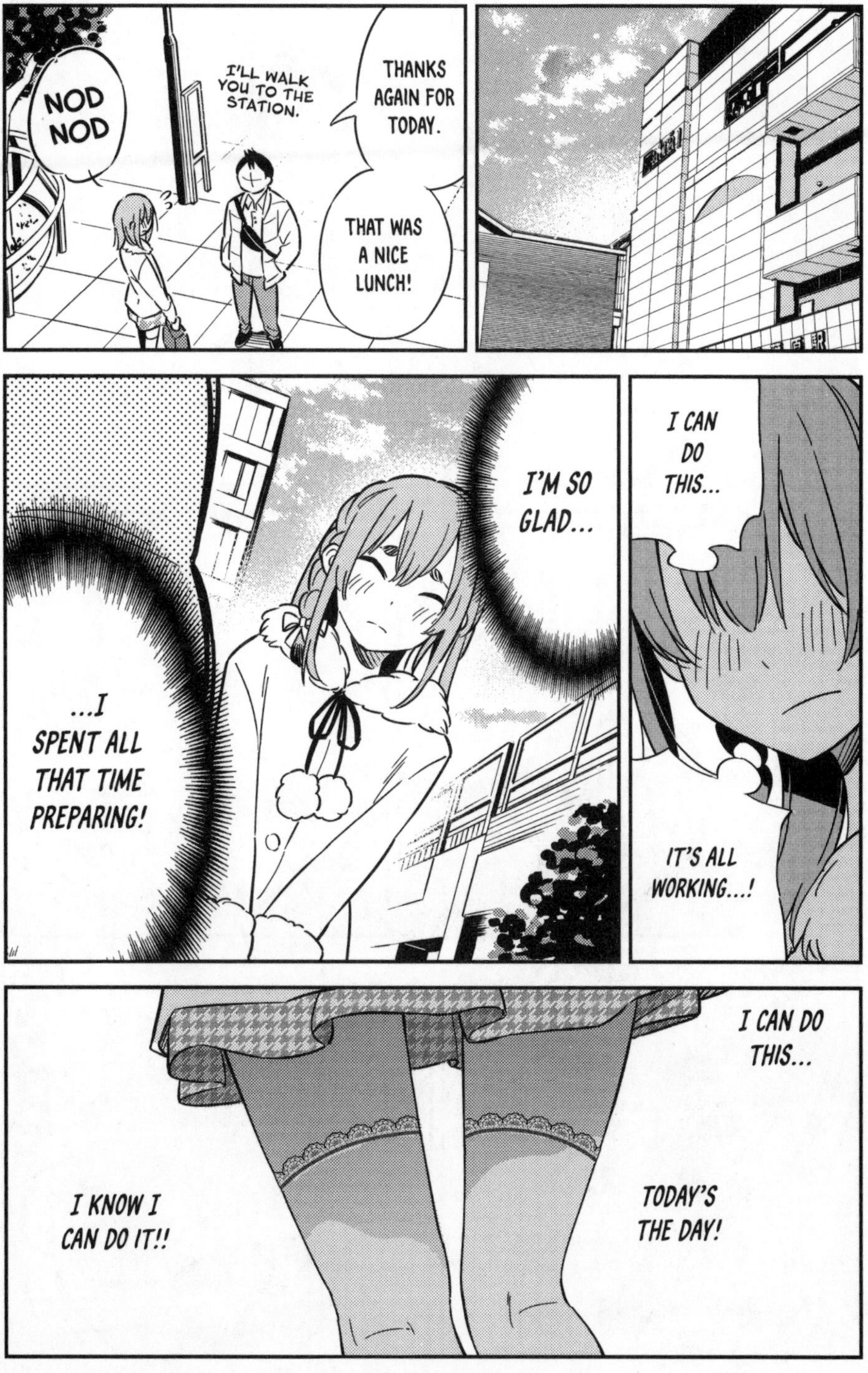
THANKS AGAIN FOR TODAY.
THAT WAS A NICE LUNCH!
I'LL WALK YOU TO THE STATION.
NOD NOD
I CAN DO THIS...
IT'S ALL WORKING...!
I'M SO GLAD...
...I SPENT ALL THAT TIME PREPARING!
I CAN DO THIS...
TODAY'S THE DAY!
I KNOW I CAN DO IT!!

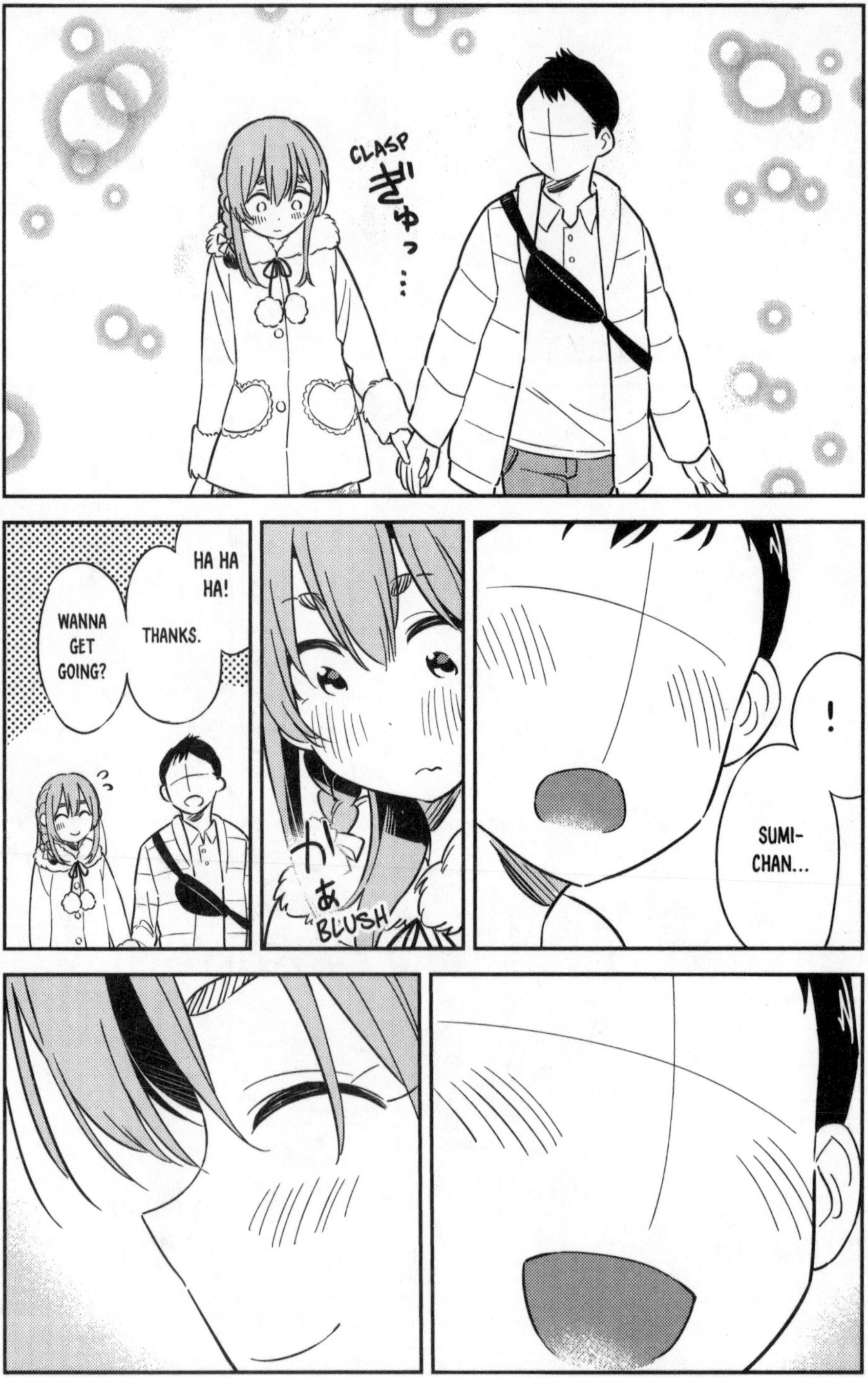
CLASP
ぎゅっ…
!
SUMI-CHAN...
かぁ
BLUSH
HA HA HA!
THANKS.
WANNA GET GOING?

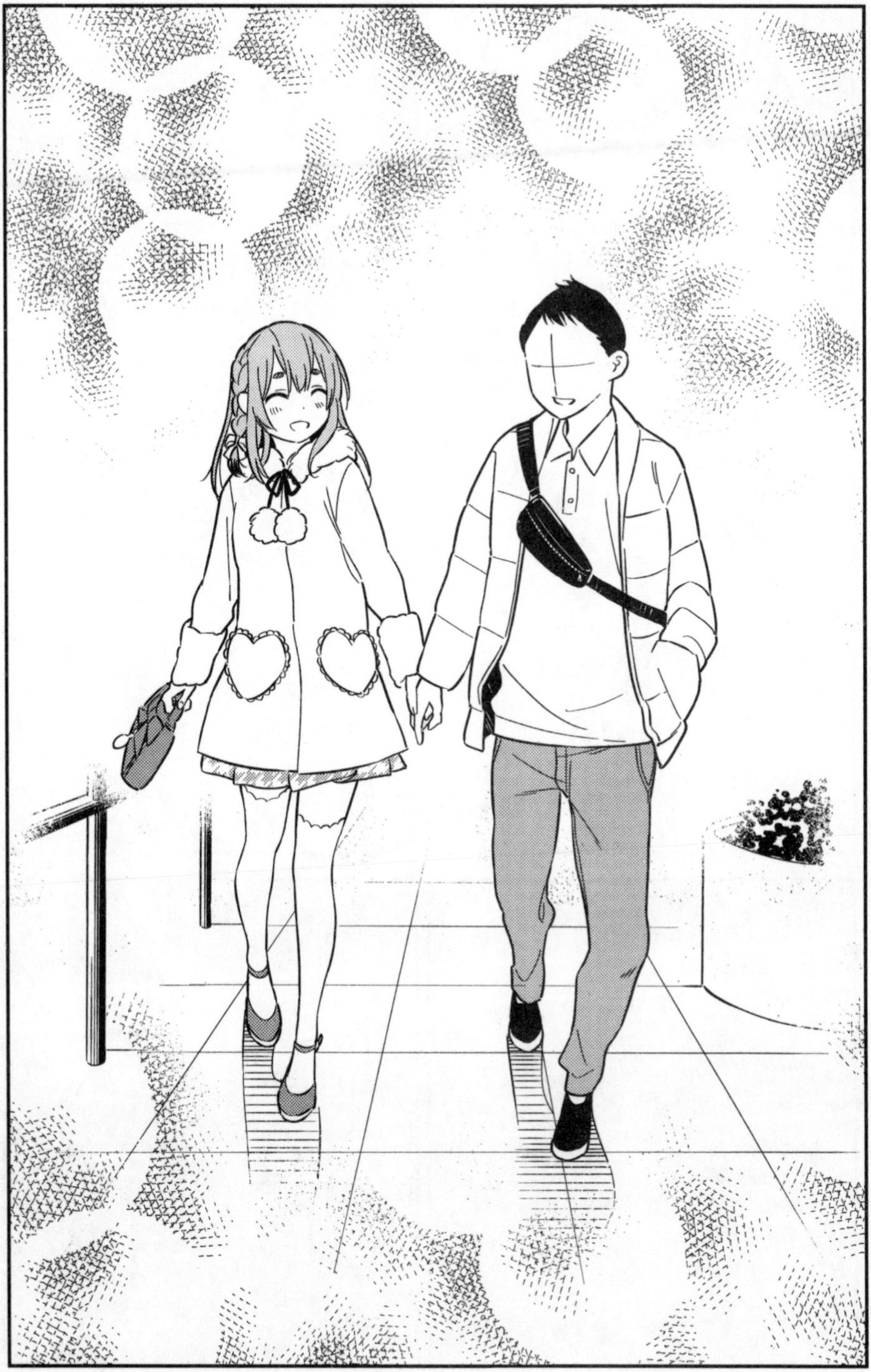

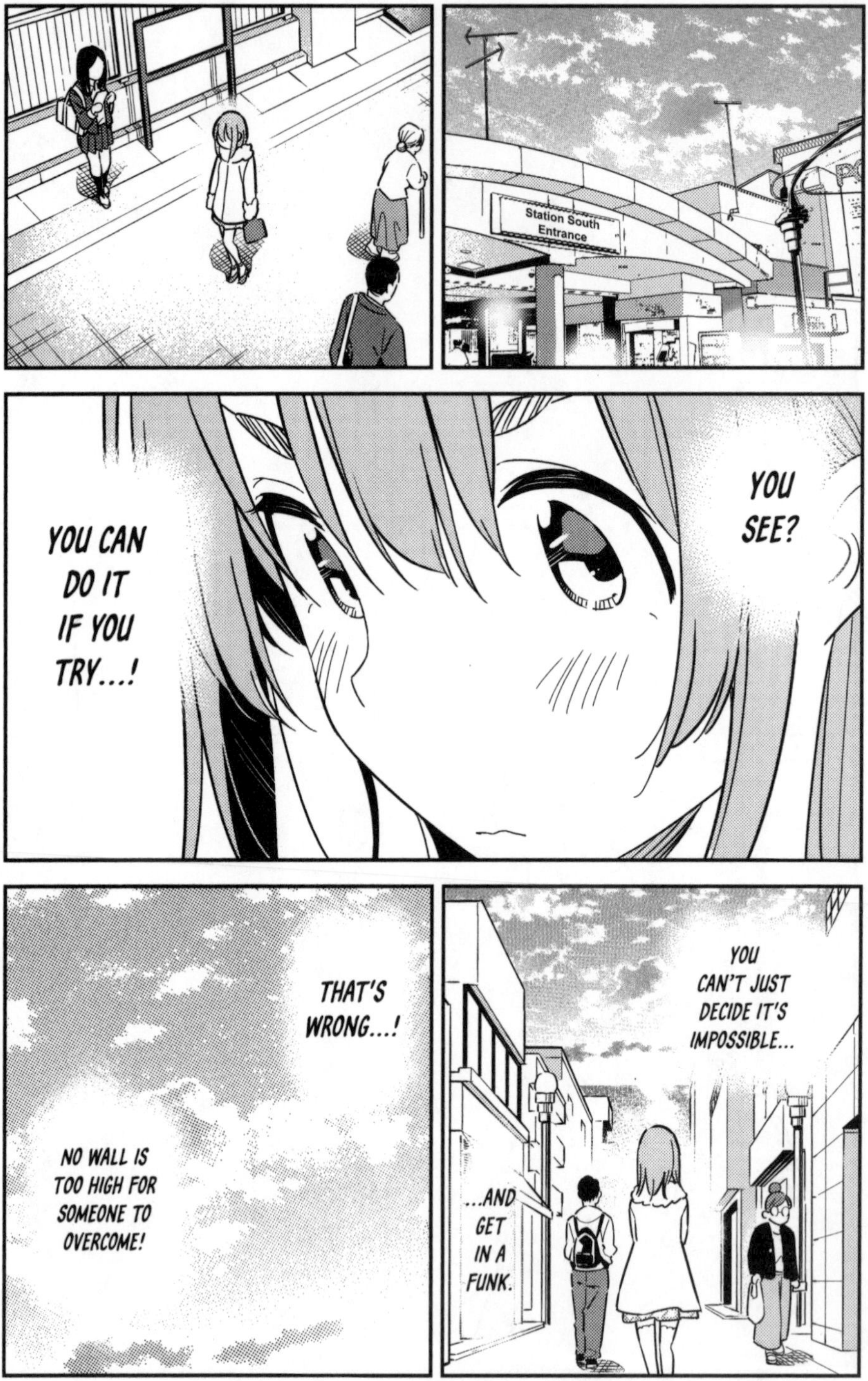
Station South Entrance
YOU SEE?
YOU CAN DO IT IF YOU TRY...!
YOU CAN'T JUST DECIDE IT'S IMPOSSIBLE...
...AND GET IN A FUNK.
THAT'S WRONG...!
NO WALL IS TOO HIGH FOR SOMEONE TO OVERCOME!

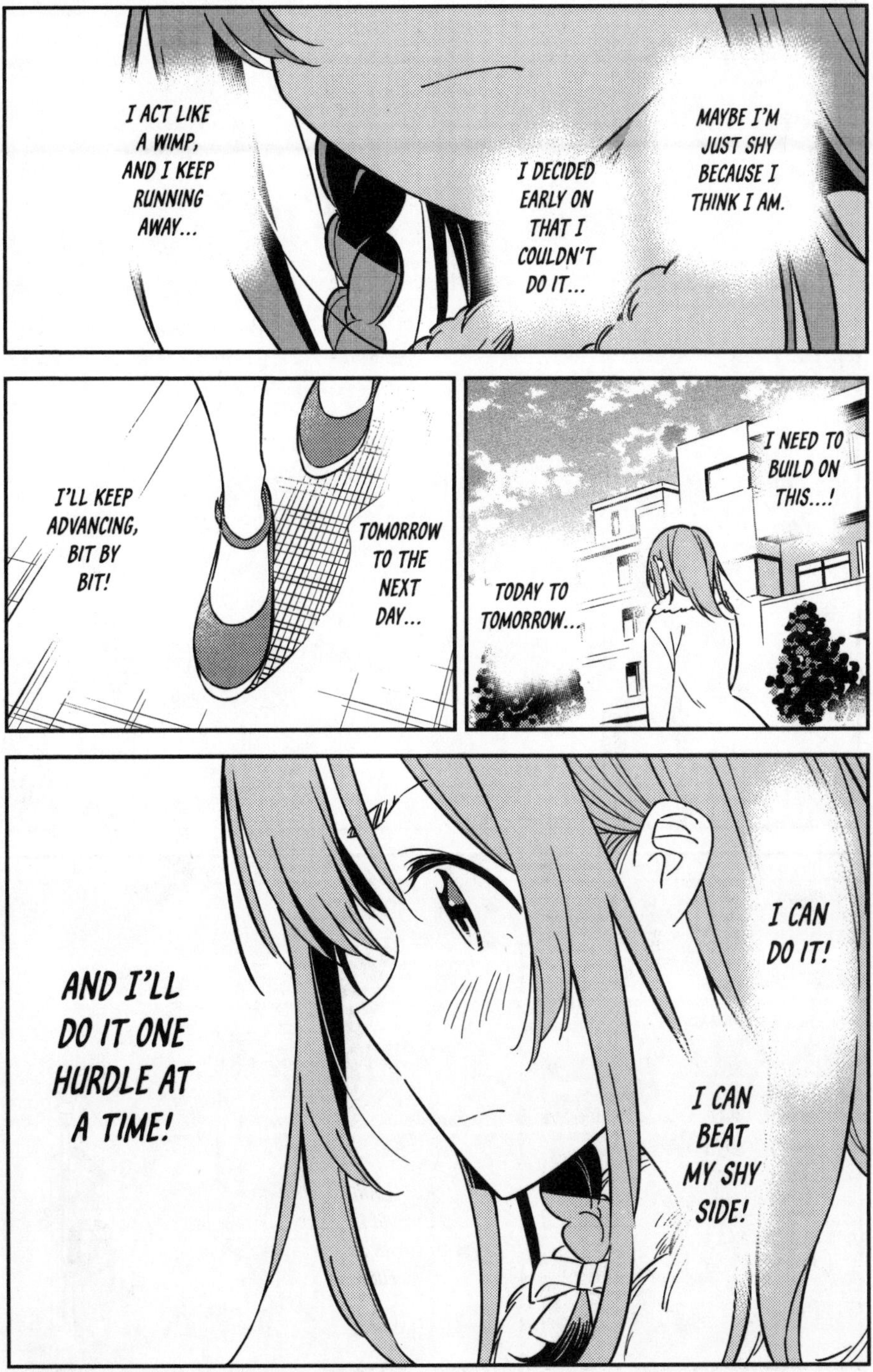

MAYBE I'M JUST SHY BECAUSE I THINK I AM.
I DECIDED EARLY ON THAT I COULDN'T DO IT...
I ACT LIKE A WIMP, AND I KEEP RUNNING AWAY...
I NEED TO BUILD ON THIS...!
TODAY TO TOMORROW...
TOMORROW TO THE NEXT DAY...
I'LL KEEP ADVANCING, BIT BY BIT!
I CAN DO IT!
I CAN BEAT MY SHY SIDE!
AND I'LL DO IT ONE HURDLE AT A TIME!

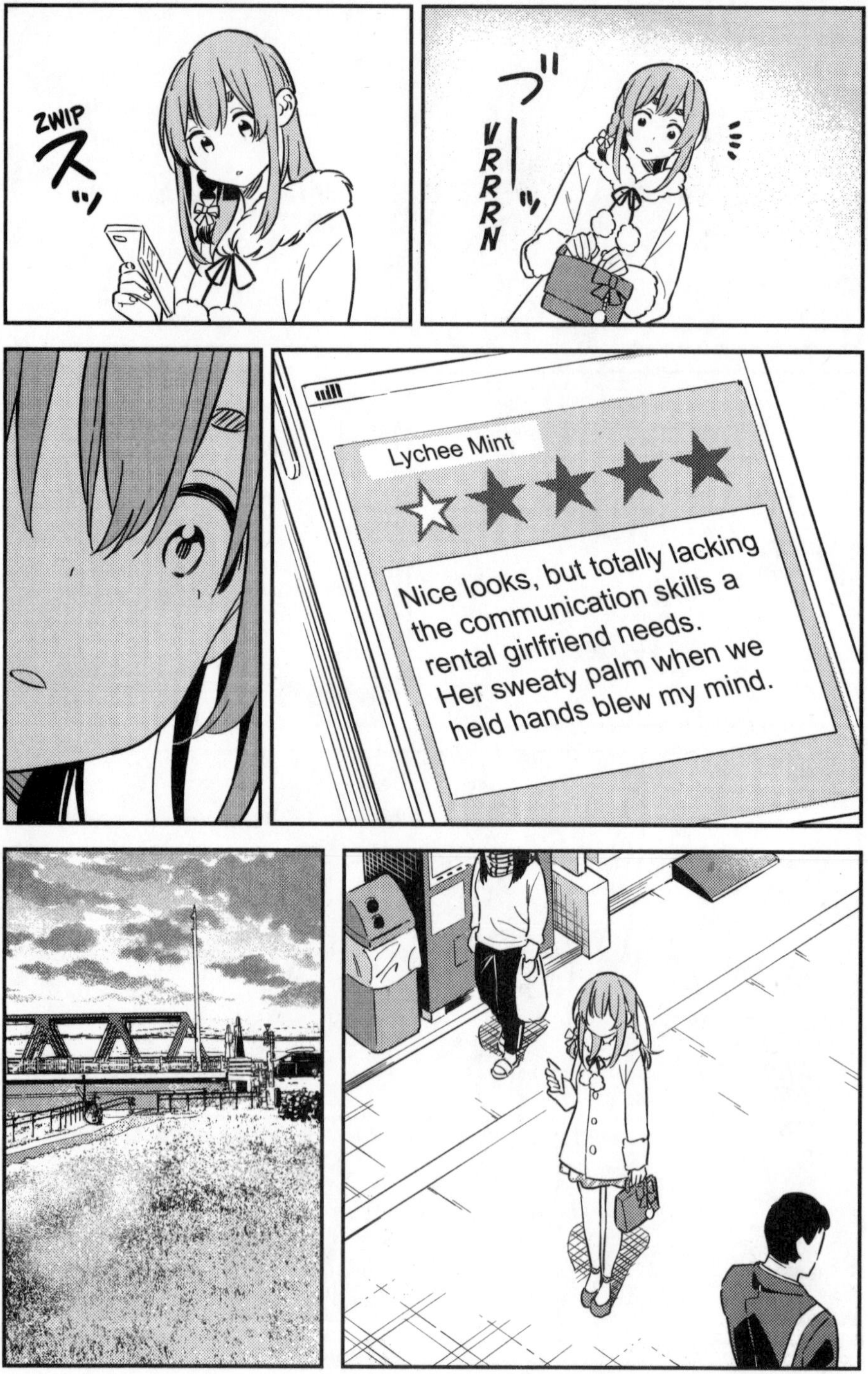
VRRRN
づーッ
ZWIP
スッ
Lychee Mint
Nice looks, but totally lacking the communication skills a rental girlfriend needs. Her sweaty palm when we held hands blew my mind.

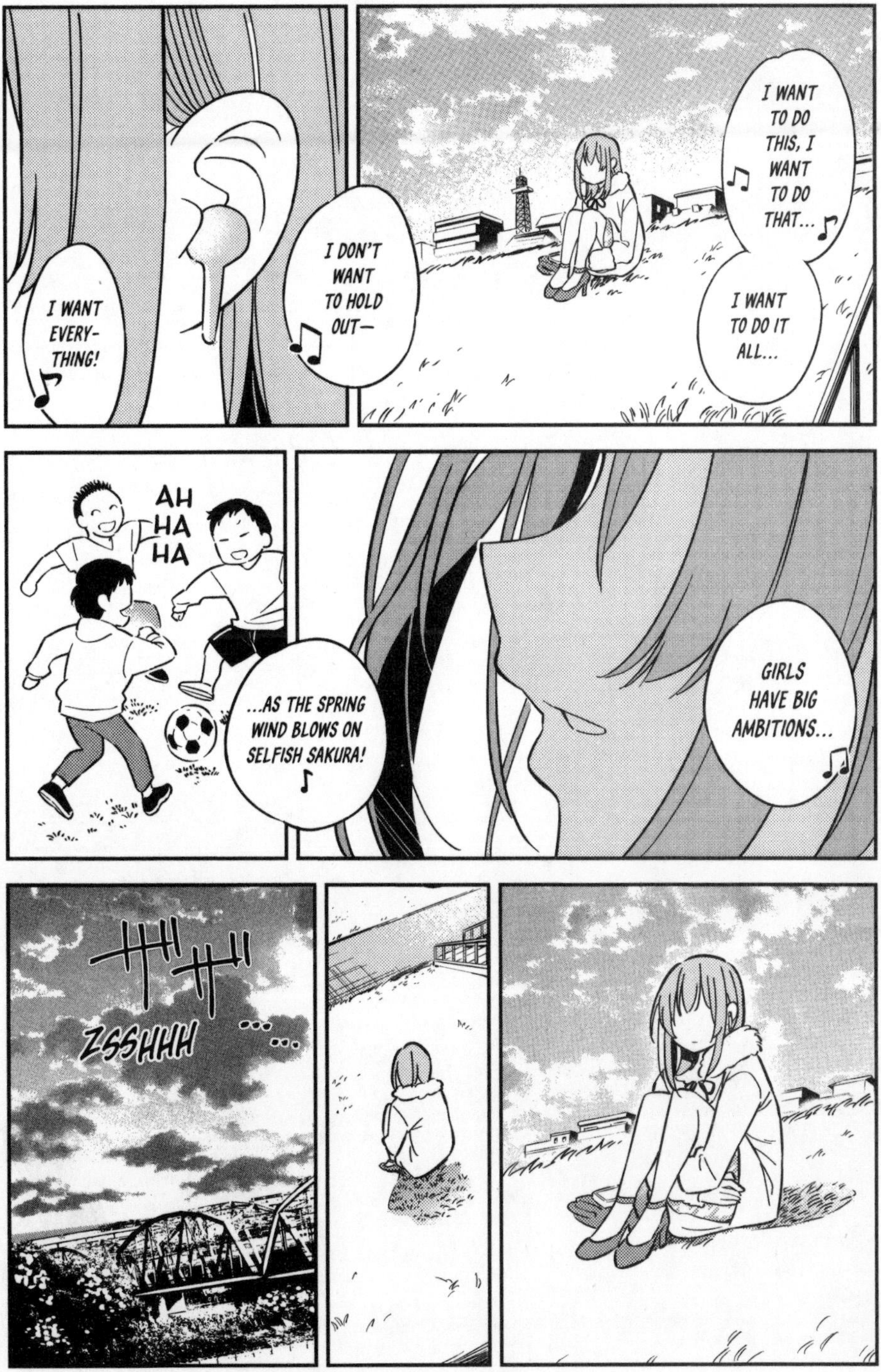
I WANT TO DO THIS, I WANT TO DO THAT... ♪
I WANT TO DO IT ALL...
I DON'T WANT TO HOLD OUT— ♪
I WANT EVERY-THING! ♪
GIRLS HAVE BIG AMBITIONS... ♪
...AS THE SPRING WIND BLOWS ON SELFISH SAKURA! ♪
AH HA HA
ZSSHHH
...

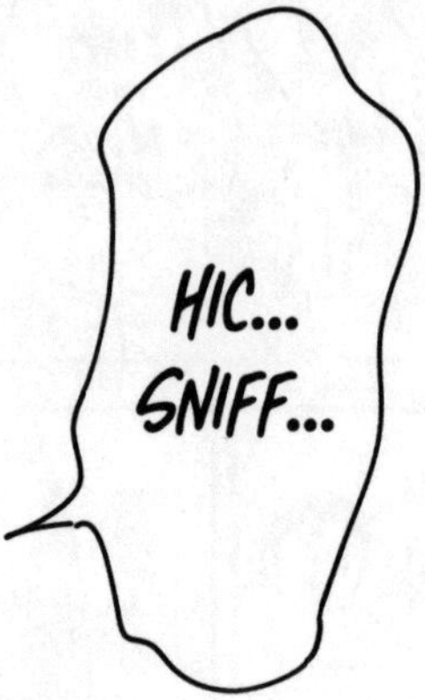
HIC... SNIFF...

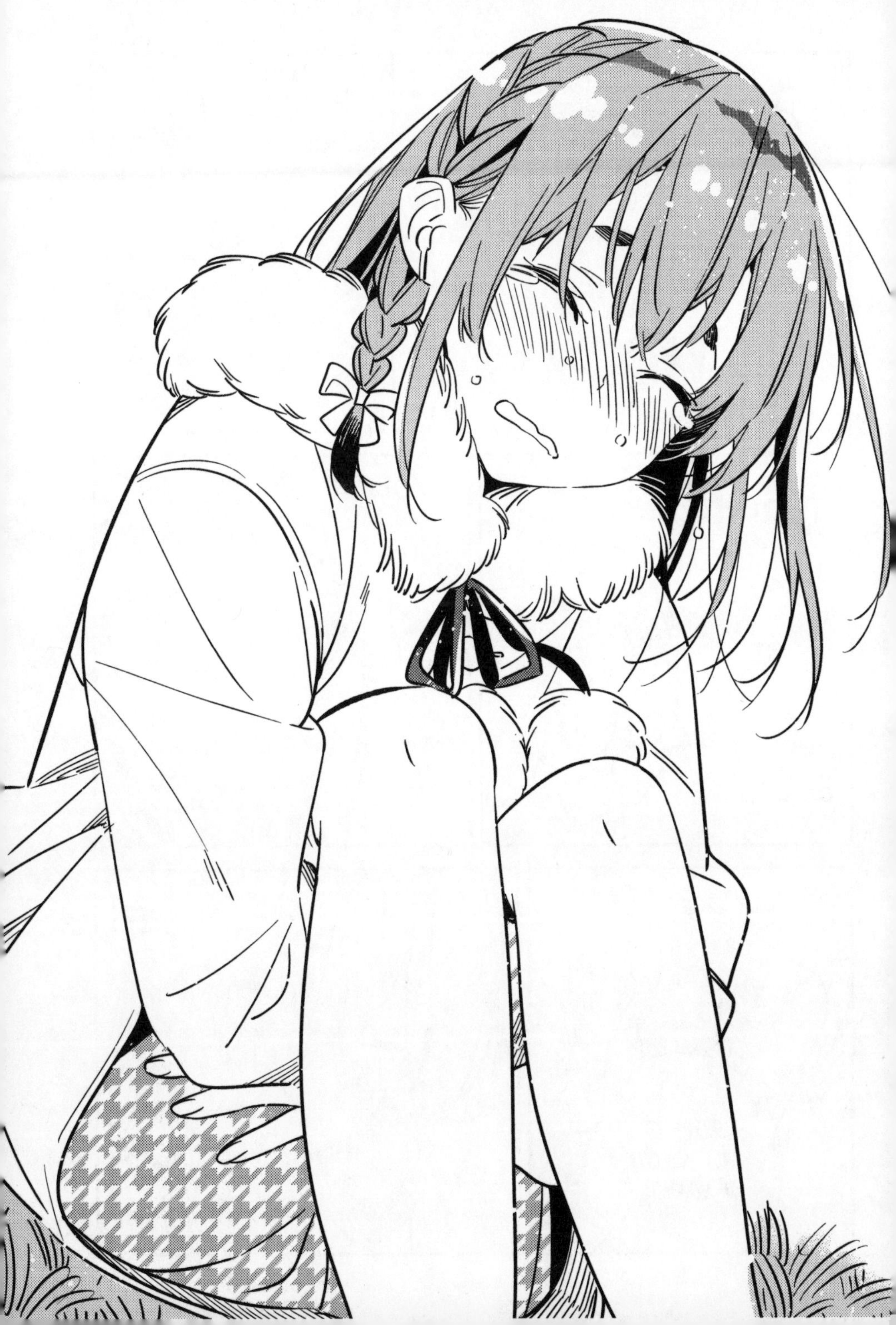

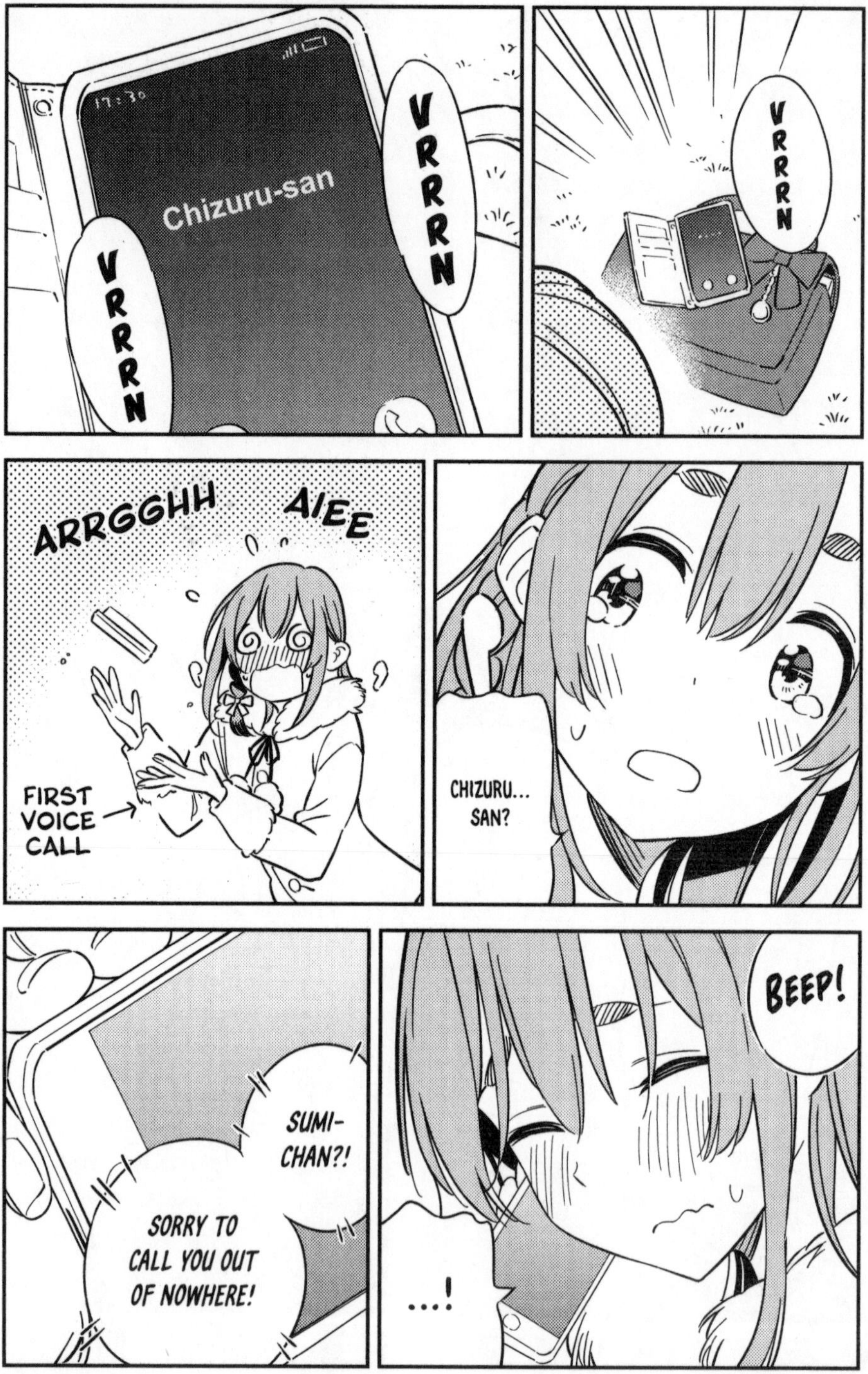
VRRRN
VRRRN
17:30
Chizuru-san
VRRRN
CHIZURU... SAN?
AIEE
ARRGGHH
FIRST VOICE CALL
BEEP!
...!
SUMI-CHAN?!
SORRY TO CALL YOU OUT OF NOWHERE!

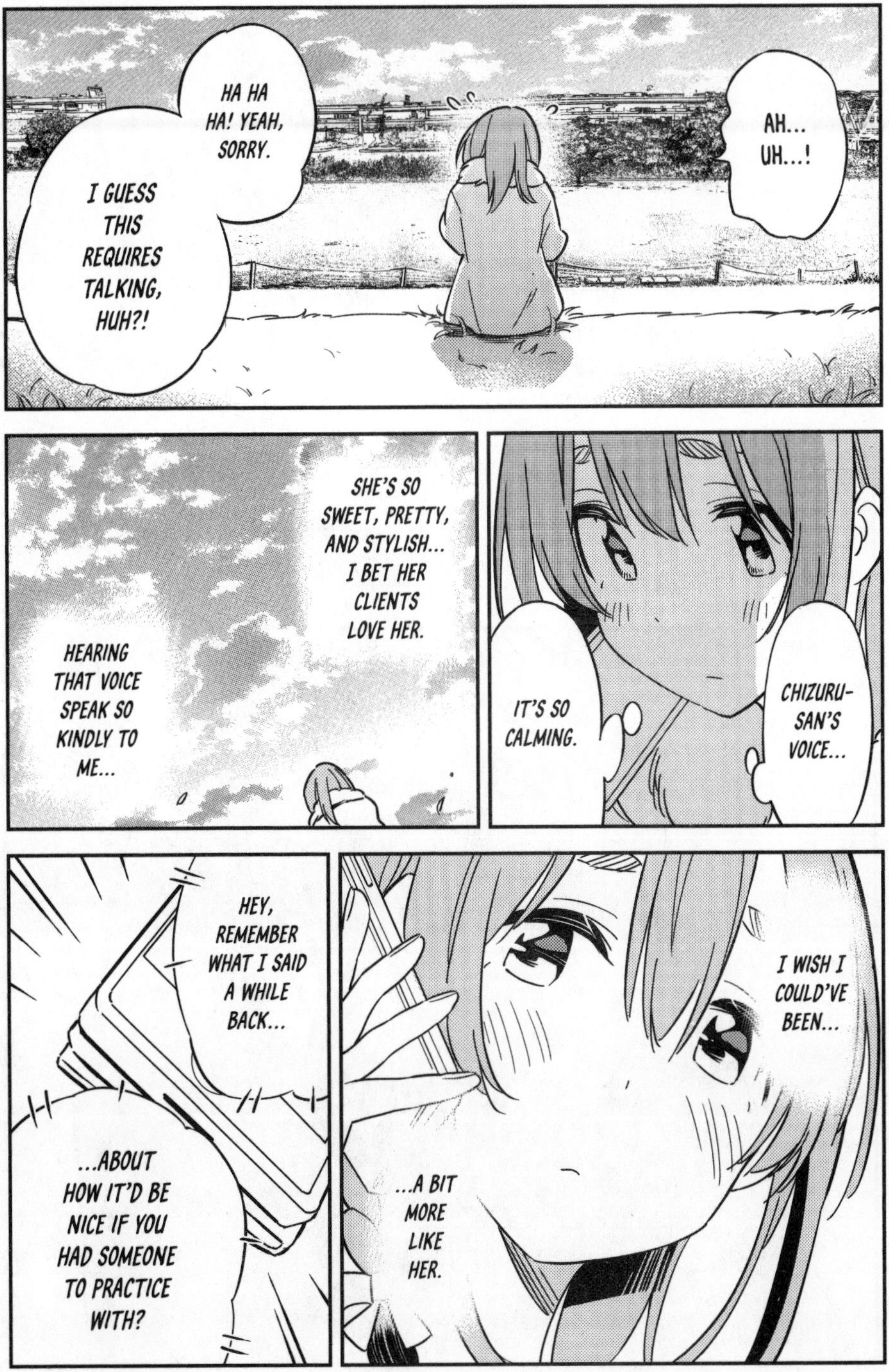
AH... UH...!
HA HA HA! YEAH, SORRY.
I GUESS THIS REQUIRES TALKING, HUH?!
CHIZURU-SAN'S VOICE...
IT'S SO CALMING.
SHE'S SO SWEET, PRETTY, AND STYLISH... I BET HER CLIENTS LOVE HER.
HEARING THAT VOICE SPEAK SO KINDLY TO ME...
I WISH I COULD'VE BEEN...
...A BIT MORE LIKE HER.
HEY, REMEMBER WHAT I SAID A WHILE BACK...
...ABOUT HOW IT'D BE NICE IF YOU HAD SOMEONE TO PRACTICE WITH?

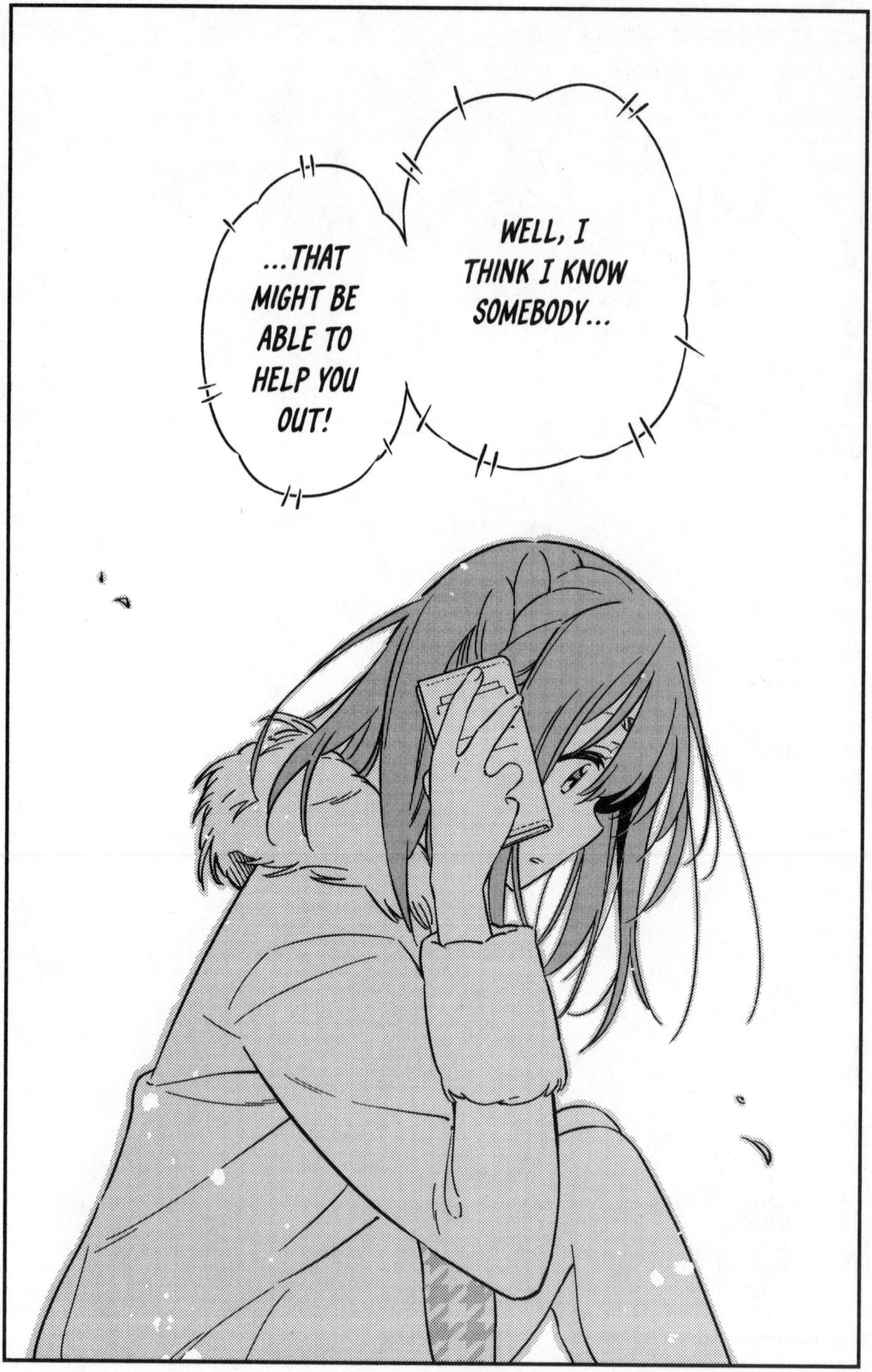
WELL, I THINK I KNOW SOMEBODY...
...THAT MIGHT BE ABLE TO HELP YOU OUT!

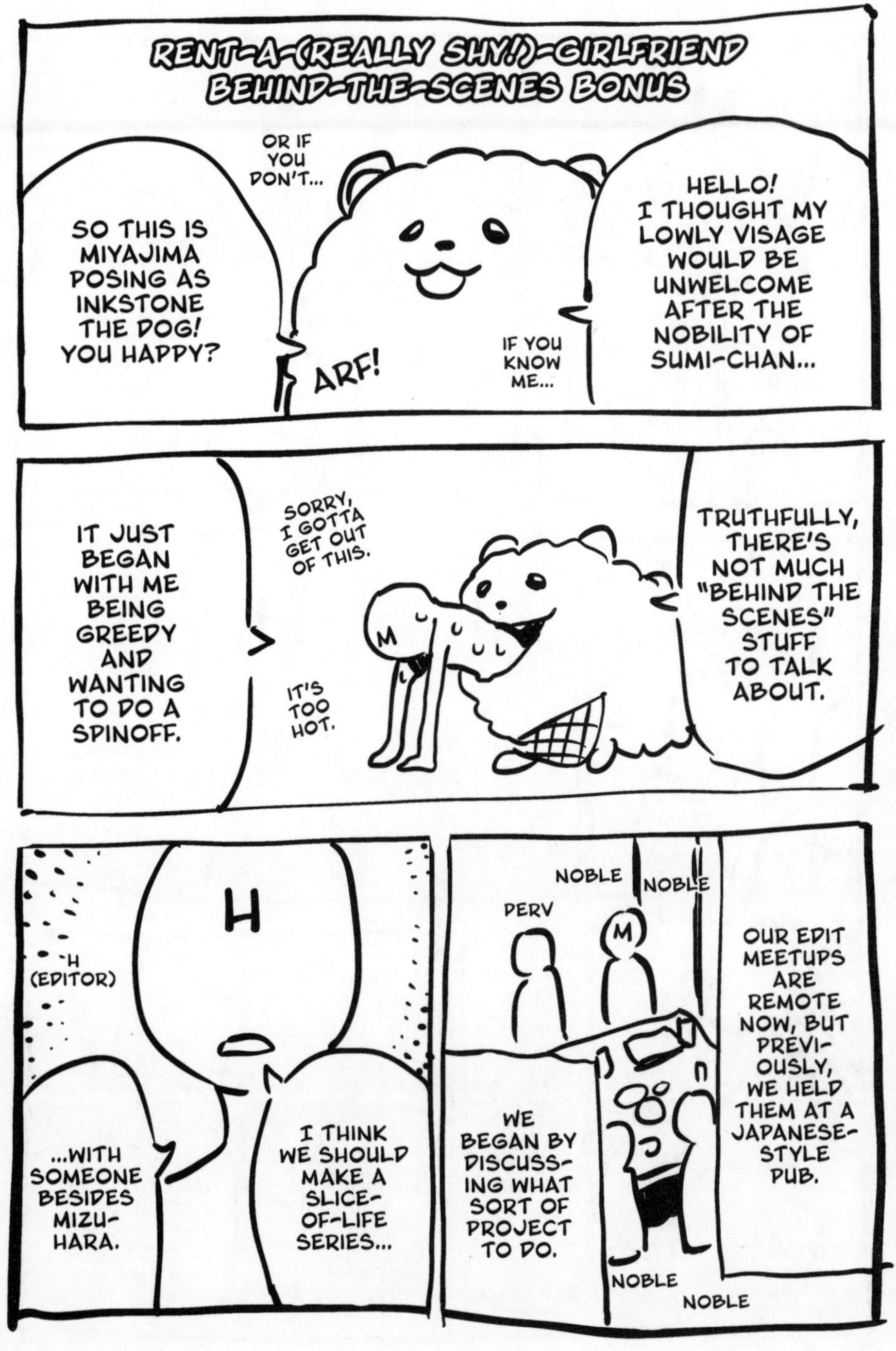
RENT-A-(REALLY SHY!)-GIRLFRIEND BEHIND-THE-SCENES BONUS
HELLO! I THOUGHT MY LOWLY VISAGE WOULD BE UNWELCOME AFTER THE NOBILITY OF SUMI-CHAN...
IF YOU KNOW ME...
OR IF YOU DON'T...
SO THIS IS MIYAJIMA POSING AS INKSTONE THE DOG! YOU HAPPY?
ARF!
TRUTHFULLY, THERE'S NOT MUCH "BEHIND THE SCENES" STUFF TO TALK ABOUT.
SORRY, I GOTTA GET OUT OF THIS.
M
IT'S TOO HOT.
IT JUST BEGAN WITH ME BEING GREEDY AND WANTING TO DO A SPINOFF.
NOBLE
NOBLE
PERV
M
OUR EDIT MEETUPS ARE REMOTE NOW, BUT PREVIOUSLY, WE HELD THEM AT A JAPANESE-STYLE PUB.
WE BEGAN BY DISCUSSING WHAT SORT OF PROJECT TO DO.
NOBLE
NOBLE
H
H (EDITOR)
I THINK WE SHOULD MAKE A SLICE-OF-LIFE SERIES...
...WITH SOMEONE BESIDES MIZUHARA.

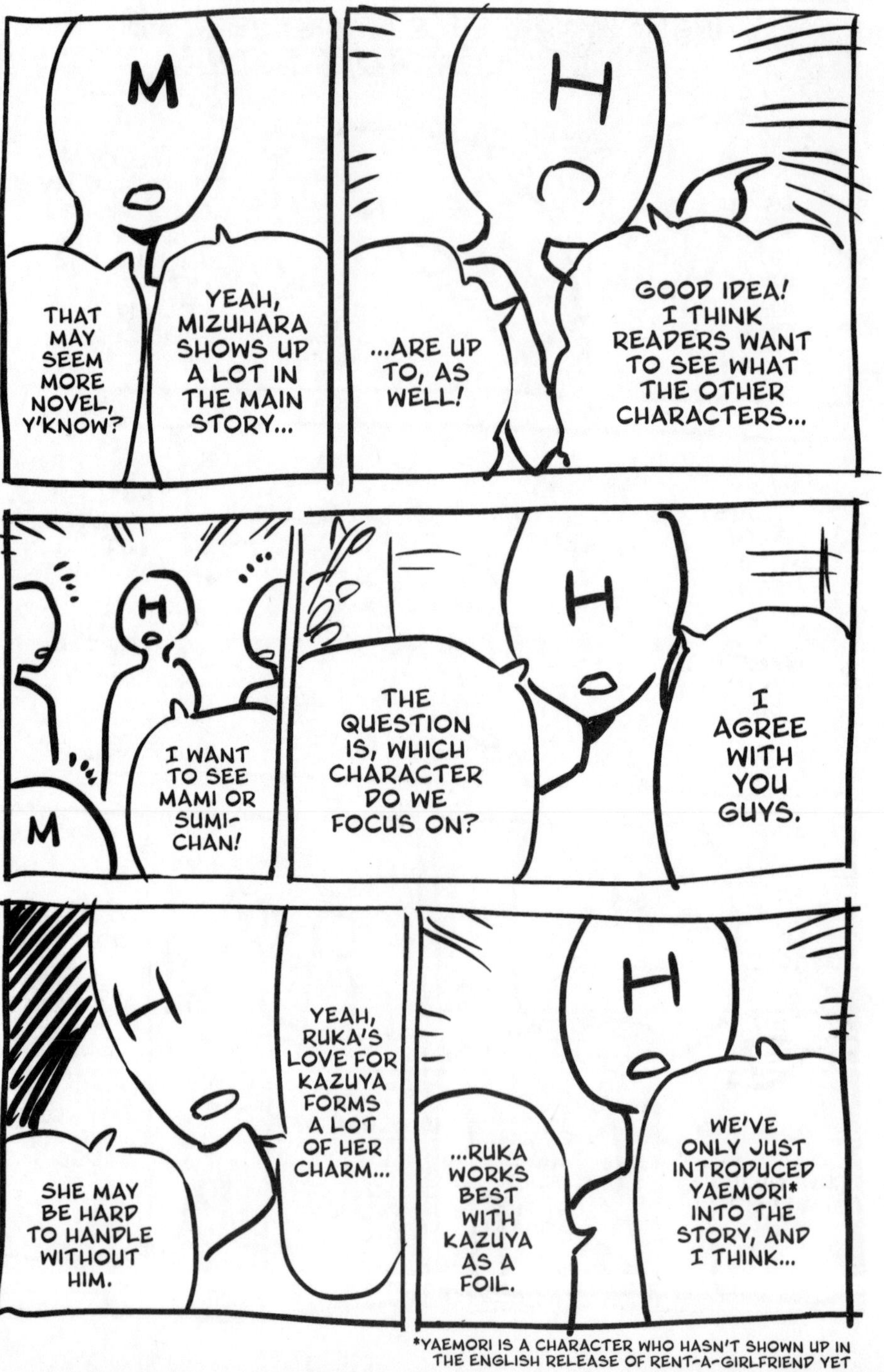
GOOD IDEA! I THINK READERS WANT TO SEE WHAT THE OTHER CHARACTERS...
...ARE UP TO, AS WELL!
YEAH, MIZUHARA SHOWS UP A LOT IN THE MAIN STORY...
THAT MAY SEEM MORE NOVEL, Y'KNOW?
I AGREE WITH YOU GUYS.
THE QUESTION IS, WHICH CHARACTER DO WE FOCUS ON?
I WANT TO SEE MAMI OR SUMI-CHAN!
WE'VE ONLY JUST INTRODUCED YAEMORI* INTO THE STORY, AND I THINK...
...RUKA WORKS BEST WITH KAZUYA AS A FOIL.
YEAH, RUKA'S LOVE FOR KAZUYA FORMS A LOT OF HER CHARM...
SHE MAY BE HARD TO HANDLE WITHOUT HIM.

*YAEMORI IS A CHARACTER WHO HASN'T SHOWN UP IN THE ENGLISH RELEASE OF RENT-A-GIRLFRIEND YET

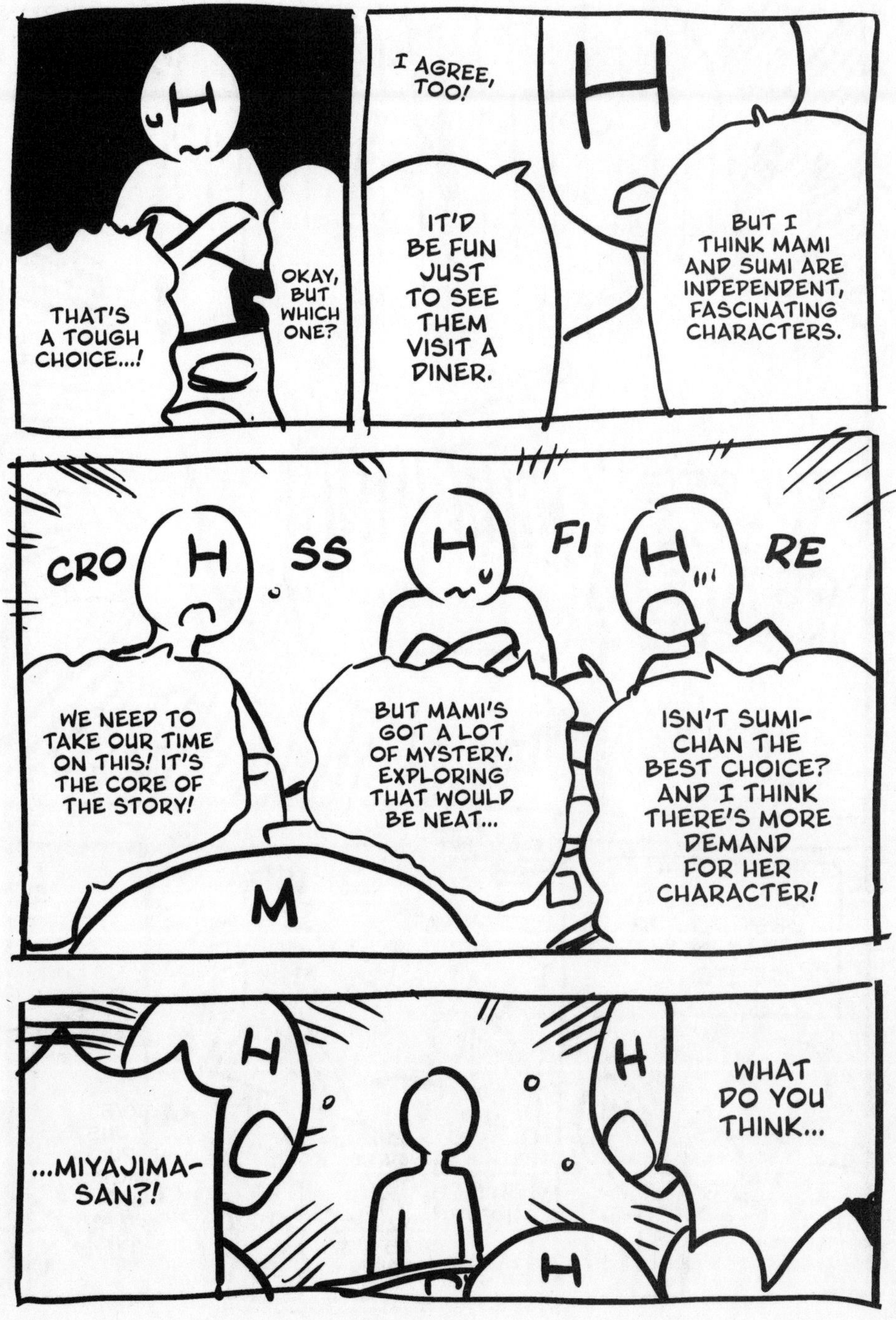
BUT I THINK MAMI AND SUMI ARE INDEPENDENT, FASCINATING CHARACTERS.
I AGREE, TOO!
IT'D BE FUN JUST TO SEE THEM VISIT A DINER.
OKAY, BUT WHICH ONE?
THAT'S A TOUGH CHOICE...!
CRO SS FI RE
ISN'T SUMI-CHAN THE BEST CHOICE? AND I THINK THERE'S MORE DEMAND FOR HER CHARACTER!
BUT MAMI'S GOT A LOT OF MYSTERY. EXPLORING THAT WOULD BE NEAT...
WE NEED TO TAKE OUR TIME ON THIS! IT'S THE CORE OF THE STORY!
WHAT DO YOU THINK...
...MIYAJIMA-SAN?!

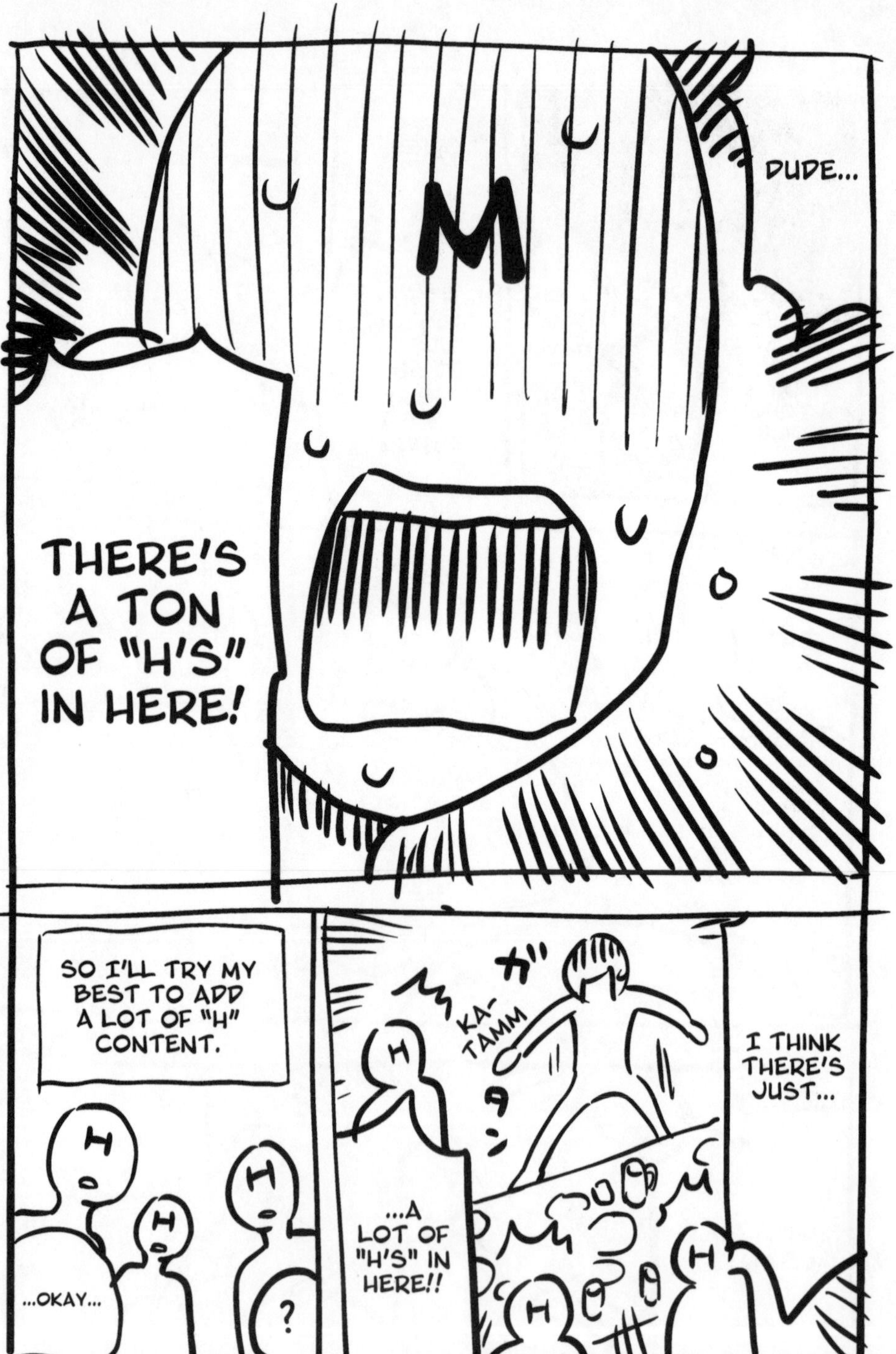
DUDE...
M
THERE'S A TON OF "H'S" IN HERE!
I THINK THERE'S JUST...
KA-TAMM
...A LOT OF "H'S" IN HERE!!
SO I'LL TRY MY BEST TO ADD A LOT OF "H" CONTENT.
...OKAY...
?

THIS IS YUKA "YUNKERU" KINAMI, ART ASSISTANT ON RENT-A-(REALLY SHY!)-GIRLFRIEND!
@KOTUPONN55

I WAS GIVEN MY OWN BONUS PAGE, SO I WENT ALL OUT DRAWING SUMI-CHAN!
^^ SWEET! ^^

EVER SINCE SUMI-CHAN DEBUTED, I'VE ALWAYS FELT SYMPATHY FOR HER... SINCE I HAVE SHYNESS ISSUES, TOO!

I LOOK FORWARD TO SEEING HOW SHE'LL DEVELOP IN THIS SPINOFF!

YOU CAN DO IT, SUMI-CHAN!!

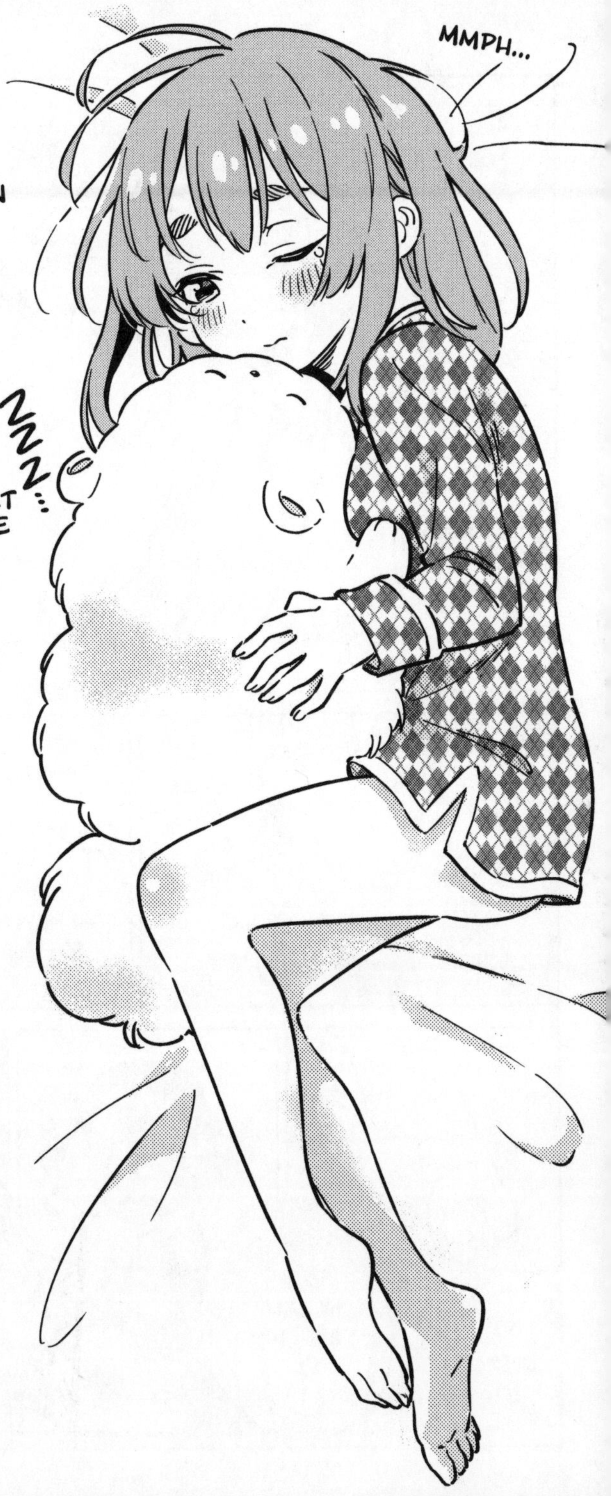
MMPH...
ZZZ...

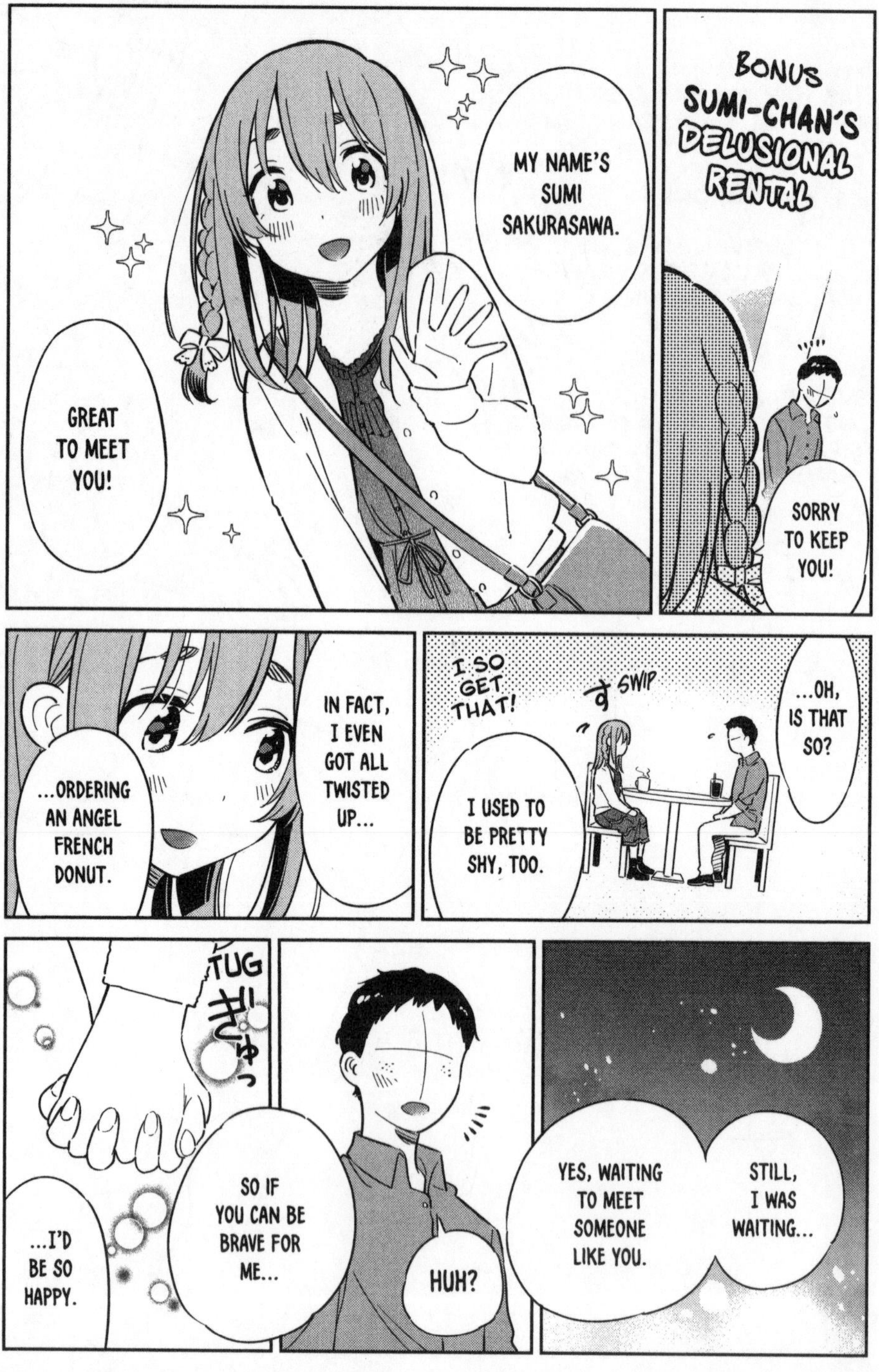
BONUS
SUMI-CHAN'S DELUSIONAL RENTAL
SORRY TO KEEP YOU!
MY NAME'S SUMI SAKURASAWA.
GREAT TO MEET YOU!
...OH, IS THAT SO?
I SO GET THAT!
す SWIP
I USED TO BE PRETTY SHY, TOO.
IN FACT, I EVEN GOT ALL TWISTED UP...
...ORDERING AN ANGEL FRENCH DONUT.
STILL, I WAS WAITING...
YES, WAITING TO MEET SOMEONE LIKE YOU.
HUH?
SO IF YOU CAN BE BRAVE FOR ME...
TUG ぎゅっ
...I'D BE SO HAPPY.

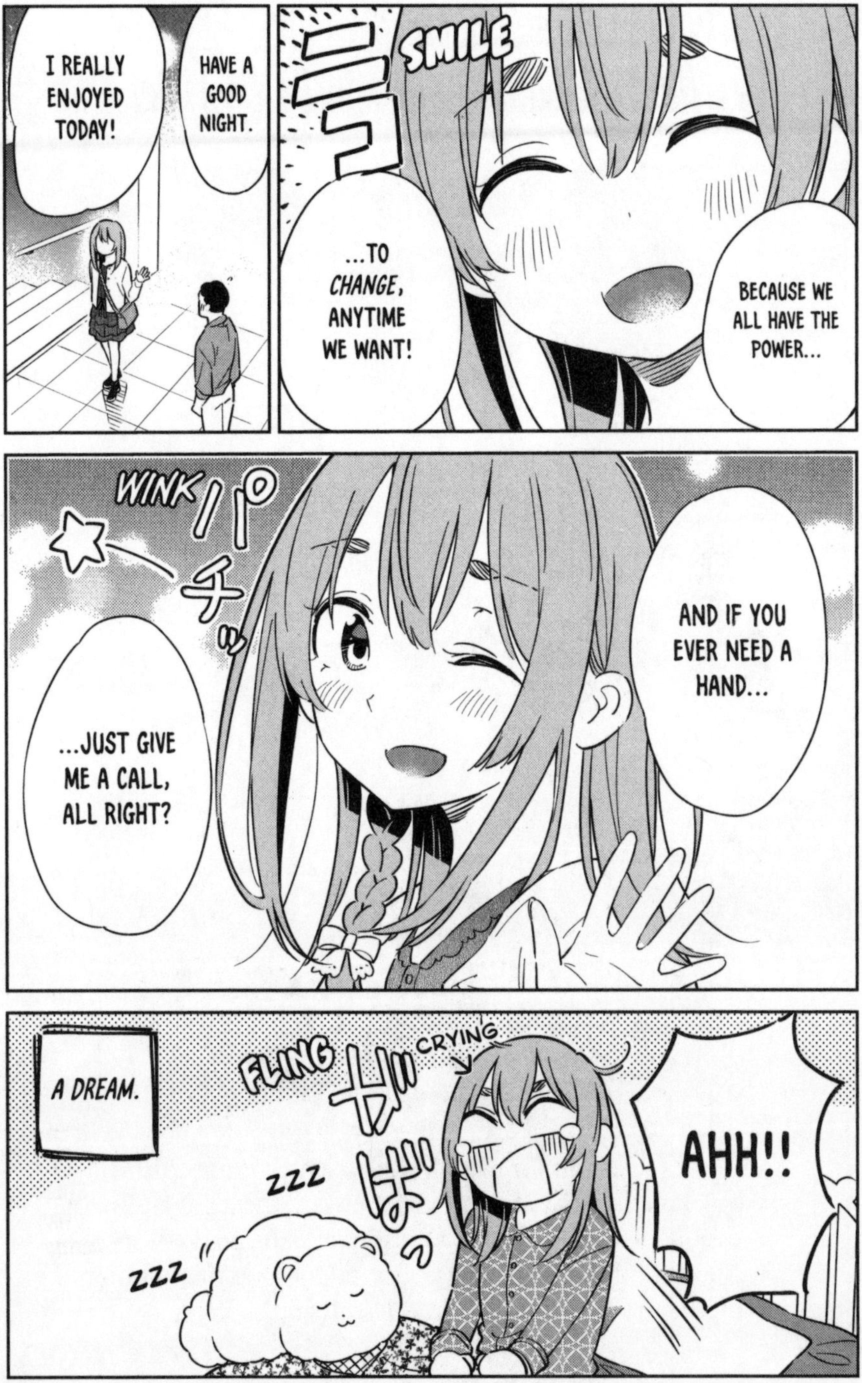
SMILE
BECAUSE WE ALL HAVE THE POWER...
...TO CHANGE, ANYTIME WE WANT!
HAVE A GOOD NIGHT.
I REALLY ENJOYED TODAY!
AND IF YOU EVER NEED A HAND...
WINK
...JUST GIVE ME A CALL, ALL RIGHT?
AHH!!
CRYING
FLING
A DREAM.
ZZZ
ZZZ

Young characters and steampunk setting, like *Howl's Moving Castle* and *Battle Angel Alita*

Beyond the Clouds © 2018 Nicke / Ki-oon

A boy with a talent for machines and a mysterious girl whose wings he's fixed will take you beyond the clouds! In the tradition of the high-flying, resonant adventure stories of Studio Ghibli comes a gorgeous tale about the longing of young hearts for adventure and friendship!

THE WORLD OF CLAMP!

Cardcaptor Sakura
Collector's Edition

Cardcaptor Sakura:
Clear Card

Magic Knight Rayearth
25th Anniversary Box Set

Chobits

TSUBASA Omnibus

TSUBASA WoRLD CHRoNiCLE

xxxHOLiC Omnibus

xxxHOLiC Rei

CLOVER Collector's Edition

Kodansha Comics welcomes you to explore the expansive world of CLAMP, the all-female artist collective that has produced some of the most acclaimed manga of the century. Our growing catalog includes icons like *Cardcaptor Sakura* and *Magic Knight Rayearth*, each crafted with CLAMP's one-of-a-kind style and characters!

Knight of the Ice ©Yayoi Ogawa/Kodansha Ltd.

SKATING THRILLS AND ICY CHILLS WITH THIS NEW TINGLY ROMANCE SERIES!

A rom-com on ice, perfect for fans of *Princess Jellyfish* and *Wotakoi*. Kokoro is the talk of the figure-skating world, winning trophies and hearts. But little do they know... he's actually a huge nerd! From the beloved creator of *You're My Pet (Tramps Like Us)*.

Chitose is a serious young woman, working for the health magazine *SASSO*. Or at least, she would be, if she wasn't constantly getting distracted by her childhood friend, international figure skating star Kokoro Kijinami! In the public eye and on the ice, Kokoro is a gallant, flawless knight, but behind his glittery costumes and breathtaking spins lies a secret: He's actually a hopelessly romantic otaku, who can only land his quad jumps when Chitose is on hand to recite a spell from his favorite magical girl anime!

A SMART, NEW ROMANTIC COMEDY FOR FANS OF *SHORTCAKE CAKE* AND *TERRACE HOUSE*!

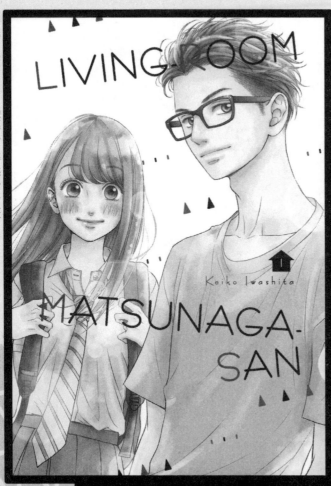

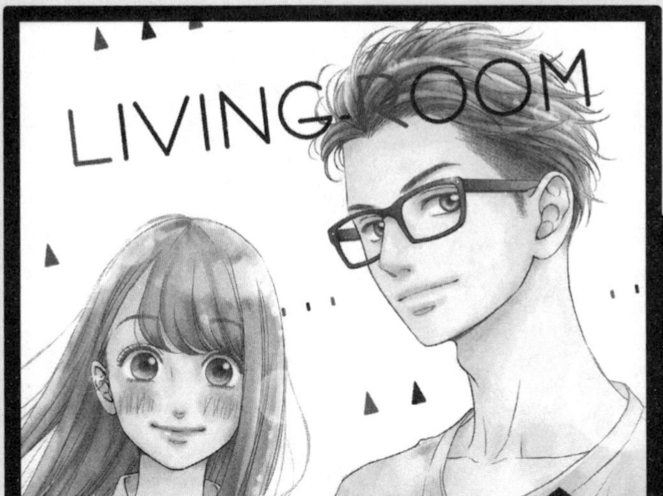
LIVING-ROOM
MATSUNAGA-SAN
1
Keiko Iwashita

KC KODANSHA COMICS

A romance manga starring high school girl Meeko, who learns to live on her own in a boarding house whose living room is home to the odd (but handsome) Matsunaga-san. She begins to adjust to her new life away from her parents, but Meeko soon learns that no matter how far away from home she is, she's still a young girl at heart — especially when she finds herself falling for Matsunaga-san.

PERFECT WORLD

Rie Aruga

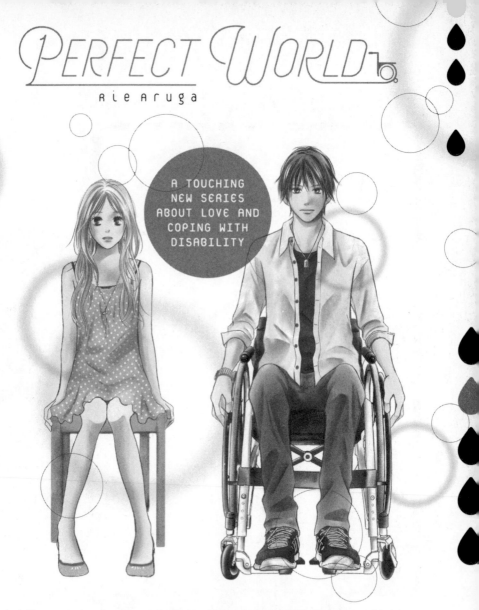

A TOUCHING NEW SERIES ABOUT LOVE AND COPING WITH DISABILITY

An office party reunites Tsugumi with her high school crush Itsuki. He's realized his dream of becoming an architect, but along the way, he experienced a spinal injury that put him in a wheelchair. Now Tsugumi's rekindled feelings will butt up against prejudices she never considered — and Itsuki will have to decide if he's ready to let someone into his heart...

"Depicts with great delicacy and courage the difficulties some with disabilities experience getting involved in romantic relationships... Rie Aruga refuses to romanticize, pushing her heroine to face the reality of disability. She invites her readers to the same tasks of empathy, knowledge and recognition."
—Slate.fr

"An important entry [in manga romance]... The emotional core of both plot and characters indicates thoughtfulness... [Aruga's] research is readily apparent in the text and artwork, making this feel like a real story."
—Anime News Network

KC
KODANSHA
COMICS

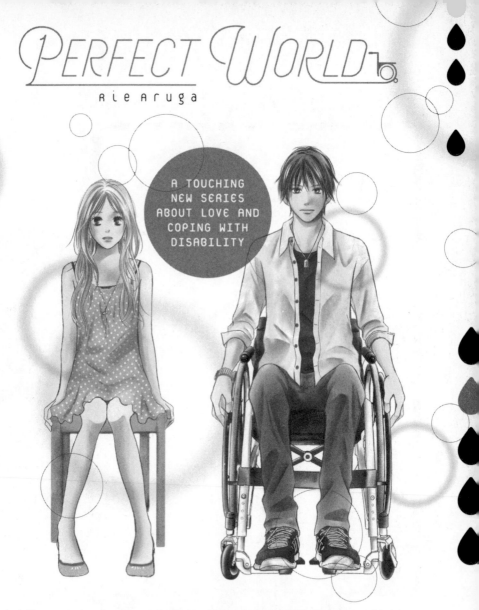

One of CLAMP's biggest hits returns in this definitive, premium, hardcover 20th anniversary collector's edition!

CLAMP

1 Chobits

20TH ANNIVERSARY EDITION

"A wonderfully entertaining story that would be a great installment in anybody's manga collection."
— Anime News Network

"CLAMP is an all-female manga-creating team whose feminine touch shows in this entertaining, sci-fi soap opera."
— Publishers Weekly

Poor college student Hideki is down on his luck. All he wants is a good job, a girlfriend, and his very own "persocom"—the latest and greatest in humanoid computer technology. Hideki's luck changes one night when he finds Chi—a persocom thrown out in a pile of trash. But Hideki soon discovers that there's much more to his cute new persocom than meets the eye.

KC
KODANSHA
COMICS

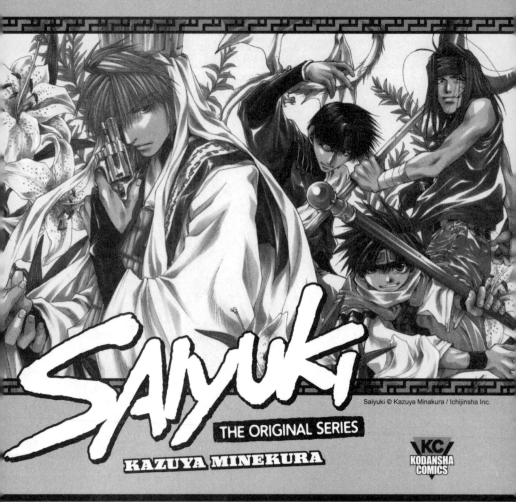

Something's Wrong With Us

NATSUMI ANDO

The dark, psychological, sexy shojo series readers have been waiting for!

A spine-chilling and steamy romance between a Japanese sweets maker and the man who framed her mother for murder!

Following in her mother's footsteps, Nao became a traditional Japanese sweets maker, and with unparalleled artistry and a bright attitude, she gets an offer to work at a world-class confectionary company. But when she meets the young, handsome owner, she recognizes his cold stare...

The beloved characters from *Cardcaptor Sakura* return in a brand new, reimagined fantasy adventure!

"[*Tsubasa*] takes readers on a fantastic ride that only gets more exhilarating with each successive chapter." —Anime News Network

In the Kingdom of Clow, an archaeological dig unleashes an incredible power, causing Princess Sakura to lose her memories. To save her, her childhood friend Syaoran must follow the orders of the Dimension Witch and travel alongside Kurogane, an unrivaled warrior; Fai, a powerful magician; and Mokona, a curiously strange creature, to retrieve Sakura's dispersed memories!

The adorable new odd-couple cat comedy manga from the creator of the beloved *Chi's Sweet Home*, in full color!

Praise for Chi's Sweet Home

"Nearly impossible to turn away... a true all-ages title that anyone, young or old, cat lover or not, will enjoy. The stories will bring a smile to your face and warm your heart."

—*School Library Journal*

Sue & Tai-chan

Konami Kanata

Sue is an aging housecat who's looking forward to living out her life in peace... but her plans change when the mischievous black tomcat Tai-chan enters the picture! Hey! Sue never signed up to be a catsitter! *Sue & Tai-chan* is the latest from the reigning meow-narch of cute kitty comics, Konami Kanata.

KC KODANSHA COMICS

THE SWEET SCENT OF LOVE IS IN THE AIR! FOR FANS OF OFFBEAT ROMANCES LIKE *WOTAKOI*

Sweat and Soap © Kintetsu Yamada / Kodansha Ltd.

In an office romance, there's a fine line between sexy and awkward... and that line is where Asako — a woman who sweats copiously — meets Koutarou — a perfume developer who can't get enough of Asako's, er, scent. Don't miss a romcom manga like no other!

"Clever, sassy, and original....*xxxHOLiC* has the inherent hallmarks of a runaway hit."
—NewType magazine

Beautifully seductive artwork and uniquely Japanese depictions of the supernatural will hypnotize CLAMP fans!

Kimihiro Watanuki is haunted by visions of ghosts and spirits. He seeks help from a mysterious woman named Yuko, who claims she can help. However, Watanuki must work for Yuko in order to pay for her aid. Soon Watanuki finds himself employed in Yuko's shop, where he sees things and meets customers that are stranger than anything he could have ever imagined.

KC
KODANSHA
COMICS

CUTE ANIMALS AND LIFE LESSONS, PERFECT FOR ASPIRING PET VETS OF ALL AGES!

YUZU THE PET VET

1

BY
MINGO ITO

In collaboration with
NIPPON COLUMBIA CO., LTD.

Yuzu the Pet Vet © Mingo Ito / NIPPON COLUMBIA CO., LTD. / Kodansha Ltd.

For an 11-year-old, Yuzu has a lot on her plate. When her mom gets sick and has to be hospitalized, Yuzu goes to live with her uncle who runs the local veterinary clinic. Yuzu's always been scared of animals, but she tries to help out. Through all the tough moments in her life, Yuzu realizes that she can help make things all right with a little help from her animal pals, peers, and kind grown-ups.

Every new patient is a furry friend in the making!

The art-deco cyberpunk classic from the creators of *xxxHOLiC* and *Cardcaptor Sakura*!

CLOVER © CLAMP·ShigatsuTsuitachi CO.,LTD./Kodansha Ltd.

Su was born into a bleak future, where the government keeps tight control over children with magical powers—codenamed "Clovers." With Su being the only "four-leaf" Clover in the world, she has been kept isolated nearly her whole life. Can ex-military agent Kazuhiko deliver her to the happiness she seeks? Experience the complete series in this hardcover edition, which also includes over twenty pages of ravishing color art!

KC
KODANSHA
COMICS

Rent-A-(Really Shy!)-Girlfriend 1 is a work of fiction. Names, characters, places, and incidents are the products of the author's imagination or are used fictitiously. Any resemblance to actual events, locales, or persons, living or dead, is entirely coincidental.

A Kodansha Trade Paperback Original

Published in the United States by
Kodansha USA Publishing, LLC, New York.

Publication rights for this English edition arranged through
Kodansha Ltd., Tokyo.

First published in Japan in 2020 by Kodansha Ltd., Tokyo
as *Kanojo, hitomishirimasu,* volume 1.

ISBN 978-1-64651-365-9

Printed in the United States of America.

ScoutAutomatedPrintCode

Translation: Kevin Gifford
Lettering: Paige Pumphrey
Editing: Jordan Blanco
Kodansha USA Publishing edition cover design by Phil Balsman

Publisher: Kiichiro Sugawara

Director of Publishing Services: Ben Applegate
Associate Director, Publishing Operations: Stephen Pakula
Publishing Services Managing Editors: Madison Salters, Alanna Ruse
Production Managers: Emi Lotto, Angela Zurlo

KODANSHA.US

KODANSHA